LIFEPRINTS

LIFEPRINTS

NEW PATTERNS
OF LOVE AND WORK
FOR TODAY'S WOMEN

GRACE BARUCH

ROSALIND BARNETT

CARYL RIVERS

McGRAW-HILL BOOK COMPANY

New York   St. Louis   San Francisco
Toronto   Hamburg   Mexico

1 2 3 4 5 6 7 8 9 DOCDOC 8 7 6 5 4 3

ISBN 0-07-052981-7

LIBRARY OF CONGRESS CATALOGING IN PUBLICATION DATA

Baruch, Grace K.
  Lifeprints: new patterns of love and work for today's women.
Includes index.
1. Women—Psychology.   2. Conduct of life.
I. Barnett, Rosalind C.   II. Rivers, Caryl.   III. Title.
HQ1206.B28   1983   305.4   82–13007
ISBN 0–07–052981–7

Book design by Christine Aulicino

55,447

For Franklin and Susannah
G. K. B.

For Amy and Jonathan
R. C. B.

For Alan, Steven and Alyssa
C. R.

PREFACE

THE THREE AUTHORS of this book come from two different traditions—the social sciences and journalism. As a journalist, Caryl Rivers has spent years asking researchers, "But what do your findings mean?" and "How can this be said so that it's clear to the nonspecialist?" As social scientists, Grace Baruch and Rosalind Barnett were trained to stay close to their findings, to interpret only with caution, to generalize only with hesitation.

Over the three years that went into writing this book, Grace Baruch and Rosalind Barnett have realized that to make their research useful to a broad audience they often must go out on a limb—dozens of limbs, in fact. Interpreting findings and explaining their implications for readers required the willingness to leap boldly—and to risk being wrong. Unless you work in experimentally controlled conditions and, for example, "create" a cause in order to study its effect, technically, you can't talk about one thing "causing" another. And, of course, we didn't do that kind of study. We didn't assign high incomes to some women and low ones to a matched group to study the effect on well-being. Nor did we give good marriages to some subjects and divorces to others. So if we find a relationship between income or the quality of marriage and psychological well-being, the reason *could* have been that women who were high in well-being were able to earn a high salary or create a good marriage. But we believe it's more likely that it works the other way around, that over time, being in a good marriage and having enough money to smooth one's way in life tend to enhance well-being.

We have relied on our findings, on the research of many other social scientists, on clinical experience, and sometimes on common sense, to come to reasonable conclusions about our results, yet we know that some will inevitably prove inaccurate. The scientific tradition reminds us to be acutely aware of the limits to which we can generalize our findings. Our data were collected in 1979–1980, a time of economic difficulty—especially inflation—and of the strengthening of the women's movement. These present conditions probably affect women differently, depending upon their expectations and prior histories. The "average" woman in our study, who was almost forty-five, had been born in 1935 to parents living through the Great Depression. Then she, as a youngster, and her family experienced the upheaval associated with World War II. When she was entering her teens, in about 1948, women who had been in the labor force during the war were being displaced, often willingly, by returning veterans, and the era of the feminine mystique and family togetherness was taking hold. But by 1979 when we began to interview our subjects, economic pressures, as well as new attitudes and opportunities associated with the women's movement, meant that many American women found themselves living in a social and economic climate for which their earlier life experiences had not prepared them. The predominant pattern for women today, even for married women with children, is working for a salary. Attitudes and practices about work, marriage, and children seem to be changing rapidly.

Thus the women who were thirty-five to fifty-five in 1979–1980, despite their individuality, are also part of a particular age group moving together through time. Their experiences cannot be identical to those of women now sixty-five or seventy, nor to young women now in their twenties. Yet despite these differences, we believe that the experiences of the women we studied are highly relevant to younger and older women.

The message of our subjects' lives is that no one pattern fits all women, no one lifeprint guarantees well-being, and no one path leads inevitably to misery. Each pattern has its own clusters of joys and problems. Being aware of the choices women have made—or failed to make—and of some of the consequences, can, we hope, light up many corners of women's lives that have been invisible and guide women who are on the brink of making those choices. In no way do we mean to suggest that the shape of one's life is always a matter of choice. But we do believe that there are more choices now than before—and that women have more choices than many have realized.

When we began our study, we had some notion of the kinds of findings we might uncover. If you have no ideas about what you might find, you can't even design the appropriate study. The work of our predecessors, who are part of what we see as a "new wave" of social scientists studying women, suggested many important questions to explore and issues to investigate.

We're delighted that other studies are coming up with similar findings. It is particularly reassuring to note this consistency when results seem startling. As a social scientist you look not for unique findings but for those that can be replicated. We've drawn heavily on the work of colleagues when it is relevant to the story we have to tell, but since this book isn't meant as a "review of the literature," many important studies aren't mentioned.

We are indebted to the National Science Foundation for generous support of the research on which this book is based. Our work could not have been completed without supplementary funding from the National Institutes of Health and from Time, Inc. through the Wellesley College Center for Research on Women. These grants were to Grace Baruch and Rosalind Barnett, who had responsibility for the study from its conceptualization through the data analyses. Caryl Rivers, in addition to her primary responsibility for the writing, joined in the process of reviewing and reconceptualizing the findings and suggesting important new questions to ask of the data.

Our appreciation goes to Robert Binstock of the Florence Heller School at Brandeis University, where the study was originally carried out, and to the School of Public Communication at Boston University for sharing its facilities and support. Of course, responsibility for conclusions or errors belongs to the three of us.

We have a special debt to the devoted and talented women who served as interviewers and research assistants: Jeanne Anastis, Myrtle Cox, Shirley Dana, Barbara Jacobs, Barbara Kraft, Regina O'Grady, Thalia Price, Lynn Spichiger, Holly Zalinger—and especially Marion Meenan. Patricia Gillis and Katherine DeMarco worked endlessly on the details of coding, typing, and retyping that require superhuman attention and patience. Our statistical consultants—Kenneth Jones of the Heller School, and later the team of Ralph Turner and David Connell—spent long hours, usually at times inconvenient for them, to complete the data analyses.

For many years now, Elaine Markson, our literary agent, has supplied us with friendship, encouragement, and a cool head; the editorial team of Gladys Carr and Gail Greene provided many valuable criticisms and suggestions. We are especially grateful for the sensitive and insightful critiques provided by two psychologist colleagues, Zick Rubin and Alexandra Kaplan. They read portions of the manuscript under great time pressure, and we profited enormously from their effort.

Our greatest debt is to the women whose lives we studied. In the long hours they spent with us and with our team of interviewers, they shared their experiences openly and became our teachers. To protect their privacy, their names and any identifying details have been altered. Those women "appearing" in more than one chapter were given last names to help in remembering them. Our only regret is that they must remain unknown, and we hope we have done them justice.

CONTENTS

	Preface	vii
	Introduction	1
CHAPTER ONE	**LOOKING IN THE WRONG PLACE**	12
CHAPTER TWO	**WHAT ABOUT ME?**	23
CHAPTER THREE	**THE WELL-SPRINGS OF MASTERY AND PLEASURE**	34
CHAPTER FOUR	**MARRIAGE**	55
CHAPTER FIVE	**CHILDREN: AND BABY MAKES THREE**	78
CHAPTER SIX	**FINDING THE CHALLENGE**	103
CHAPTER SEVEN	**RISKS AND DREAMS**	121
CHAPTER EIGHT	**OVERLOAD AND UNDERLOAD: WHO HAS MULTIPLE ROLE STRAIN?**	139
CHAPTER NINE	**DIVORCE: COMING APART, GETTING IT TOGETHER**	164
CHAPTER TEN	**MOTHERS AND DAUGHTERS**	192
CHAPTER ELEVEN	**BY MYSELF**	208

CHAPTER TWELVE **TOWARD A NEW THEORY OF WOMEN'S LIVES** 233

Epilogue 246
Notes 253
Appendix: Survey 265
Index 285

INTRODUCTION

THIS BOOK, and the major new study of women it is based on, began by trying to answer one central question—what contributes to a woman's sense of well-being?—and ended by recognizing that there were two questions that needed answering: first, what makes a woman feel good about herself as a valued member of society who is in control of her life? Second, what makes a woman find pleasure and enjoyment in her life? The special message of this book, and of the study, is that for many of today's women, these two questions are indeed separate, and the answers to each are different.[1]

In our culture, the sources of what we call a sense of "mastery"—feeling important and worthwhile—and the sources of what we call a sense of "pleasure"—finding life enjoyable—are not always identical. But that doesn't mean women have to choose between the two. Women are often told, "You can't have it all," but sometimes what the speaker is really saying is: "You chose a career, so you can't expect to have close relationships or a happy family life," or "You have a wonderful husband and children—what's all this about wanting a career?"

But women need to understand and develop *both* aspects of well-being, if they are to feel good about themselves and their lives.

The behavioral sciences have contributed a great deal of information to help women reach such understanding. During the past decade a new wave of scholars in the traditional areas of social science and in the new field of women's studies have laid the foundation for the study of women's lives. Our study is part of this exciting effort to create a new framework for understanding the lives of women. Throughout this book we will refer to the work of our many colleagues.

We are seeing significant changes in the lives of women today. As the social and political status of women change, as women move into new roles, these new roles in turn exert powerful forces on the women who occupy them. It is vital for all of us, and women in particular, to understand the nature of those forces and to look at what is happening to women—and why.

Many people will be surprised by our findings, which quite often contradict the conventional wisdom about what a woman is supposed to "want." But the old answers are no longer sufficient, and some of the current rhetoric is too simplistic. We believe a new vision of women's lives is emerging, and one of the primary tasks of this book is to contribute to that vision.

Perhaps the most useful tools we have for building a new framework are our core concepts of Mastery and Pleasure, which we explain in more detail in Chapter One. The ingredients in life that provide a sense of Mastery for today's women typically center around involvement in the work of one's society. Most often—but not always—this means paid work. A sense of Pleasure usually comes from intimate relationships—feeling lovingly connected with others. This doesn't necessarily require marriage and children!

With these insights, we can begin to understand why the needs and wants of women have seemed so mysterious. "What does a woman want?" Sigmund Freud once asked in frustration. "How can I love my husband and children and be so miserable?" wondered the women in Betty Friedan's *The Feminine Mystique.*

If you think there is only one ingredient in the recipe for the good life—what social scientists call "psychological well-being"— you are doomed to a search like that for the Fountain of Youth or the Holy Grail. If you are like most women, you will wonder what is wrong with you if you have a successful career yet feel dissatisfied, or if you have a gratifying family life yet feel depressed.

In seeking to understand the sources of well-being, women have been given answers so clouded with myth and misinformation that they were often of little practical help. Today, the answers are more varied than ever before—and more confusing. Some say that the sure road to happiness for women lies in becoming the "Total Woman"—the submissive wife who uses her skills at seduction to wheedle the new washer-dryer she wants out of her husband. Other voices, while denying they are describing "superwoman," hold up as a model the chairperson of the board who dashes home from the annual meeting to prepare a gourmet dinner for her husband and twelve dinner guests, while at the same time turning out a batch of homemade cookies for the children.

To which voices should a woman listen? What criteria can she use to evaluate her own life and to decide which choices to make? It has been difficult to get reliable information about which paths lead to a rich, satisfying life. A woman's life has often been perceived—by novelists, behavioral scientists, and society in general—in contradictory ways: either as a mysterious territory impossible to chart or as a precut pattern which is more or less the same for every woman.

Today, despite the spate of books on women, despite the obsession with adult development and its "crises," the details of women's lives remain unclear. Women wonder how their lives will turn out if they make certain choices. If they do not marry, will they be lonely, pitied spinsters? If they marry but don't have children, will they be haunted by regrets when they are past the childbearing years? If they follow the traditional path of marrying and remaining at home, how will they feel about themselves at midlife? Does a high-powered career lead to "burnout"? Does the career woman-wife-mother combination lead to stress and an early coronary? Can a woman pick up the lost threads of a career when she is past thirty-five?

One aim of the study on which this book is based was to discover how, and in what ways, the major areas of life affect a woman's sense of well-being. We looked in detail at a whole range of issues in different areas, or domains, of life: work, marriage, homemaking, children, parents, finances, sexuality. We also looked in depth at issues associated with being single, with divorce, and with childlessness. We asked women about turning points, regrets, and crises in their lives, about how they saw the future, about growing older.

The study, a major research project funded by the National Science Foundation, has several special characteristics. First, it was specifically and carefully designed to avoid looking at women as one large, homogeneous, undifferentiated mass. In the past, studies have tended to focus on one type of woman—married women with children—simply because they are the largest group. Too often it is assumed that what is true for these women is true for all women. As a result, there are many women that behavioral scientists are just starting to learn about—the never-married woman, for example.

Our study was designed so that we could examine women in different roles. We believed that it made a profound difference whether a woman was employed or not, married or not, a parent or not, but we learned along the way, as the reader will find out, that other things also make a difference—a woman's salary, her sexual relationships, her relationship with her mother. We all assume that the life of a married woman with children is different from that of a woman who has never married, but exactly *how* is it different? We wanted to investigate that question. We also wanted to examine the difference that paid work and particular kinds of employment made in a woman's life.

We want to be absolutely clear on an important point. Women "work" whether or not they have paid jobs. But it proved awkward in writing this book always to use the terms "paid work" or "employment"; therefore on stylistic grounds we often use "work" to mean a salaried job.

In the past, most researchers skimmed the surface of the work aspect of a woman's life, considering it to be less important than her family role. Fortunately, this attitude, which often limited the usefulness of previous research, is changing.

We'll be referring often to an excellent new study of the mental health of Americans carried out in 1976 at the University of Michigan. This national study of about 2,300 subjects, reported in *The Inner American* by Joseph Veroff, Elizabeth Douvan, and Richard Kulka, is a replication of a similar study done in 1957. Looking back on their views at the time of their earlier study, the authors of the new volume confess, "We felt that work was a minor part of the experience of women in our study . . . and did not warrant special examination."[2]

The employed women in our study included enough women in a wide range of occupations so that we could analyze the effect of certain aspects of their jobs on their well-being. We wanted to understand, for example, the impact of having a high-prestige job, which, of course, includes the converse: the impact of having a low-level job. The *prestige* of a job, as social scientists use this term, refers to its social standing, determined by asking large numbers of people to rank particular occupations. While high prestige and high pay often go hand in hand, this is not always the case. When people judge the prestige of a job, they are usually thinking about such qualities as its social value, level of responsibility, and whether it is "clean." Being a minister is "cleaner" than being a truck driver, even though it doesn't pay as well. So the pay is clearly not the only factor.[3]

The women in our study range in age from thirty-five to fifty-five. These are the years in which, for most women, the major aspects of life have settled into a stable pattern. Since we intended to study adult life patterns, we needed to look at the period of a woman's life that is most typical of her life as a whole. We wanted to go beyond the crises of young adulthood, during which women are often preoccupied with career choices and with such decisions as whom to marry or whether to have children; we wanted to examine the outcomes of such decisions. So the youngest women in our study are thirty-five. We ended our study at age fifty-five, before issues of aging—retirement, widowhood—begin to dominate women's concerns.

The age cutoffs in our study were, of course, arbitrary. A woman in her early thirties or a woman who is sixty will probably find that the research applies to her life too. Younger women will gain insight into what they can expect in the next stage of their lives. This glimpse into the future should be informative, valuable, and probably in many ways reassuring.

Whereas in the past it was middle-aged women who were found to be the least happy and most anxious, more recently it is younger women who seem to be more distressed. Studies show that younger people in general are worrying more about their future than they used to, and young women in particular are faced with options and dilemmas around life choices—career, marriage, childbearing—that did not exist for most women twenty years ago. According to psychologist Harold Dupuy, "There is now no well-defined prescription to guide young women through their twenties. They are suffering from the effort to locate themselves in society without direct role models."[4] While we certainly have no "prescriptions," we believe that we do have important and useful information that can offer new insights into what kinds of choices are likely to have the greatest impact on their lives.

Because we designed our study to look at particular groups of women, not all women in our age range are represented. Our study was limited to Caucasian women, partly because we did not feel competent to focus on the lives of nonwhite women, and partly because their lives have been different enough to require a separate study.

Also, we did not include widows in our study. A sound study of this group requires a different age range, one including women older than fifty-five, when widowhood becomes a less unusual life event.

About 300 women participated in our study. Of these, 238 were in the major phase, a random-sample survey.[5] The women represent the subgroups in the population that we believed could help us most in understanding women's lives: never married, married without children, married with children, and divorced with children. All the never-married and divorced women were employed, as were half of each of the two groups of married women. This design created the six groups that we will often refer to in this book.

What were the characteristics of the women in our study? The average age was 43.6 years; the average educational level was four-teen years—two years beyond high school. The six groups differed in educational level with the never-married women being the highest; the average woman in that group had completed about a year of schooling beyond her bachelor's degree.

The range of what we call "total family income" was from $4,500 to over $50,000. Total family income includes monies from all sources brought into the woman's family unit in the year prior to the study. The family unit, of course, could be composed only of the woman herself, as in the case of the never-married women. The average figure for the whole sample was $21,600, but there was wide variation among the groups. Never-married and divorced women were lower ($15,200 and $16,400 respectively) than married women. Married women in one-earner families had lower average total family incomes ($22,600) than did women in two-earner fami-lies ($30,700).[6] For twenty-nine percent of the women, total family income was $18,000 or less; for twenty-three percent, it was between $18,000 and $24,000; and for forty-eight percent, it was over $24,000.

We consider a major strength of our study to be that before we undertook our random-sample survey, we interviewed about ten women from each of the six groups at great length to help us determine the right questions to ask. In designing our survey ques-tionnaire, we didn't want to simply make up our own list of what the important concerns and gratifications in women's lives were and then ask only about those. So we spent more than a year doing this "snowball" study. By *snowball* we mean we asked women we knew to suggest other women as interviewees; these women, in turn, led us to more subjects. We asked the women to collaborate with us as experts on their "lifeprints"—the pleasures, the problems, the conflicts, the issues. As we have noted, the domains and range of topics about which we asked our subjects covered such areas as feelings about themselves, work, sexuality, homemaking, finances, relationships with husbands and children, relationships with parents, experiences with growing older, with menopause and the "empty nest," and so on. These 60 women helped us to identify important topics and issues we might otherwise have missed as we developed the questions for our survey. The reader will find our survey at the end of the book.

An important feature of the survey was that it deliberately asked women in great detail about the rewards and pleasures in their lives. Too many prior studies have been problem oriented; researchers, concerned about the bad things in women's lives, set out eagerly to examine them. Now, if you ask people about their problems, they will usually tell you. They may never tell you about the good things in their lives, however, unless you ask about those as well. Too often, in the past, those vital questions were not asked. Yet without knowing what a woman finds gratifying, as well as what she finds troubling, any portrait of her life will be distorted.

Thanks to the generous funding we were able to obtain, our study continued where a great many studies are forced to end— after intensive interviews with a small group of subjects. We gained many valuable insights from our initial in-depth interviews with women, but we needed to know whether our impressions would stand up using more rigorous scientific methods. Many studies of middle adulthood, although exciting pioneering works that make people think in new ways about adulthood, have been limited to small nonrandom samples. Several other studies that have received wide publicity have involved large numbers of subjects, but the subjects were selected in a nonrandom way, making it impossible to generalize from the findings. If you send out 100,000 questionnaires and get 10,000 back, you have a huge sample, but 90 percent of the prospective subjects never responded, so the 10 percent are a special group, probably not typical. You don't really know if the people you study in this way resemble the rest of the population.

If you study women and their mothers and find a large number of troubled relationships, for example, perhaps the people who talk to you do so precisely because they have a problem with that relationship, and are eager to share their thoughts. But if you studied more representative groups of women, the picture might turn out to look very different. Findings from these kinds of studies are too often presented as scientific facts, not as intriguing—but untested—hypotheses.

To generalize beyond the people you actually studied requires selecting subjects randomly, so that your sample will be unbiased. In a random sample, subjects are chosen by "the luck of the draw"— every prospective subject has an equal chance of selection—not by any particular interest on the part of the subject, or any bias, even unconscious, on the part of the researchers. A description of how we set up our study gives an example of this process, including how real-life limitations shape research decisions.

Our first decision was to work within our own geographic region rather than conduct a national study. This approach allowed us to be in close and constant touch with our own staff of interviewers; to talk personally with subjects; to stay on top of the daily questions, problems, and issues of conducting an interview study of this scope.[7]

To stay within our funding resources, we needed to locate a community that, according to census data, contained large enough numbers of each of the different groups of women we were looking for. Some groups are relatively rare in the general population, but are of great importance in understanding adult women today—divorced women in high-prestige jobs, for example. Based on population characteristics, we selected a large town adjacent to Boston that had the necessary characteristics: both urban and suburban areas and a wide economic range among its residents. To find our random sample we took the official voting list—a complete roster of adults eighteen years of age and older—and looked at the names and ages of every voter to identify women in the thirty-five to fifty-five age group. Every woman in this group of over 6,000 was assigned a random number from a computer-generated list of such numbers. For example, the first eligible person we came to might get the number 7193, and the second 0094. For each person we filled out a sheet containing her number and other information from the voting list. Next, those 6,000-plus sheets of paper had to be put in numerical order. Only then could we proceed to approach our subjects, starting with those with the lowest numbers.

Since our sample was to be composed of specific numbers of women in various family roles and work categories, our trained interviewers next had to telephone and ask tactful questions to elicit personal information from potential subjects. The interviewer then determined whether the woman she was screening was eligible. For example, a woman might say she taught piano two days a week and played in a band in a nightclub two nights a week. Was she eligible for our "employed women" category? Our guidelines stated that to qualify a woman had to be working a minimum of seventeen and a half hours a week for at least three months prior to the telephone contact. Of the women who were eligible to participate, 76 percent agreed to take part—which is a very respectable response rate.

Once the women who fit our categories were identified, our team of interviewers fanned out, meeting each woman individually for a lengthy survey procedure. Our interviewers asked questions carefully and took down the answers verbatim, probing with prearranged questions when necessary to clear up any ambiguity in the statements of the subjects. They were instructed to offer to meet subjects at any time, any place—and wound up doing their work not only in homes and offices but in libraries and restaurants and, in one case, by a pool at a YWCA. The hazards of scientific research are sometimes unexpected. One team member, while conducting an interview with a woman who worked at a church, left her good winter coat in the pastor's office. She came back to the office to find that her coat had been shipped off with a bundle of other clothes to Cambodian refugees.

When the surveys were completed, we had a mountain of data to be processed. In assessing this information, we used a concept which we call "balance." To examine how women experience certain areas of their lives, we needed a concrete way to assess the quality of their experiences. In the area of work, for example, it is rare that a person finds that experience either constantly joyous or unrelievedly grim. Each area, or "domain" of life, as we call it, offers both rewards and concerns. At work, a woman may be pleased with her salary, her chances for advancement and her co-workers. But she may dislike her boss and feel overloaded. There are distressing and rewarding aspects for almost every woman in every part of life. What is crucial is the balance between the two, because well-being in no way means an absence of problems in one's life. Rather, it means a life in which, for most domains, the rewards outweigh the problems. The analogy to a bank account is a good one: for your account to be economically healthy, you don't need an absence of withdrawals. You just have to have your deposits outweigh them by a reasonable margin. By subtracting concerns scores from rewards scores, we were able to assign each woman in the survey a balance score in the domains of life relevant to her: work or homemaking, children or childlessness, marriage, singleness, divorce, and so on. We will be talking about these scores often in the book, because we found that the balance between rewards and concerns in every domain of life we measured did indeed affect a woman's well-being.*

Perhaps the best news to come out of our study is that there is no one lifeprint that insures all women a perpetual sense of well-being—nor one that guarantees misery, for that matter. Adult American women today are finding fulfilling and satisfying lives in any number of different role patterns. None guarantees happiness, and none is problem free. Most involve tradeoffs at different points in the life cycle. A woman who is deriving great pleasure from being at home with young children may still suffer, at least temporarily, from feeling devalued and unimportant. Knowing that her pattern has such risks can help her find ways to minimize and cope with them. The woman immersed in building a high-powered career, while feeling very much in charge of her life, may also at times feel deprived of the pleasure deep involvement in close relationships brings. Again, knowing what to expect helps in tolerating periods of discontent—or in making changes that increase well-being.

For women who are just starting to make crucial choices in their lives, or for those who have made choices but now wonder about veering off in a different direction, sharing the experiences of women in different roles can help them consider their futures.

Today, the possibilities for women are more diverse than at any time in the past; women are more able to shape their lives as individuals. In the long run, these choices can create a lifestyle tailored to individual needs and talents and thus offer more opportunities for well-being. Clearly not all life decisions are a matter of deliberate choice. But to make informed decisions when choice *is* possible, women need to know more about the lives of other women who have made similar choices, about how their lives turned out.

---

* The reader interested in determining her balance scores will find the appropriate scales in the Appendix.

They need facts, not myths—data, not stereotypes. They need some idea of what life will be like on the road they have started down, and also, what it has been like for women on the other paths. Only then will they be able to see the future not as vast uncharted territory but as a place where others have gone before and described the landscape. In the next chapter we begin the task of interpreting the experiences of the 300 women who shared their lives with honesty and eloquence.

CHAPTER ONE

LOOKING IN THE WRONG PLACE

Women are much more like each other than men; they have in truth, but two passions, vanity and love; these are their universal characteristics.

—The Earl of Chesterfield, from a letter to his son, December 1749

Woman has a head almost too small for intellect but just big enough for love.

From a lecture by a physician at the Jefferson Medical College in Philadelphia, January 1847

"WOMAN" AND "LOVE" are two words that are inextricably linked in our culture, though not always in a complimentary manner. But it is not only sages and poets who sound the theme; some behavioral scientists have preached this conventional wisdom as well, though hardly with a romantic flourish. In the language of research, traditional social scientists sketched out a theory of behavior which offered women a very passive role. In this view, there are two basic realms of human behavior, the *instrumental,* doing, and the *affective,* feeling. The former has been thought to be the specialty of men. Men must wrestle with and subdue the earth, forge their identities through action. The aging Ulysses, in Tennyson's epic, still believed that "Some work of noble note may still be done/not unbecoming men that strove with gods."

Feeling, however, is woman's forte; so much so that it consumes her whole being. As Lord Byron put it: "Man's love is of man's life a thing apart; 'tis woman's whole existence."

Women have often accepted this message, whether it came from poets, philosophers, or social scientists. When internalized, this belief can lead women not only to inaction, but to the notion that it is *impossible* for them to act. Columbia University professor Carolyn Heilbrun[1] reports that when two of her colleagues once asked twelve groups of women students in small workshops to invent stories in which a woman was the central character, only one of the twelve groups was able to do so. The others told fantasies in which a woman was loved by or rescued by a man, the true protagonist of the stories.

If one assumes that the "affective" side of life is the only one that really matters to women, then a series of other ideas logically follows. Women should feel good, content with themselves and their lives, only if their relationships with others, particularly their erotic relationships, are flourishing. Conversely, when women aren't involved in a love relationship, they should almost automatically become depressed. If a woman wants to be happy, this view implies, then the "true" route is to work hard on those all-important relationships. The conventional prescription has been: find a man, have children, and if you are still miserable, figure out how to be a more supportive wife to your husband and a more loving mother to your children.

Advice aimed at women is nearly always focused on how women can improve their relationships and on how they can improve themselves in the process. Advice columns for men usually deal with the instrumental, or the "doing" side of a man's life. How can he get a better job? Manage his money? Improve his sexual performance? But for a woman, it is what she feels that counts. In the classic "women's pictures" of the thirties, Katharine Hepburn and Joan Crawford may have been tough lady executives through three reels, but they found true happiness only when they gave it all up to fall into the arms of Tracy or Gable at the fade-out. And today, this conventional wisdom runs as a steady current through our social mores, despite the acres of newsprint devoted to women's ambitions and career plans. "Aim high!" and "Be serious about your work!" say some voices. But others, perhaps more insistent, sing the irresistible siren song whose lyrics warn that when women leave the domain of feeling for the world of doing, they run tremendous risks. We hear the dire warnings all around: women are starting to feel too much stress; they are having heart attacks just like men. Women will ruin their chances of happiness with a man if they get too involved in work. If women don't marry and have children, they will be condemned to a life of loveless misery. Men are becoming impotent because women are getting too ambitious. Society is falling apart because women have stepped beyond their traditional niche of home and hearth.

Often even the bravest words about women's "liberation" and need for self-discovery are tinged with anxiety. Women who are successful in the business world and who have a husband and children are displayed in magazine pages as heroines, proof that, yes, yes, a woman can succeed at work and not abandon the all-important world of feeling. It's the old idea dressed up with 1980s chic. What it says is that a woman's job is a fine accessory, an appetizer for the main dish, the warm-up act before the star comes on. If work is no longer taboo for a woman, it is still peripheral to her well-being, the "new-old" message reads: if you really want to know about the state of a woman's life, you need only look at her relationships with others, especially with men. They are the key ingredient in her well-being. The things that are happening in other areas of her life are not nearly so important. Love is what counts in this one-dimensional approach—and if things aren't going well in a woman's love life, that's where repairs are needed.

That's the conclusion you reach if you buy the conventional wisdom.

A word of caution: don't!

If that statement sounds flip, it isn't meant to be. It grows out of our study of the well-being of women and recent research by other social scientists. Some of our most important findings are:

• A woman who works hard at a challenging job is doing something positive for her mental health.

• Marriage and children do not guarantee well-being for a woman. Being without a man or being childless does not guarantee depression and misery.

• Doing and achieving are at least as important to the lives of women as are relationships and feelings. If that side of a woman's life is neglected, her self-esteem is endangered.

We are not saying that loving relationships with others are not extremely important to a woman's life. In fact, they are crucial to a full, rich life for both men and women, and to ignore this is to substitute a new inadequate one-dimensional approach for the old one.[2] But while a man is expected to temper his concern for love relationships with respect for the importance of his work, a woman who does so is suspect. Edward VIII gave up his throne for "the woman I love" and people still write of him with pity. It is assumed that the duties of being a king would have given him a more fulfilling life than the one he led. The possibility that he made the right choice is rejected out of hand, but a woman who gives up a career to marry is assumed to have chosen well.

Women too often tend to misunderstand the sources of their own well-being. The problem is one of proportion. People have assumed that feelings and relationships loom so large in the lives of women that virtually nothing else really matters, and many women have internalized this message. So, when they are depressed and want to feel better about themselves, they usually start looking in the wrong places. Often, they become obsessed about relationships: Will I meet the right man? Am I giving enough to this relationship? Do I love him enough? Should I be a better mother?

It is not that these are "wrong" questions, or that women—and men—should not be concerned with such issues. The problem is that for a woman, these questions may not always hold the key to her self-esteem, her pride, or her sense of being in charge of her life.

Our study documents the fundamental importance of both love and work—what Sigmund Freud saw as the twin pillars of a healthy life—to a woman's mental and emotional well-being. When either is ignored, a person's development becomes lopsided. The man who shuts off the emotional side of his life and throws himself entirely into activity becomes the workaholic. But we hear less about the other side of that coin—the woman who only pays attention to the feeling side of her life, and who becomes what might be called a "lovaholic." The workaholic can wind up overworked, exhausted, and emotionally sterile. The lovaholic risks feelings of worthlessness, dependency, and depression.

This is vital information for women today, because it comes at a time when powerful voices are urging women to return to a more limited sphere than the one they have begun to carve out for themselves. We hear once again that the home and the private world of family and emotions are the proper place for women. Only when women return home, abandoning the public domain and their career ambitions, the argument goes, will women be happy and society be whole again. The speakers are many, and often well-meaning. Some are from the fundamentalist religious movements gaining strength in this country. Some are politicians who ignore women in the political arena. Some are scientists who sound the alarm that women are in a sorry state, and that when women work, both the family and society suffer. In fact, there is a great deal of evidence to show that the marriages—and the children—of working mothers are no less and no more stable and happy than those with mothers at home. As for the problems of society, well, there is a long tradition in our culture of blaming women in eras of social change. When women campaigned for the vote, opponents of suffrage claimed that if women were given the power of the ballot, they would lose their privileged positions as queens of the home, would become tainted and corrupted by the evils of politics, and the family would be destroyed as a result.

The issue of the proper role of women in society is vital to the individual lives of every American woman. Should she listen to the voices that are calling for retreat and return, for a new triumph of the traditional role? Or should she ignore those voices, and continue on with a course that will carry her into unfamiliar territory? To answer those questions, she will first have to ask more basic ones. What makes a person happy? What are the ingredients of a full, rich life? What is well-being all about, for women?

Those were the fundamental questions we attempted to answer when this study was conceived. They are not simple questions, nor are there easy answers. Our first task was to develop a working definition of well-being. This task has concerned behavioral scientists for some time, and there is a substantial record of thought, study, and research in that area.

Well-being is something intangible. It can't be touched or seen or weighed. It is abstract like the idea of good health. Health is defined by a combination of things: normal blood pressure and temperature, absence of disease, a good energy level. To determine the state of your health, the doctor takes your blood pressure and temperature, gives you blood and urine tests, and then combines all the results with your report about how you're feeling to draw a conclusion about the state of your health.

In much the same way, psychologists base their assessment of a person's well-being on a variety of items and scales. In our study, the items and scales (found in the survey at the end of the book) measured a set of components crucial to our conception of well-being. We give here definitions of these components with some examples and with the number of the question(s) so that the interested reader can see exactly how each was measured:

• *Self-esteem: a high regard for oneself.*[3] Items measuring self-esteem ask about such feelings as confidence and inferiority, competence and incompetence, pride and shame. (Question #113)

• *A sense of control over one's life.* These items ask to what extent a woman feels able to shape her life as opposed to feeling helplessly carried along. (Question #104)

• *Absence of symptoms of anxiety and depression.* Items measuring symptoms ask how often in the past week a woman was bothered by such problems as crying easily, temper outbursts, feeling trapped or caught. (Question #85)

The next three well-being elements were each measured by simply asking a direct question. For optimism, for example, we asked: "When you think about the future, how do you usually feel—extremely hopeful, somewhat hopeful, not at all hopeful?"

• *Happiness: feelings of joy and delight.* (Question #109)

• *Satisfaction.* More deeply rooted and less transient than happiness, it comes from "stacking up" what has actually happened in one's life against expectations and desires. (Question #111)

• *Optimism.* A positive expectation about the future; the feeling that things will turn out well. (Question #112)

Studies of psychological well-being usually rely on what the person says in answer to researchers' questions. Although people can certainly distort or lie—even if their intent is to tell all—asking people about themselves is still the best way to study a person's sense of well-being, even if it is not a perfect way. The distinguished psychologist Gordon Allport made this point a long time ago. He often said, "If you want to know something about a person, ask." If you are able to create an atmosphere of rapport and trust in your interviews, you have a good chance of learning how a woman really sees herself and her life.

Subjects received scores on each of the well-being measures.

Our analysis of the relationships among these scores revealed a two-dimensional picture of well-being. We found a strong statistical relationship among self-esteem, control over one's life, and levels of anxiety and depression. For example, a woman who had high self-esteem and felt in control of her life typically had low scores on the depression scale. Because of this statistical relationship, we were able to identify the first dimension of well-being, which we called "Mastery."[4] We'll see that Mastery is strongly related to the doing side of life, the "instrumental" side.

That finding went hand in hand with another. We found a similar strong relationship among three other measures of well-being: happiness, satisfaction, and optimism. These scores also rose and fell together, giving us our other dimension, which we labeled "Pleasure." Pleasure is closely tied to the feeling side of life—the quality of one's relationships with others.[5]

Now we had a two-dimensional picture or model of well-being, one that was statistically based and that helped make sense of our data.[6] The two major components of well-being, then, are: 1) Mastery (self-esteem, sense of control, low levels of depression and anxiety), and 2) Pleasure (satisfaction, happiness, optimism). Why is this two-dimensional model of well-being so helpful to understanding women?

The answer is that this model gave us a way of looking at how a whole range of issues affect women. We can understand better why women feel good—or distressed—in certain circumstances. For example, why does the career woman who takes a year off to have a baby sometimes report she feels intense joy but is fighting feelings of worthlessness? Often it's because she is nourishing the Pleasure side of well-being, while Mastery is temporarily being neglected. What about the woman struggling through law school while trying to raise a family, who finds she and her husband have too little time to spend together? Why does she feel new waves of self-confidence but at the same time experience less enjoyment in her life? Because she is paying attention to Mastery, while Pleasure is for the moment at least, being short-changed.

The concepts of Mastery and Pleasure can help us pinpoint the sources of well-being for women, and answer important questions. For instance, what impact does having a paid job have on Mastery? What impact does it have on Pleasure? We can ask the same questions for marriage, children, income, sexuality, and so on. One of the most important tasks of this book is to describe how, and in what ways, all these affect the two components of a woman's sense of well-being.

In this book, we are going to focus heavily on Mastery, because its importance to women's well-being has been so often overlooked. As we've noted, Mastery is tied to the doing and achieving part of life. But women have often been encouraged to downplay the importance of achievement and to concentrate solely on emotions and relationships. This is what we mean when we say that women "look in the wrong place" for sources of good feelings—and for the roots of bad ones as well.

Women often experience a puzzling malaise that they express by asking, "Why am I unhappy? or "Why am I depressed?", usually followed by "What is wrong with me?" What they may be missing is a sense of Mastery, but they don't often say, "I need to feel more important" or "I'm upset because I am not running my own life." When they seek help, often they are told only to take a hard look at their relationships. For example, a depressed housewife is asked how she feels about her husband, or how she relates to her children. Rarely is she asked "What do you do all day?" and "Does it use your talents?" Yet, her central problem may be that she is grappling with a lack of structure and challenge in her daily life. Lack of structure, we know, can be murderous. Men are expected to have enormous problems when they leave the structured environment of work at retirement or when they become unemployed; many feel useless, empty, unmotivated. But the woman at home who feels the same way is too often advised to focus only on her relationships, which may not be the issue at all. Betty Friedan spoke in *The Feminine Mystique* of "the problem that has no name" to which women at home are uniquely vulnerable. When women who adore their husbands and love their children still feel depressed and useless, they are often surprised. They "know" they are supposed to be perfectly happy because the emotional side of their lives is in good order. Often they don't realize that it is the doing side of their lives that is the problem. A woman in this situation could work harder on her relationships but it would change little. It's like pumping air into the left front tire when the right rear one is flat.

But, of course, it is not only the housewife who falls victim to the "wrong place" syndrome. An unmarried working woman often experiences the same feeling of something missing. She too might focus only on examining her relationships, sure that her discontent is due to what is or is not happening in her love life. But an equally important problem may be that she is in a job that gives her little sense of pride or self-esteem. Perhaps getting a better job or going back to school may be the key to feeling better, not just a change in her love life. Many women, when they feel unhappy, automatically think of improving their relationships or improving themselves, and fail to pay attention to the instrumental side of life. They think:

"Things would be fine if only I could meet a man."

"Things would be fine if only I could marry this man I am going with."

"Things would be fine if only I had a child."

But when the real problem is in the area of Mastery, such a woman would find that a changed relationship wouldn't really change her life. She would go from being a woman *without* a man who felt bad about herself to being a woman *with* a man who felt bad about herself; or, she would change from an unhappy non-mother to an unhappy mother. Often women in this situation not only fall into the trap of exaggerating how wonderful their lives would be "if" only they had a man (or a wedding ring, or a child), they also tend to exaggerate the unhappiness of their lives.

Many women who are not married have had unrealistic notions of how wonderful married women must feel. When psychologists Veroff, Douvan, and Kulka looked at attitudes toward marriage in *The Inner American,* they found that women who had never married had a rosier picture of marriage than did women who were married, or who had been married. It's the old truism: the grass always seems greener on the other side of the fence.

An exaggerated view of marital bliss is not surprising, given that women have been told that true happiness comes from love relationships. But these relationships can only enrich and deepen a person's life—they cannot transform who a person is. If love is woman's whole existence, then women don't exist at all. One must bring a self into a relationship, one is not created by it. A healthy life demands the integration of both the instrumental and the affective domains. Yet in today's atmosphere of backlash on "women's issues," we see a renewed emphasis on the importance of traditional family life and relationships, and a devaluing of other needs and goals, especially those on the instrumental side. For women, we believe, there is a danger of sliding into the lovaholic syndrome, and this, we believe, can further aggravate the looking-in-the-wrong-place phenomenon. Several recent bestsellers by writers trying to help women reflect this bias. In Maggie Scarf's *Unfinished Business,* a painstaking study of depressed women, the major thesis is that depression is related mainly to loss of relationships. While Scarf's advice to women—that they have to learn to be more independent—is certainly sound, we have serious questions about her main premise.[7]

In her study, Scarf saw women who were disturbed enough to seek medical treatment for depression. These were clinically depressed women, not women who were experiencing, as all of us do at times, feelings of unhappiness or loss. These women had a great many problems in their relationships. One question is: were these women depressed because of problems with their relationships, or were their relationships in shambles because they were depressed? Scarf assumed that the former was the case, but as we've seen, women who feel bad about themselves often mistakenly think love is the problem; a woman who tells you she is depressed because of problems with her husband may not be giving you the right diagnosis. Were there other issues in these women's lives that, in fact, might have been more central to their depression?

Another question is, what relevance do the cases of clinically depressed women have for the lives of women in general? This is part of a much larger question: can you learn much about people who are well by looking at people who are not? Is "abnormality" simply an extension of "normality?" Because these women were depressed and had problems with loss in relationships, does that mean that women in general risk depression mainly, or only, when their relationships are not going well? Our data suggest that this is not so. We found symptoms of depression and low self-esteem among women with few difficulties or deprivations in their relationships but with major problems in their work life. Conversely, many women—for example, divorced women with satisfying jobs—reported serious problems in relationships yet were not depressed. When one's sense of selfhood and role in society is intact, one can usually tolerate a reasonable amount of unhappiness or dissatisfaction in relationships without developing symptoms of depression and anxiety. In an important study done in England,[8] researchers found that among women experiencing major stress in their lives, merely being employed, regardless of the kind of job, helped protect women from developing psychiatric symptoms. We would argue that this is because work can provide a sense of self-esteem, meaning, and control often hard to come by in the thorny area of human relationships. It's not that work should replace love as *the* fountain of well-being. Our study and the work of many other researchers document the critical role relationships play in our lives and the devastating effects loneliness can have. Rather, it's that any one part of life can become problematic, and if that's all you have, your vulnerability is intensified.

The best "preventive medicine" for women against depression is fostering their sense of Mastery. The confident, autonomous woman is likely to be less vulnerable to depression. If we continue to insist that we will find the answers to a woman's problems— and a source for all her joys—only in the realm of her feelings toward others, we will keep on looking in the wrong place.

CHAPTER TWO

WHAT ABOUT ME?

CAROLYN STONE, at fifty-three, is the coordinator of women's programs for a small foundation. She married in her twenties and thought that she would have the ideal American family: "I would be the perfect mother, the kind who would create elaborate birthday parties where you make all the food and the decorations yourself. I thought my whole life would be focused around my family."

But when her two daughters were preteen-agers, her marriage broke up. She went back to school to get an M.B.A. and later married again. The funding for her present job is running out, but she is optimistic about the future:

"It is marvelous to be fifty-three. I just love being the age that I am. It represents everything that I've been through. I have no desire to be thirty again, or forty. I look to the future with great enthusiasm. You know, there is the underlying anxiety of whether someone will hire a fifty-three-year-old woman, but I think they will and I think this is a great age."

For thirty-eight-year-old Marilyn Walker, her twenties were rocky years. She came from a poor and troubled family; her father was abusive when he was drunk. She married a man she thought was different from her father, because, she says, he came from an affluent background, lived in a nice house, and drove a nice car. Even though he abused her physically at times during their courtship, she believed him when he said things would be fine when they were married. But the abuse continued. It took her thirteen years to leave him, because, "I was scared to death of him."

Now she supports her two children as a bookkeeper. She likes her job because it gives her independence. "It makes me feel good.

I'm liked and respected. Sometimes I get aggravated because there isn't enough time to keep the house the way I want it, but I've learned, who cares?"

Her relationship with her children is very close, and she says, "I feel very good about myself, better than I ever have in my life. I feel I'm handling something that's big and I guess a lot of people didn't think I could. . . . Maybe I feel this way because I showed them—but I don't think it's just that, because that would have passed. It's within myself that I feel darn good about it."

Carolyn and Marilyn, two women who are near the opposite ends of the age spectrum of our study, echo a new theme that is being heard among American women today. It is the resounding cry of "I feel good about myself!"

This is not to say that we didn't find women who were depressed, who had little self-regard, or who thought their life hadn't turned out very well. We did find such women; but on the whole, the women in our survey scored high on our measures of well-being. And one of our most important findings was that among women thirty-five to fifty-five level of well-being was not related to age. Women in their fifties reported feelings about their lives similar to those of women in their thirties. The two components of well-being—Mastery and Pleasure—do not decline as a woman gets older. In fact, many women find that the years of middle adulthood are turning out to be much better than their youthful years. As one forty-five-year-old mother of two puts it: "I never felt like anything when I was younger. I never felt attractive, never felt as sure of myself as I do now. When I think of the future, I think positive. People are listening to me now. They never listened before."

The fact that women in their fifties seem as positive about their lives as do women in their thirties has important implications, both for young women looking ahead and for older women making decisions about the present course of their lives. Women in the middle years haven't always presented a glowing picture of health: as we've noted, studies in the 1950s showed these women to be a particularly depressed group, often anxious and pessimistic about the future.[1] The contrast between the women in those studies and today's midlife women raises the question, why such a dramatic turnaround in thirty years?

We believe that it is not so much that women have changed as individuals, but that the society around them has changed. There were earlier attempts to challenge and change the situation of women, but today new ideas about women's roles have permeated our whole culture. Doors previously barred are swinging open. The fences around the small piece of turf—home and family—where so many women were confined, are coming down. The world beyond the front stoop is no longer an alien landscape for women. The events, ideas, and attitudes known collectively as "the women's movement" have created a new social climate for women. Given the data on women's psychological well-being before and after the advent of the movement, we would argue that no other phenomenon seems adequate to account for the change.

Why are women—especially those in middle adulthood—feeling better off? The new social climate, we believe, by giving women more choices, also gives them more opportunity than ever before to enhance their sense of Mastery. For most women, there is more freedom today than at any time in the past to explore and develop the "doing" side of their lives, their instrumental capabilities.

In their search for a sense of Mastery, which depends so heavily on a sense of self-worth and of control, women must ask a very important question: what about me? It is a question that until quite recently was taboo. A woman who had the temerity to ask it was more often than not branded as selfish and narcissistic. It is still not an easy question for most women.

But the ability to say "What about me?" is vital to the well-being of women. Why has it been so difficult? The answer is embedded in our culture and in the ways women have been socialized from childhood through their adult years. They have been expected to find their own joy and satisfaction primarily through giving to others.

This belief is so ingrained that it has colored not only society's attitudes, but its language as well. To choose a name for our second well-being factor—made up of happiness, satisfaction, optimism—we searched through the dictionary, seeking an appropriate word. Under the word *pleasure,* this sentence was used to illustrate its proper use: "She took pleasure in seeing her son succeed." But when we decided to also check the word *joy,* the usage of that word was illustrated this way: "He found joy in writing his poems." The old attitudes not only haven't vanished, you can't escape them.

These attitudes create what might be called a "nurturant imperative" for women. Its constant pressure inevitably influences a woman's behavior, thoughts, and feelings, often creating guilt if she even *starts* to examine her own needs. Social scientists have only recently begun to examine the power of such attitudes; to discover how deeply ingrained the idea is that women exist mainly to nurture others. In fact, psychologist Carol Gilligan of Harvard tells us that concern for others is central to the way in which women make moral decisions about their lives.[2]

All of us make many such decisions in the course of a lifetime. We do it every time we face a choice which sets our needs and desires against those of others and requires us to figure out how to juggle those needs: Should I accept a new job that takes me further away from my widowed mother? Is my desire to return to school going to hurt my children? Must I give in to my husband's corporate employer who wants us to move our family for the fifth time? The *way* we make decisions, not just the actual decisions about what is right and wrong, has a great impact on our life, and, according to Gilligan, men and women often make these decisions very differently.

The scientific study of moral decision-making is fairly new. It was pioneered by Lawrence Kohlberg of Harvard, who developed a method of scoring the basis on which people make moral judgments.[3] He found that people can be classified according to "stages" of decision-making. Those at the lower end of his scale make decisions in the least autonomous way—because an authority figure says it is right, or because of peer pressure, for example. Young people who follow the dictates of some cult group fall into this category.

Those at the other end of the spectrum, at the highest stage of moral reasoning, are people who have internalized a set of principles and act on the basis of those principles rather than being guided by what others think or feel. Many Russian dissidents, who defy the political and moral power of the state, and who face ostracism for standing up for what they believe to be right, are such people.

But interestingly enough, when women were tested on Kohlberg's scale, they seldom reached the highest level of decision-making. They rarely saw an abstract principle as the only basis for making a moral decision. Therefore, women did not score as "high" in moral decision-making as did men. Does this mean that women are simply not capable of the highest level of reasoning? Are their brains so clouded by fuzzy emotionalism that they can't achieve moral greatness?

Carol Gilligan says this is not the case at all. Rather, women view moral situations in a complex way. They tend to give great weight to the impact a decision would have on the people involved. Making a decision on principle alone seems too bloodless, too narrow, for most women. A decision that would be in accord with a principle, but would bring great sorrow or harm to others, would be anathema to most women. Gilligan argues that women's moral decision-making is not inferior to men's; it is just different, bringing to bear an intense awareness of the needs and concerns of others. When Kohlberg developed his theory and his measures and scoring system, he used only male subjects. Because women were not included, his approach therefore lacks validity not only for women, but for human beings as a whole. Rethinking this area of moral decision-making is an important task which brings together scholars from many disciplines and in which both women and men have a stake.

The moral imperative that girls learn from their earliest days— care for others—is one of the qualities that psychoanalyst Jean Baker Miller calls a hidden strength of women.[4] It is a quality that is too scarce in our society, she argues. Because men too often are not encouraged to grow up with the sense of "I must care for those who are not me," they are short-changed; as a result, the lives of too many men can be sterile and alienated. Belief in the moral value of caring for others, Miller points out, creates the sense of community and wholeness that makes society something other than a savage battlefield.

But if the nurturant imperative is one of women's strengths, when overdone it can become self-destructive. Women have to "include themselves," as Gilligan puts it, in the list of people who are to be nurtured. If they can give only to others and never to themselves, they fail to develop their own sense of self and the results are feelings of low self-esteem. After all, if you see yourself as the last person on the list of those who "get," how valuable can you be? And when you can't ask for things, you have little control over what you get, and often wind up feeling powerless and cheated.

The new self-interest that women are reporting today is a crucial

part of why they are feeling so good. But it is often hard to talk
about self-interest on the part of women without setting off an alarm
buzzer in the heads of many people, particularly women themselves.
The word "self-interest" conjures up images of the neglectful
mother, the self-centered wife, the competitive co-worker. The
"ideal" woman is supportive, self-sacrificing, always giving. She is
the woman you see in the TV commercials, happily dispensing lem-
onade to all the kids on the block, getting up in the middle of
the night to fetch the cold tablets for the husband who has the
sniffles, rushing to the washing machine to scrub the ring out of
her husband's shirt collar. She is the Joan of Arc of self-sacrifice,
immolating herself with everybody else's needs. She is also the
woman who is a good candidate for the psychiatrist's couch or
the Valium bottle, who complains of low energy levels, feelings of
hopelessness, and nameless anxiety and dread. The woman who
always puts others first, who can't see that she deserves some of
the "goodies" of life herself, may be particularly susceptible to depression.

There is a particularly compelling need today for women to
keep this in mind, because we are seeing an increasing level of
attacks on the "selfishness" of women. There are allegations that
all kinds of social ills, from runaway children to the neglected elderly, are due to the fact that women have left their "rightful" place
in the home. Such arguments are simplistic and wrongheaded, but
women are especially vulnerable to the accusation that if society
has problems, it's because women aren't nurturing enough. The
influential voices of the "neoconservative" movement speak of a
golden age when people had respect for authority, country, and
duty. They fail to mention, however, that the times of which they
speak were golden only for a white, male, affluent elite.

A case in point is the concept of "narcissism," popularized
by Christopher Lasch's book *The Culture of Narcissism*. Lasch argues that we, as a nation, have become self-obsessed and selfish,
looking inward while neglecting others and the body politic. He
cites as evidence the growth of "pop" psychology, the rush to evan-
gelical religion, the drug culture—and the women's movement. His
arguments may have merit when applied to some aspects of societal
behavior, but to lump the women's movement into the culture of
narcissism is to misunderstand profoundly what is happening to
women today. The women in our study bear little resemblance to

the caricature of the self-obsessed, selfish woman who is saying, "All for me and to hell with everybody else!" In fact, for most women, it is a tremendous struggle just to arrive at a point where they can say, "Me too."

The gains made by women in the past decade may seem impressive, but it is easy to forget how tenuous they can be. History shows that advances made by women in one era can vanish in another. Many young women may assume that the rights and opportunities they now possess can never disappear. To believe this is to underestimate the power of the ideas that even today are beginning to erode the momentum of women's progress. There is a seductive nostalgia surrounding the world that neoconservatives such as Lasch evoke. They celebrate a society in which, as Carolyn Heilbrun puts it in *Reinventing Womanhood,* "all that is noble in civilization—order, peace, honor, and beauty as well as the family and community—these values and institutions are maintained at the price of women's labor." She says that whenever men yearn for a lost culture, they forget the cost of that culture to women. It is understandable that some men sing the praises of a time when men were free to fight glorious wars, build towering edifices, and write great poems because women subsidized their efforts by keeping the workaday world going—minding the children, cleaning the house, and putting meals on the table. Women did not disturb the rhythms of the male world by daring to ask the question, "What about me?" Today, however, women are not remaining silent.

"There are only twenty-four hours in a day, and if you try to do too much, be everything to everybody—the ultimate mother, the perfect housewife, and the devoted daughter to your parents and the perfect wife to your husband—well, there isn't enough of you to go around," says a fifty-four-year-old mother of six, who has recently found a job as a physical education instructor and who has taken up painting as a serious hobby. "I did try to do too much," she says. "I had a period there where I began to think, When am I ever going to have time for myself? What about me?"

It is a question women must consider seriously if they are to reach the state of good mental health we call "well-being." That may seem obvious, but where women are concerned, too often it isn't. If this were a book about men, we wouldn't have to make the point that a person should be concerned with his own personal development and welfare. But with women, the nurturant imperative is so strong that they often hear this message and reject it because it sounds like selfishness. Yet the woman who feels good about herself and her life, who has high self-esteem and is able to see that her own needs are met, as well as those of others, is more able to relate to others in a healthy way. The woman who feels that she is nothing unless she is constantly giving, who is in constant need of reassurance, or who falls into the martyr role—getting what she wants by stirring up guilt in those around her—creates misery for others as well as herself. But in the past, there has been far too little emphasis on self-development as being crucial to a woman's life.

When a woman allows herself to ask "What about me?" she sets in motion a chain reaction of consequences. She allows herself options, which means that she must make choices: Should I marry? Have children? Go to graduate school? Questions that seem settled may get reopened: Should I change jobs? Get a divorce?

The more a woman is able to choose for herself the roles and activities that suit her individual needs and desires, the more she will increase her well-being. One of the most important findings to come out of our research is that being where you want to be is good for you. We found a very strong correlation between preferring the role you are in and well-being. The homemaker who is at home because she likes that "job," because it meets her own desires and needs, tends to feel good about her life. The woman at work who wants to be there also rates high in well-being.

It may seem like plain common sense to say that people will feel good if they are doing what they want to do. But in the past, women often found themselves in life roles not because they, as individuals, made choices for themselves, but because they were doing what *all* women were supposed to do. For too many, the fit between "woman's place" and their own abilities was poor. In an important, large-scale national survey, *The Quality of American Life,* published in 1976 by a team of social scientists at the University of Michigan, the researchers compared employed women and women at home, and found generally similar levels of satisfaction among the two groups—with one striking exception. College-educated homemakers scored lower on satisfaction than both workers and other homemakers. Not only were they lower in well-being, these women often had marital problems as well. "It is the highly educated housewife who does not have an outside job whose marriage seems most likely to be beset by disagreements, lack of understanding and companionship, doubts and dissatisfaction," the researchers concluded.[5]

These were women who possessed skills and abilities perhaps best used in the workplace, but because they were not using those skills, their well-being—and their marriages—suffered.

Some women, aware of society's views on woman's proper role, try to blot out their own needs and force themselves to do their "duty." But in the long run, this won't work. The consequences of being where you don't want to be often spill over and affect other lives as well as your own. For example, when a team of researchers at the National Institute of Mental Health studied mothers of elementary school children in 1962, they took into account whether or not the women were in the roles they preferred. The researchers scored the women on a complex "adequacy of mothering" index and found that the lowest scores on that index were those of full-time homemakers who were at home because it was their "duty" to be there.[6] The message is clear: the women who were bending their own needs out of shape to do the "right" thing for their children were, unknowingly, hobbling their ability to be good mothers.

A major message of this book, then, is that making one's own choices about the future is crucial for well-being. For women, there are greater opportunities to do so now than at any time in our history. But sometimes opportunities are mixed blessings; when you have the power to make your own decisions, you also have the opportunity to make mistakes. The outcome can't be guaranteed. While having options is crucial, being in charge of your own life isn't easy. It's important to be aware that it's hard and sometimes feels lonely and downright scary. You might not make the right choice. You might fail at something you choose to do.

So women do give up something when they take control of their own destinies—they give up the security of being dependent. While dependency has negative long-term consequences, in the short run it can be very comfortable. It's easier to let other people make decisions for you than to make them yourself. When you make your own decisions, you give up the right to be a victim, since you can't blame others for your life if it is one you have chosen. It's very human to want to blame somebody other than yourself when things go wrong. There is a certain comfort in saying, "My life is rotten because my boss is an unfeeling cad!" or "If my husband made a decent living, I would have a good life."

Some women feel pressured or resentful when they realize they have to choose. As one woman in her thirties put it: "I think in some ways I'm angry about the women's movement because it has forced me into thinking about things that I would have been more comfortable not thinking about. It's hard to make choices in your life. But women's liberation has taken that away from women. You can no longer be home and play a martyr role, because now you have a choice—it's blatantly there. But it's been good for me, because now I know I'm not at home with my children because I feel I have to be, but because I've made that choice. It's what I want to do, and I'm enjoying it."

In fact, while making choices may seem—and in fact may be—risky, the "old way" may have been even riskier; the aura of safety in having others decide for you is simply an illusion. There is no such thing as a "sure bet" in this life. Well-reasoned, thoughtfully made plans can still go astray, but there is less risk in shaping a life to your own individual abilities than there is in simply accepting a one-size-fits-all life pattern. When you drift into a style of life because it is what others think you should do, you may end up feeling at the end of a leash—powerless and out of control. And, as we've seen, these feelings are linked with the malady that has been called the "woman's disease"—depression.

When we give workshops and seminars on women's issues, one theme emerges very often during question and answer sessions. Women often ask, "What exactly should I do to make sure things will come out right?" It's as if women are searching for a new version of the old magic formula, which was: "Just get married and have children and you'll be happy." That formula didn't guarantee well-being and neither will any other. We all live with some degree of risk and uncertainty.

But it isn't only women who are looking for certainty. There is a deep human longing for a world in which things come out right, virtue is rewarded, well-laid plans never go awry. This wish runs so deep that it often leads to a distorted view of reality.[7] People look around and see that the divorce rate is high, crime is on the rise, families are having problems. Because of their wish to believe in a well-ordered world, they view this as a temporary aberration: the times are out of joint. It is hard to accept the fact that the times are always out of joint. Instead, people look backward to some nonexistent Eden, where there was tranquility and justice, and ask, "What went wrong?"

The next step, unfortunately, is to look for a villain, and today, as we've noted, women are handy. "If only they would return to their proper place, things would be fine again!" cry the voices. Women, with their selfish demands, are disrupting the Eden in which all was well with the world. If women would only go back to being what they were, chaos would end and we would all live happily ever after.

We have to see this illusion for what it is: nostalgia, not reality; wishful thinking, not a solution for social problems. Women will accomplish nothing for society—and will only harm themselves and those closest to them—if they can't let themselves ask, "What about me?"

THE WELL-SPRINGS OF MASTERY AND PLEASURE

I feel like one of the things that has been happening to me recently is the sense that I have a great deal more control over what happens. I feel more in touch with the factors in myself that cause things to happen. I would say that ten years ago, or perhaps even two years ago, I would have felt more as if things happened to me.

Roseann Marshall, 39, an actress who is single

As WOMEN GAIN more control over their own destinies, as they begin to take different directions in their lives, an interesting change is occurring. They are becoming less alike. In the past, when women had little freedom to choose the roads they would travel, they undoubtedly seemed, on the surface, very similar. Perhaps that's why too many mental health professionals have tended to treat all women the same way, assuming that one role pattern would fit them all. But today, as women begin to look for ways to meet individual needs, it becomes much harder to ignore the differences, to say that what holds true for one woman is equally true of another.

We are now beginning to look closely at women in different

roles, to find out what elements of these roles contribute to—or hamper—the sense of well-being. We can no longer simply assume that any particular role is "good" or "bad" for women. We should apply what might be called a "cost-benefit analysis" to each one. There are advantages and drawbacks to every lifeprint, and to understand how life turns out for women in different roles we must first understand these pluses and minuses.

Our study gives us a good opportunity to weigh the advantages and drawbacks of the various lifeprints available to women. The women who participated have felt the impact in their own lives of many of the changes that Americans are experiencing and that will continue to affect us in the forseeable future. Their lives have been influenced by the large number of women moving into the labor force, the women's movement, the new self-awareness created by the rising educational level of the population, and changing attitudes toward sexuality, marriage, and divorce.

They have also experienced a major shift in the predominant pattern of life roles for women that has taken place over the past decades. Whether or not many other people in society are doing what you are doing can be critical to your sense of support and approval. When the women in our study were growing up, working women were the "deviant" group, and they often felt isolated and stigmatized. Today, however, it is the homemakers in our sample who often feel alone and misunderstood by those around them, while working women are experiencing a newfound sense of support. These trends are not likely to be reversed in the years ahead; the lives of the women in our sample are therefore highly relevant to women who are now in their twenties or early thirties.

One of the most important aims of our study was to examine different groups of women to see what their lives are like. What are the well-springs of Mastery and Pleasure for women in different roles? What are the areas of risk and vulnerability? The sources of stress? Are some roles a "good bet" for well-being and are others particularly problematic?

One way to get answers to these questions is to focus in turn on each of the six separate groups of women in our study. We've devised a set of symbols for each of these groups, so that we can show how they stand on a visual "map" of well-being. The six groups with their sets of symbols are:

Never-married,
employed

Married with
children, at home

Married without
children,
employed

Married without
children, at home

Married with
children,
employed

Divorced with
children,
employed

We wanted to discover the sources of well-being for these groups of women and in the process, of course, also learn about the opposite, about what diminishes Mastery and Pleasure.

To do these crucial analyses, we started with a set of items and scales that measured components we believed would have a significant impact on well-being. We based our expectations about what affects well-being on prior research, clinical experience, and, most of all, on the long interviews with the sixty-two women in our "snowball" sample. Some components, or "variables," were "classic" ones that researchers often ask about, such as age, income, and education. Others are from a more clinical tradition: the quality of a woman's marriage, her relationship with her mother. Because our funding enabled us to take advantage of sophisticated computer technology, we could ask what impact, if any, each of these many items had on a woman's sense of Mastery and level of Pleasure.

The computer analysis gave us a composite picture of each of our six groups of women and allowed us to determine not only how high or low each of these groups were in Mastery and Pleasure, but also what specific elements were most responsible.

Perhaps the best way to understand the differences among the six groups is to actually see them, on a map of well-being. Below is a computer-based picture that shows at a glance the relative positions of our six groups. The vertical line represents Mastery; the horizontal line represents Pleasure.

The groups inside the circles are our four groups of employed women, the two groups inside the triangles are the homemakers.

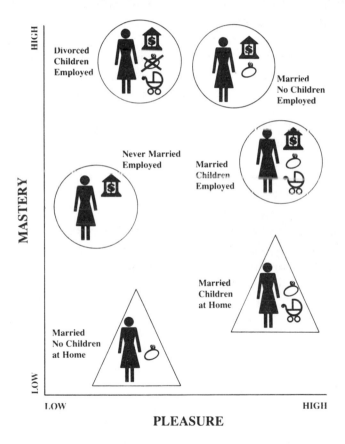

The circles and triangles highlight how our groups look on Mastery. What is dramatically illustrated on the map is that the groups of working women are all in or near the top half of the

Mastery scale. Whether married or not, whether they have children or not, they are all higher than the groups of homemakers. As we'll see, homemakers are doing well with respect to Pleasure, but Mastery is a problem area for them. So, paid work is the element that best determines whether a woman ranks high or low in the area of Mastery. Because of this, we will pay considerable attention to the role of work in women's lives throughout the book.

It is also important and intriguing to note that divorced women are the highest group of all in sense of Mastery. When Gail Sheehy[1] looked for what she called "pathfinders"—people who had undergone major changes in their lives and were high in well-being, she found that divorced women often fit that description. What's the reason for this? We think it's that the divorced women in our sample, all of whom have been divorced for at least a year, and on average, seven years, have for the most part been able to get their lives on track again after a very rocky period. They have encountered and dealt with a difficult challenge. They have coped with being both a single parent and breadwinner; many reported having to do this with little outside support. As one thirty-eight-year-old woman put it: "I found out a few things about myself that I didn't know were there. And in the last few years I've taken care of the home, the kids, handled a job. It makes me feel proud. I often say, there's nothing I can't handle as long as I'm healthy!"

It is also intriguing to note the high well-being—Mastery and Pleasure—of the busiest women in our study, the employed, married women with children. These are the women so many people worry about, assuming they have high levels of stress and conflict and overly full lives. But as we can see, these women are doing very well indeed. In our chapter on multiple roles (Chapter Eight), we will examine why these women are thriving despite busy and hectic lives.

Let us focus now on women's sense of Pleasure. Is there some key to the level of Pleasure similar to the role of paid work in enhancing the sense of Mastery? Looking at the Pleasure scores of all our groups, we see a pattern there as well: whether employed or not, whether mothers or not, the four groups of married women are all higher in Pleasure than the two groups of nonmarried women. Why is this so? The answer is not simply that the status of "married woman" brings Pleasure. Rather, we believe that Pleasure is tied to what we will call "arenas of intimacy."

   All of us function in a number of close relationships in our lives. We are the children of parents and sometimes the parents of children. We are spouses, lovers, friends. Each of these relationships is a small world unto itself, an "arena," if you will. We all know that such relationships can enrich our lives, but what our study tells us is that the more of these arenas in which you function, the more opportunities you have for deriving Pleasure. We don't mean that the greater the number of relationships you have, the happier you are—it's not a matter of quantity and score-keeping. But opportunities for meaningful close relationships do grow out of these arenas, in the sense that being a spouse, a parent, a daughter offers chances for intimacy that might otherwise be hard to find. Taking a look at the next map of well-being, you can see graphically how this works.

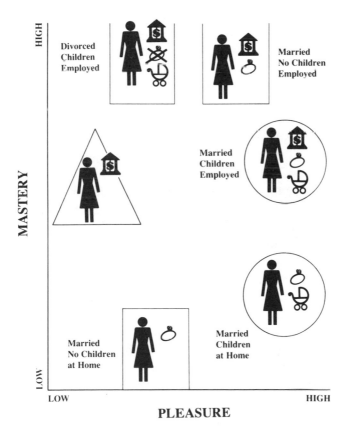

Inside the circles are the two groups of women, the married working mothers and the married homemakers with children, who function in two major arenas of intimacy. The women in these groups are both spouses and parents, and their Pleasure scores are the highest in the sample—nearly identical.

Inside the boxes are the three groups having only one arena of intimacy; two of these groups of women are wives—married, working women without children, and married childless women at home—and the other group is made up of divorced women who are mothers. The Pleasure scores of these groups are similar. In the triangle is the one group that has no "built-in" arena of intimacy, the never-married women; their Pleasure scores are the lowest in the sample.

For women who are both mothers and wives, one reason for their high levels of Pleasure, we believe, is that these roles, by their nature, build in arenas of intimacy and thus opportunities for gratifying relationships. One certainly doesn't have to be married or be a mother to have long-term satisfying relationships, but marriage and parenthood make it more likely.

These are group data, of course, and there are many exceptions to the general rule. Many women who are wives and/or mothers do not find satisfaction in their relationships; many women who are neither build close relationships they find very satisfying. But those don't automatically come with the lifestyle they have chosen.

Examining our findings, we began to notice an important phenomenon. When we looked at married homemakers both with and without children, for example, we noticed that their sense of Mastery, compared to other groups, was heavily dependent on their husbands' approval. We wondered why this was so, given that Mastery tends to be affected more by "doing" issues—employment, income—rather than by relationships. As we looked at the different groups, an explanation seemed likely to us, one that we have labeled "out-of-step anxiety." When women feel that they are defying the dictates of society, they often feel self-doubt and are in need of support for their threatened sense of self-esteem.

We are all affected by what others expect of us. When we are doing what society says we're supposed to do, we feel reassured. When we aren't, we often feel anxious. Women have probably been more vulnerable than men to this "out-of-step" anxiety. We've seen that women make moral decisions that put great emphasis on the needs of others. We think that they also evaluate their own lifestyle choices in much the same way. Their concern about how others view their choices and how these affect others may heighten their awareness of disapproval. Men are often told to put their heads down and charge—"damn the torpedoes and full speed ahead." Women aren't supposed to act this way, and often they are alert for signs of approval—or disapproval. So it is understandable that feeling out of step can be more distressing for women than for men.

When we thought about which groups of women might be vulnerable to out-of-step anxiety, we made an unexpected discovery. They all were vulnerable, but in different ways. Never-married women can feel out of step because they are not married; divorced women can feel that way because they aren't married any longer. Childless women often feel different because they don't have children, and employed women who do have children often feel anxious because they have departed from the "proper" role they were socialized to play. And the one group of women that did follow the expected route of marrying, staying home, and raising children now find that the rules have changed—suddenly, society is questioning the value of what they are doing. It's nearly impossible to be a woman today and not feel out of step.

If you feel out-of-step anxiety, it helps to have someone to validate your lifestyle, someone to say, "You're an okay person." It's precisely at this point that relationships can bolster the sense of Mastery. The most recent research on "social supports," that is, on helpful relationships in times of stress, shows that people help most by maintaining the self-esteem of the person feeling the strain.[2]

The maps of well-being illustrate where our groups of women are in terms of Mastery and Pleasure, but can't tell us how they got where they are. What best accounts for their levels of Mastery and Pleasure? To answer this question, we looked at each group separately in terms of our analyses of the variables thought to affect well-being. Based on these analyses, we'll highlight what seems most important in understanding the six groups, what makes the most difference to Mastery and Pleasure. Let's begin with what has been the most frequent role pattern for adult women, married homemakers with children.

Married with children, at home

Looking first at Mastery, we found that for women in this group there were two variables that made a major difference in a woman's Mastery score. One was the sense that her husband approved of her role choice—in other words, he liked the fact that she was home. The other was his help in doing household and child-care jobs usually thought of as "feminine," such as cooking and laundry.

It was interesting—and a bit disturbing—to see how closely the self-esteem of these women was tied to their husbands' approval. The women appear to be judging themselves by how their husbands see them—or more precisely, by how they *think* their husbands see them. Of the six groups in our study, only the two homemaker groups were so tied to their spouses' attitude for sense of Mastery.

This brings up an important concept: the risk factors and "vulnerable zones" associated with different role patterns. As we looked at the groups of women, we wanted to learn what aspects of their lives might leave them vulnerable to distress. For homemakers, what we call the "zone of vulnerability" is clearly their dependence on their husbands' approval. But another person's approval is often unstable, particularly over long periods of time. The following letter to Ann Landers is a grim illustration:

> I promised my husband I would return to work when our daughter was 6 months old. I figured by then I would be ready to take her off the breast and put her on the bottle. Well, she will be 6 months old in two weeks and I am NOT ready.
>
> I have this tremendous feeling of guilt because I am not contributing financially. It is very difficult to make ends meet with one paycheck. We do manage if I cut corners, and I'm trying, but my husband has told me I must keep my word and go back to work.
>
> How can I convince him that I need to stay home at least another month or two? Emotionally I am so torn. Please help.
> *Boston Globe,* December 10, 1981

One of us recently went to a dinner party, and listened with dismay as a man said, loudly enough so his homemaker wife could hear, "I wish she would go out and get a good job like yours." This man was probably delighted with the time and attention his wife gave him in earlier years, but now, with the kids getting older and college expenses looming, with inflation making a dent in his income, he had suddenly withdrawn his approval of her lifestyle. A woman in this position is in a terrible bind. She did what her husband wanted her to do all these years—and suddenly the rug has been pulled out from under her. Of all the women in our sample, the two groups of homemakers had the fewest years of education and are probably the least equipped to enter the job market, find challenging work, and command a good salary.

When her husband's approval is suddenly withdrawn, such a woman is in real trouble as far as self-esteem and sense of control are concerned. And the homemaker whose sense of Mastery is so tied to her husband is also in trouble if she should lose him by death or divorce. Statistically these are not unlikely events.

Why should a husband's sharing tasks around the house that are usually seen as "woman's work" contribute to a homemaker's sense of Mastery? In the past, women sometimes guarded their "jobs" fiercely and shooed away husbands who tried to help, viewing home and family as private turf, not to be violated. But today, with society casting doubts on the value of the homemaker role, women may see a husband's sharing as a concrete sign of approval— proof that her job is a serious one that needs to be done. So a husband can function to bolster a homemaker's sense of Mastery, protecting against the out-of-step anxiety we've discussed.

When we looked at homemakers with children in relation to the other dimension of well-being, Pleasure, we found again that their well-being was tied to husband and marriage. The most powerful determinants of Pleasure were how well things were going in the marriage—the balance between rewards and concerns—and the husband's occupational prestige. The importance of the quality of marriage is no surprise, but why do homemakers experience heightened Pleasure when a husband has a prestigious job? And conversely, why does Pleasure suffer when a husband isn't doing so well? Psychologist Jean Lipman-Blumen[3] calls this phenomenon "vicarious achievement." In other words, these women tend to identify with their husbands' achievements and to derive satisfaction from their accomplishments. But the problem, of course, is that this leaves such a woman highly vulnerable should a husband falter or fail.

For both Mastery and Pleasure then, a homemaker's dependence on the state of her marriage and on her husband's approval, support, and accomplishments leaves her with a very narrow base for her sense of well-being. It is important that such women make an effort to find sources of self-esteem and satisfaction that are not husband-centered. That may not always be easy to do. For instance, husbands are often critical of the time wives spend with friends. "What do you want to yak with those women for?" a husband will bark. He has his work to occupy his time, and when he's not at work, he wants his wife to spend her time with him. But a woman must realize that friendships and outside activities are essential to her well-being—just as they are for unmarried women—that they are not "silly" or trivial, but are vital to the building of a support network outside of the couple relationship. Recent research emphasizes the importance of this often-neglected part of life, and homemakers need to pay attention to it, if only because of the later years, when a husband may be gone and children scattered.

Married without children, at home

We focus next on the second group of married homemakers, those without children. This was the smallest group of women we studied, because there were very few in the community we surveyed and probably elsewhere as well. In the past it was much more common than it is today to find a woman in the role of homemaker when she did not have children. The women we studied who were in this role tended to be in somewhat special circumstances. On the average, they are older than women in other groups. Some worked for many years, married late, and retired from working. Some were married to much older men who did not want children. Others were married to busy and affluent husbands and devoted their time to traveling with and entertaining for their husbands. This group is the most difficult to generalize about because their situations vary so much. We do know that they are at rock-bottom relative to others on Mastery. There's no doubt that this role is risky for a woman's feelings of self-esteem.

Overall, married homemakers who do not have children are similar to those who do; their sense of Mastery is also closely tied to their husbands' approval. One such woman who had been thinking about going back to work worried that it would take too much time away from her relationship with her husband: "Could I work and be a good wife to Walter? I do just about everything for Walter. I take a great deal of pride in his coming home and seeing what I've done around the house. I ask him, 'Is this okay?' He loves me very much and I feel very special when I'm around him."

Almost all the elements that contribute to Pleasure for these women also center around their husbands and their marriages: the husband's income, his attitude toward her being home, how well the marriage is going, sexual satisfaction, and how happy she is with the way decisions are made in the marriage. Clearly, this second group of homemakers is extremely vulnerable to problems in the marriage or to the loss of their husband. As we've noted, building other people and activities into one's life can help reduce this vulnerability.

We turn next to the pattern most younger women can expect to be in for a major part of their life: married women who are employed and who have children.

Married with children, employed

These women, we've noted, score very high in both Mastery and Pleasure. Do they have a zone of vulnerability that is tied to out-of-step anxiety?

Married, working women who have children can feel out of step because they are doing what a woman was not supposed to do, at least according to society's message when they were growing up. They heard dire warnings that a working wife and mother was unfair to her family, that her marriage was bound to be unhappy and her children neurotic. For married working mothers, we found, how the marriage was going—marriage balance—made the difference in Mastery. Unlike homemakers, such women's sense of Mastery wasn't dependent on a husband's approval, income, or the prestige of his occupation. But the quality of her marriage *was* crucial. If it is going badly, she probably isn't getting that comforting assurance that helps her feel, "I'm okay." In this sense, for married working mothers, as for other married women, marital issues can constitute a vulnerable area for their sense of Mastery, even though they are less dependent on a husband's success and stamp of approval. Of course, younger women today who have not been socialized in traditional ways will probably be more comfortable as employed mothers than women now in their fifties, and for them marital problems, however distressing, may be less threatening to their self-image.

An area separate from marriage that also strongly affects the sense of Mastery of working married women with children is what is often called the "social ties" area. Our index of social ties included items measuring friendships, volunteer and community activities, leisure interests, and hobbies. A busy woman could easily neglect these, given her pressing schedule at work and at home. But if she does so over the long term, there can be a cost to her well-being. We've already suggested that homemakers can increase the "insurance" for their sense of Mastery by involvement in social ties.

On the Pleasure side of well-being, major contributors for this group of women include sexual satisfaction, marriage balance—the same as for homemakers—but also the balance between rewards and concerns at work. Unlike homemakers, these women have two distinct sources of Pleasure: love and work. So when things aren't going well in their marriage, good experiences at work can help offset distress at home, and vice versa—a satisfying marriage keeps one going when there are problems at work. Many researchers think that it is precisely because most men function in both spheres—family and work—that their mental health has tended to be better than women's.[4] Here again, we are seeing changes that should benefit younger women, whose patterns will combine love and work more consistently—and perhaps more comfortably.

Married without children, employed

Our second group of married employed women are those with no children. Of particular importance to their sense of Mastery was whether or not they preferred being childless.[5] A woman who finds herself married but without children is clearly in a pattern contrary to society's dictates. If, in addition, she would prefer to have children, she may be particularly vulnerable to out-of-step anxiety. It seems important to both her sense of self-esteem and control that she come to feel that her lifestyle suits her—and to the extent that other parts of her life are satisfying, she is more likely to find that it does. For whatever reason a woman is childless, if she arrives at a point where she prefers being childless to having children, her well-being is enhanced compared to women who regret their situation. So women who consciously chose not to have children; women who were infertile (or whose husbands were); women who drifted into permanent childlessness by putting off their decisions—all do well if they reach the point of seeing the positive side as stronger than the negative. We'll have more to say about childlessness in Chapter Five.

When one isn't involved in child rearing, life at work may take on a special importance, and in fact how things are going at work *does* contribute to both Mastery and Pleasure for this group. The right job, then, is a particularly important element in well-being for these women, and conversely, a bad work experience seems particularly risky. On the Pleasure side, in addition to the quality of work, sexual satisfaction is very important. The sexual aspect of marriage may be particularly critical when a couple is not held together by parental responsibilities; we saw that sexual satisfaction was also especially important to childless women who were home-makers. For employed women, however, their enjoyment of work provides another source of Pleasure, so that they are not solely dependent on their marriages.

Never-married, employed

Turning now to the two groups of nonmarried women—never-married and divorced—we give only a brief overview here, since each group is described at length in a later chapter. The never-married women in our study are perhaps more intensely vulnerable to feeling different and out of step than any other group. After all, they aren't involved in either of the two roles our society has always prescribed as essential to women, marriage and motherhood. Here it's important to note that the women in our study were born in the 1930s and 1940s to parents experiencing the Great Depression and the Second World War. They were raised with the traditional social attitudes about women's roles. A fifty-year-old subject, for example, was born in 1929 and turned twenty-one in 1950, when the "feminine mystique" was entering its heyday. As a young woman, she was presented with a narrow prescribed path that would bring social approval. For those who did not marry, the road has often been difficult. To whom do they look for affirmation about their lives?

For many, we found, the answer is that they look to what social scientists call one's "family of origin"—to their parents and siblings. The quality of their relationship to these family members, their "parent balance," was the major contributor to their sense of Mastery. This means, of course, that relationships with parents (and siblings) can be not only a source of support, but a zone of vulnerability. One barrier for many never-married women in getting this support is that they have often moved away from the world of their parents. Not only are they not married, and not mothers, they are also the best-educated group in our sample, having often surpassed their parents in educational achievements. When a woman knows she has moved in a direction radically different from that of her family, she may be sensitive to any sign of disapproval from parents and siblings, even though their approval can make a big difference in how she feels about herself. One woman who is thirty-five and single finds that her relationship with her parents has improved over the years. She says of her mother: "It seems that in being close to her I am back in the family in some way. She's been supportive of me and my life." But when support is lacking, self-esteem suffers. A troubled relationship with parents can make life particularly difficult and lonely for never-married women.

Work is another critical area for single women. Having a high-level job, and preferring to be employed rather than be a homemaker, were both very important for never-married women's sense of Mastery. As we've noted, the prestige of a job reflects its social standing, so high-prestige work can bring precisely that social approval never-married women tend to need. And such jobs also are usually well paid; the money they bring also helps enrich one's life. The reason that preference is important, we believe, is that a never-married woman who really wants to be a married homemaker, who doesn't feel that she's working because she wants to, can feel particularly discouraged about herself and her life. Clearly, the woman who finds that her lifestyle suits her is better off than the woman who feels that her life was imposed on her because she was never "chosen."

For single women, Pleasure, like Mastery, was affected by work-related issues. The quality of life at work—work balance—was crucial, as it was for other employed women, but in addition, whether they preferred to work also affected Pleasure. For single women, this part of life is central as a source of enjoyment as well as of self-esteem. The lesson is clear: since no young woman can be sure she will marry (and stay married), seeking out the most challenging, satisfying work is the most reliable "well-being insurance."

Divorced with children, employed

Divorced women are strikingly different from the other groups of women in our study. It is particularly intriguing that only for divorced women did the quality of relationships with children have a strong impact on both Mastery and Pleasure. For them, a positive balance between the rewards and concerns children brought was a major contributor to Mastery, as was whether they preferred to have children. Why are children so central to these mothers' sense of Mastery and not to that of others? We think it is because how their children are doing, and how they are doing as mothers, constitutes a "stamp of approval." It is the one built-in intimate relationship. If the kids are doing well, they can feel they are doing well. As one woman told us: "I feel as though I've saved myself and by saving myself I'm doing okay with the kids. I've traded one set of problems for another, but I'd much rather have the ones I've got than the ones I had when I was married and felt trapped and miserable."

When there are problems with children, a mother, particularly a single parent, can feel out of control and anxious. A divorced woman expressed it this way: "I'm very concerned about my boys. They don't really respect me as an authority. I can't really threaten them physically, and sometimes that's the only thing that will work with boys. I feel very strongly about my responsibility and commitment to them."

Problems with children present a major zone of vulnerability for divorced women.[6] But when things are going well, divorced women feel especially good about themselves. One woman told us: "I never derived an awful lot of satisfaction from the kids when they were little. I've felt the greatest rewards from them since the divorce. They've been very close, very caring, and very supportive of me as a professional."

In addition to issues concerned with children, occupational prestige is a major contributor to Mastery for divorced women. (We saw that this was also true for never-married women.) Perhaps it's because money is such an acute problem for most divorced women that a prestigious job is so important to them. Money is particularly important in preventing the "out-of-control" feeling when one is the only breadwinner.

For divorced women the same areas are critical for the Pleasure side of well-being as contributed to Mastery: children and work. The major determinants of Pleasure for this group are the balance of rewards over concerns in the domains of children and work.

So, more than for any other group, divorced women's well-being seems linked to their children. This isn't surprising, since a major concern women have about divorce is, will it harm their children? But like homemakers who are narrowly focused on husbands and marriage, divorced women can encounter problems. Intense reliance on any one area of life can leave a woman vulnerable to great distress when things go wrong in that area—and things inevitably go wrong at times in each part of our lives. It's not that divorced women should neglect their children—but that they need to seek other arenas of intimacy and other sources of enjoyment and self-esteem—friendships as well as romantic relationships. Issues involving children can loom so large in the lives of divorced women who are mothers that they forget how necessary other relationships are. But how children turn out is not something we can control. A divorced mother's too intense involvement with her children only increases the likelihood that their problems will diminish her own well-being.

Total Sample

While it is important to focus on each separate group in specific detail, it can also be useful to take a "wide-angle" picture of the sample as a whole to examine patterns that apply to all the women in our study. To do this analysis, we had to leave out many of the scales and items that applied only to particular groups and examine only areas relevant to all the women. For example, we couldn't consider balance scores in the area of marriage because some of our subjects weren't married, and we couldn't look at the effects of how things were going with children, because some of the women weren't mothers. But the variables we could examine in this analysis yielded findings that were revealing and very much worth discussing here. Total family income, for example, turned out to be an important contributor to both Mastery and Pleasure for the sample as a whole.

Research consistently shows the importance of income, and it is tempting to say that this finding documents what folk wisdom has always alleged: money buys happiness. But it is not that simple.

By itself, of course, having a high income can't guarantee happiness. A high income alone accounts for only a small part of well-being— a small slice of the pie, if you will. But money may function in life rather like a bulldozer does on the landscape. It flattens out the obstacles—the hills and ridges—that can make for a bumpy ride through life. When psychologist Abraham Maslow did his pioneering work on "self-actualization" in the 1930s, he found that people who were preoccupied with survival simply did not have the time or energy to devote to developing their fullest human potential.[7] The struggle to survive the debilitating effects of poverty is an all-consuming one. Our sample is somewhat weighted against inclusion of extremely poor women, because it included only women who were either employed or married (or both), and because we designed our study to include many in high-prestige jobs. For women at below-poverty level, the impact of family income on well-being is so strong that it's hard to study the effects of other variables.[8] But for our subjects, we could gauge the impact of the "beyond survival" aspects of life.

The importance of income to well-being is a clear sign that we can no longer afford to ignore serious career planning in the education of young girls. The time-honored advice that mothers gave to daughters, "It's as easy to love a rich man as a poor man," is hardly adequate when the divorce rate stands at 40 percent. Diamonds may have been a girl's best friend in an era when a woman's only hope of having a high family income was to marry a man who was well-off, but today, marketable skills that will enable a woman to command a good income over her lifetime are a better investment.

The second major finding to emerge from our analysis of the whole sample of women was that the most powerful contributor to Pleasure in a woman's life was sexual satisfaction. We were surprised by the strength of the impact that sexual satisfaction had on a woman's well-being, so it's interesting that recent studies are coming up with similar findings.[9] We have come a long way in recent years from the Victorian era, when it was thought that a woman's only proper sexual role was to lie on her back and think of England, but there is still a strong belief that while women are captivated by the gossamer haze of romance and courtship, sex itself is not a central issue with respect to their well-being, or at least not after age forty or so. Our findings show that feeling satisfied with the sexual side of one's life is associated with Pleasure across the whole age range of our sample, even though Madison Avenue portrays older women as obsessed with dentures or arthritis remedies. It's interesting that at least for women thirty-five to fifty-five, level of sexual satisfaction is unrelated to age. The other side of this coin, of course, is that as women grow older, sexual partners become increasingly scarce. Men die earlier, and those men who are alive and unattached tend to turn to younger women. A major unanswered question is whether and how older women can find solutions for this "numbers" problem.

Our data also contradict another popular stereotype—that of the sexless career woman. Intelligent women of any age are often portrayed as unattractive. When she is young, the "brain" is the girl in the glasses wearing the shapeless dress; her older counterpart is the cold, man-eating lady executive. Neither one is expected to have much interest in sex. But we found a positive relationship between occupational prestige and sexual satisfaction: women who have good jobs tend to have satisfying sex lives. This bears out what Abraham Maslow found in the 1930s, that achievement-oriented, assertive women were more sexually satisfied than the more passive, typically "feminine" women. His findings didn't make much of a dent in the popular culture of the times, however. People kept on believing that "sexy" women were passive, unambitious—and dumb. Marilyn Monroe caricatured the "dumb blonde" in her movie roles, and eventually became entombed in the role. She became a national laughingstock when she announced she wanted to play a Dostoevski heroine; no one could believe that a woman who symbolized joyous female sexuality could possibly be intelligent or ambitious.

It is not only having a prestigious job that is related to a woman's sexual satisfaction, but also the proportion of money a woman contributes to her family income. While total family income is important to overall well-being—to both Mastery and Pleasure— how much of that a woman earns herself has a strong impact on her sense of sexual satisfaction.

Obviously, this does not mean that money somehow buys sexual satisfaction. But it does mean that when a woman earns a good income, it gives her positive feelings about herself, and the better you feel about yourself, the more you are able to take steps toward enjoyable sexual relationships. Maslow's "self-actualizing" women were probably high in sexual satisfaction because they brought those good feelings about themselves into the sexual arena. Married women who earn an income comparable to that of their husbands, for example, are less likely to feel unequal and intimidated in their relationship. It may be foreign to our thinking to see that when a woman is engaged in serious training for a career, she is at the same time doing something good for her sex life, but our data suggest that this may very often be the case.

For women, and for men too, we believe, sex is not something that happens in a vacuum. Sexual satisfaction, we found, is closely tied to how a woman feels about what is happening in the rest of her life. If a woman is married, and if her marriage is a source of gratification, sexual satisfaction is enhanced. If she is a homemaker, how rewarding she finds that role affects her sexual satisfaction. The woman who is unhappy being at home will find her unhappiness spilling over into her sexual life, and an employed woman will find that satisfaction with her job affects her satisfaction with her sexual relationships. The point is that when you feel good about the rest of your life, your chances of feeling good about your sexual situation is enhanced. For some women, this may mean that other areas of life provide enough sources of self-esteem and happiness so that they can feel satisfied with sporadic sexual relationships or even with celibacy. So the woman who is where she wants to be, in a role that suits her desires and talents, is a woman who is also doing something positive to protect her lifelong sexual satisfaction.

Knowing the importance of income and sexual satisfaction to a woman's life helps to explain one of the major findings that we've reported—that the groups of married women in our study all score higher on Pleasure than unmarried women. This pattern, found in many other studies as well, is often interpreted to mean that the institution of marriage is good for women and carries with it some magic guarantee of a satisfying life. Perhaps some of what accounts for the well-being of married women is that they have, as a group, a higher family income and better conditions for a satisfying sexual relationship than do unmarried women. If so, then young women today who can provide for themselves financially and who are able to establish a close intimate relationship with a sexual partner need not be unduly obsessed with whether or not a wedding ring is in their future.

MARRIAGE

He's very interested in what I do, and it's very gratifying to me. He's proud of my work and he loves it when people consult with me or say "Ask your wife" about how to do something. He gives me support—it gives him a kick.

Irma Finn, 38, a therapist

When I complain, he complains with me. When I'm happy, he's happy. It has worked out very nicely.

Lena Barnes, 44, a teacher

Neither my husband nor I ever interfere with what the other is doing, as long as it doesn't interfere with us. I mean, my husband would never tell me, "Don't cut your hair." His idea is, "If you like it, do it!" And I feel the same way about him.

Flo Curtis, 50, a receptionist

THESE THREE WOMEN, in talking about their marriages, each selected a different aspect of the relationship to praise. They are typical of married women today: they like their husbands and find that being married heightens their good feelings.

The married women in our sample, whether they had children or not, whether they were employed or at home, scored very high on our measure of the quality of their marriage—that is, the balance between the rewards and concerns of marriage. While most women would hardly claim that their marriages were made in heaven, all in all things seemed to be going very well.

Today's marriages look particularly good when compared to those of three decades ago. You might expect that marriages in the 1950s were happier than marriages are today. After all, the fifties were the "togetherness" years, as a leading women's magazine put it. But the major national study by researchers at the University of Michigan compared the attitudes of Americans in the fifties with those today and found this was not the case. Data on marital satisfaction show that couples in the nineteen-seventies reported greater satisfaction with their marriages than did their counterparts in the fifties.[1]

These findings may surprise you. After all, aren't we supposed to be witnessing the Decline of Marriage? Every day, it seems, we hear new reports about the rising divorce rate, the uncertainty of young people about the desirability of getting married and the prospects of staying married. Are all these gloomy assessments unfounded?

The answer is not a simple one. Certainly, the statistics on divorce rates are real, but we tend to look at those figures and see nothing but disaster. There is a bright side to those statistics, however. With divorce readily available, and its stigma largely erased, couples no longer feel tied together in mutual misery. While bad marriages come apart, those that endure tend to be happy ones. Today, Americans expect more—*demand* more—from their marriages, and the price of the "good" statistics on happy marriages may be the "bad" ones on divorce.

It's important to look at marriage in a realistic light, and in the context of the society around us. We must not fall into the trap of imagining a past that was some kind of matrimonial Eden. We are a profoundly different people as a nation than we were in the fifties. The American character was assessed in those years by Harvard sociologist David Reisman in *The Lonely Crowd.* He found a trend toward conformity, toward "going along" and seeking the approval of others, rather than setting and working toward internal goals. Americans often were impressed by authority, status, the need for doing the "right" thing. While in retrospect that era may seem like one of sunny tranquility, social critics at the time railed against what they saw as widespread complacence. "The Man in the Gray Flannel Suit" too easily surrendered to the mores of his employers, while his wife derived her status from his. The only real path to upward mobility for most women was marrying well. A woman's marriage was, quite literally, all she had. No wonder she clung to even a bad marriage with tenacity. And, when things were not going well, she often thought there was something wrong with *her*—in fact, social scientists told her that was the case. As the authors of *The Inner American* put it, "Failure to assume and maintain the spouse role was taken to be a symptom of psychological problems."

How did women thrive in such circumstances? Too often, they did not. Their problems were largely ignored in the 1950s, but by the sixties and seventies social scientists began to view the mental health of the American housewife with considerable alarm. When sociologists Walter Gove and Jeanette F. Tudor looked at the statistics on psychiatric problems in Western societies, they found the highest rates among married women.[2] As the evidence rolled in, it prompted sociologist Jessie Bernard to conclude that marriage was a health hazard for women.[3]

In the early days of the women's movement, the institution of marriage drew fire from many feminists, who saw it as inevitably a bastion of male privilege and power. Many women followed the example of Nora in Ibsen's *A Doll's House* and stalked out of their marriages, slamming the door behind them, perhaps because they could not imagine a different form of marriage.

There may be fewer doors slamming today. A new view of marriage is one that sees the institution as territory to be occupied, not a fortress to be abandoned. Many women, including many feminists, are perceiving marriage as a more flexible institution, one which can change to accommodate the well-being of *both* partners. More and more, Americans may be constructing their own marriages, rather than accepting old patterns and roles. While this is never an easy process, it seems to fit the character of the Americans of today, who are characterized in *The Inner American* as better educated, more psychologically aware, and more prone to look inward. Some of the traits that now seem to be characteristic of Americans fit the description of Abraham Maslow's "self-actualizing" personality: striving to reach one's full potential, being able to set inner standards, not being slavishly dependent on authority.[4]

In spite of the new conservatism of the 1980s, we believe strongly that the clock won't be turned back for women. Marriage is not the same institution it was thirty years ago, and the trends in society—particularly the growing number of women entering the labor force—make it unlikely that the old forms will return in the near future. We are in a "transitional" era as far as marriage is concerned, and the experiences of the women in our sample should be very instructive to younger women. When the women we studied were growing up, the winds of change that were to rattle the windows and doors of American society in the sixties were yet unknown— and probably impossible to imagine. The women's movement, the sexual revolution, the counterculture—all hit these women with the force of a tidal wave. The issues they dealt with and are still grappling with are not very different from those today's young women will confront, although it will probably be easier in the future to find solutions; many of these ideas that seemed so new and radical in the sixties and seventies are now part of our everyday vocabulary. But the issues have not gone away, and young women need to be alert to them.

What do we really know about how marriage affects women, and what is it about the experience of marriage that heightens or depresses their well-being? Too often it's assumed that marriage is a wonderful thing for women—any marriage, for any woman.

But we wanted to take a critical look at what it is about being married that contributes to well-being in women. Is it sex or security, romance or companionship? Is marriage a safe haven or an adventure? Is it, as some theorists have suggested, the core of a woman's sense of self?

Our survey gave us some intriguing answers to these questions. In effect, we were able to break down the ways in which women experience marriage into their components and examine many different facets of marriage to see how, and to what degree, they affect women's well-being—that is, their Mastery and Pleasure.

Perhaps our most important discovery about marriage was this: whether a woman was married or not affects only the Pleasure side of well-being, not the Mastery side. That's crucial information, because it says a great deal about what marriage can't do for a woman:

Being married won't insulate a woman against depression.

Marriage can't guarantee a sense of self-esteem.

Marriage won't make a woman feel in control of her life.

In the past, marriage was expected to be like an all-inclusive "package plan," a complete source of happiness and well-being for women. This sentiment was reflected in the popular culture—in movies, books, and a seemingly endless series of song lyrics of the make-him-your-reason-for-living variety. What might be called the "marriage myth" put an impossible burden on that institution. A woman was led to expect from a marriage—and from an individual man—all sorts of good feelings about herself that we now know don't, and can't, come simply from being married. It is not surprising that many marriages cracked up under the strain. But despite the changes in our society, despite the woman's movement, the myth lives on. One has only to look at the magazines aimed at young adolescent girls, which feature scores of articles about young male TV and movie stars. These media personalities are not only offered as fairly safe objects of sexual fantasies for young girls, but are portrayed as the means to a sense of identity and a fulfilling life. The message is "if you were John's girl friend, life would be wonderful," or "a whirlwind romance with Matt would make all your dreams come true." The syndrome that we have called "looking in the wrong place" is alive and well in the messages aimed at today's teen-agers.

Knowing that being married may not significantly affect their sense of Mastery can help women avoid the trap of inflated expectations. If you think Mr. Wonderful is going to transform your life and your image of yourself when he slips on the wedding band, disappointment is inevitable. And knowing that marriage is not essential to Mastery should relieve the anxieties of young women who worry, "What if I never get married?" Since self-esteem and a sense of control over your destiny function *independently* of whether you are married or not, at least for women thirty-five to fifty-five, you are clearly not doomed to a life of misery as a single woman.

But if we know what marriage *doesn't* do for well-being, we can now ask, what *can* it do? As we've seen, being married has a significant effect on the sense of Pleasure. What this may mean is that marriage can do for women what it traditionally was supposed to do for men. No one ever supposed that men found their identity in marriage, or that an unmarried man couldn't feel good about his life. But marriage gave him an opportunity for intimacy, and for sharing, and added richness and warmth to his life.

What facets of marriage enhance or detract from level of Pleasure? In our initial in-depth interviews with women, we asked them to talk at length about the things they found both gratifying and distressing in their marriages. We used their answers to draw up a specific list of rewards and concerns for the second phase of the study, to which our married subjects responded. So, our survey was based on information from women *themselves*—not simply on what we assumed women would find as the good and bad parts of marriage.

When we examined women's answers to the rewards and concerns items, we found that some of the individual items seemed to move together, like constellations or "clusters" of the good and the bad facets of marriage. We then looked at these clusters to see what impact each had on a woman's sense of well-being—her scores on Mastery and Pleasure.

We found that the view of marriage given to us by our subjects reflected many of the observations about our culture reported in *The Inner American*. Many of us see marriage not as an end in itself, but as having the potential for increasing our happiness and well-being. We are focused more on internal reality than exterior symbols. In the 1950s a woman considered herself lucky if she landed a professional man with a high income who could provide a lovely house in the suburbs and the other good things in life. If he was preoccupied with work, if he rarely talked to her about the things she cared about, if he left all the children's crises to her, those were *her* problems. He was a good breadwinner, and thus a good husband.

Today's women, by and large, would reject that notion of what a marriage should be. Since this generation has more psychological awareness, it comes as no surprise that communication and support are what they find crucial to the success—or failure—of their marriages.

The new patterns of family life encourage this "interpersonal" focus. Today, there is a longer gap between marriage and the birth of the first child than there was in the fifties.[5] Three decades ago, young couples tended to move rapidly into parenthood, and the "couple" phase of the relationship was quickly obscured by the demands of parenthood. Couples today have more time alone together, without the demands of children. Smaller family size also makes a difference. In the past, when large families were the rule rather than the exception, parents were often too busy coping with day-to-day life to be concerned with their own communication as a married couple. But today, the two major rewards clusters women value in marriage hinge on that issue.

The first was one we call the "caring husband" cluster. Women with high scores on this cluster find these items rewarding:

Your husband backs you up in what you want to do
Your husband sees you as someone special
You can go to your husband with your problems

The second cluster, which we call the "cooperation" cluster, includes these two items:

Your husband is willing to share in child care
Your husband shares the housework

Taken together, these two clusters give a picture of the good things about American marriages today that is very different from the historical "ideal" marriage of the nineteenth century in which the woman was supposed to be a virtuous, submissive handmaiden to her husband. A nineteenth-century cleric described a wife's duties this way: "She makes it her daily joy to lighten his cares, to smooth his sorrows; like a guardian angel, she constantly endeavors to render him more virtuous, more honorable, more useful and more happy."[6] This ideal wife seems to us like a combination of a valet and a nagging conscience.

If today's marriage is nothing like the Victorian clergyman's prescription, neither does it resemble the 1950s marriages described by sociologist Talcott Parsons. In his description, the man took care of the "doing" side of life and the woman tended to feelings.[7] As Parsons saw it, marriages consisted of two separate, fenced-off territories in which husband and wife had completely different functions. One of this model's many inadequacies was that it did not take into account the emotional capacities of men and ignored the fact that women were constantly using their instrumental capabilities in the home.

Today the marriages that women describe as highly rewarding are ones that are more like partnerships between loving friends than they are like teams of oxen yoked in gender-harnessed roles. In these good marriages, husbands see their wives as something special, and there is a loving regard between the two partners. At the same time, these husbands often support their wives in activities outside the home, and they are confidants, men who can listen to problems. Interestingly, the husbands described by so many of the married women in our sample seem very little like the "male chauvinist pigs" who were the targets of radical rhetoric a decade ago. The women in our study talk of men who can be supportive as well as assertive, who can dry a dish and tend to a child's cry. Perhaps men have become more flexible than women expected ten years ago, or, more to the point, the men who have successful marriages may be the ones who are able to be flexible. In the wake of the women's movement, many couples split apart over these issues. Many others not only survived, but thrived. Change does not have to create chaos and confrontation; in an atmosphere of mutual respect, it can be an opportunity for growth. Sue Ross, thirty-seven, a college administrator with three children, and her husband Bud are an example of that "graceful" change.

For Sue, Bud is her strongest supporter. They met when she was a college student and he was a young professor. She finished her master's degree in sociology but decided, when her children were young, that she would not go on to get her Ph.D. The marriage fell into a traditional pattern, rather by accident than by design.

The demands of the children fell mainly on Sue, and she remembers: "In that whole process I began getting very irritated and angry with things always being left to me. There was always this lip service—sure, go ahead and do this or that—but the demands were always there. Now, to be fair, Bud never cares particularly whether the house is clean; I'm the one who likes a clean house. Nor would he care if I didn't shop at different stores to keep the budget down—which I need to do. So it isn't that he ever made those demands, but I saw what had to be done."

Sue eventually decided that the situation badly needed changing. "It got to be sort of a joke. I'd bring another book home from the library and Bud would tell the kids to watch out, because their mother had the latest title, so there would be another shake-up before the end of the week. And it was true. I'd read something that would really strike me and I'd say it was true of us. I started to read a lot, because at that point I was trying to decide whether to have another child or to go back to work. While I never went to any group, I did bring home all the books about women's issues.

"I think the whole business of looking at sex roles made me see how easily we'd fallen into the traditional definition of roles. I think it [Sue's awareness] changed things and both of us have grown enormously. I'm surprised at how well my marriage has turned out. I expected to have one kind of marriage and I think I'm lucky to have ended up with another kind. The one thing I've always been able to count on is Bud's integrity. All I have to say is, 'Look, you may say you believe in this, but here's what's really happening.' He makes every effort to understand. Now, it's my role to speak out. If I don't say it, the issue dies. But if I do say it—and this is true of any issue at all—he is always willing to be open and listen and have good arguments. We've learned how to argue over the years, and in this I've been lucky."

When Sue talks about Bud, she illustrates two components of what we've called the "caring husband" cluster: being seen as special and being supported in one's endeavors.

"My husband has always been encouraging. No matter how discouraged I got the year I went out to look for a job, he always had this feeling that I'm so terribly special the world is going to reach out and grab me—which is lovely. If you ask me who it is who understands me best, it's my husband."

The two rewards clusters, like the concerns clusters we'll describe below, have much more effect on the level of Pleasure a woman reports than on her sense of Mastery. The good news is that for women today marital issues may affect their enjoyment of and satisfaction with life, but they aren't enormously threatening to a woman's sense of self. As we'll see in Chapter Nine on divorce, women whose marriages have failed completely still end up with high levels of Mastery even though the Pleasure side of their lives is sometimes not all it could be.

The caring husband cluster has a very strong relationship to a woman's level of Pleasure. Without that encouragement and support, her sense of well-being will be diminished. But to be a supportive husband, a man can't insist on his traditional status as number one in the family. At times he needs to put his own career concerns on the back burner and give time and attention to hers. Many men have been able to do this; others have not been so flexible.

Ironically, the sort of man women have always been urged to find—the hard-working professional in a high-status job—may be least likely to share the spotlight. Men with a strong drive for power often don't want any competition from wives. In 1974 when psychologists David McClelland, Abigail Stewart, and David Winter studied graduates of a prestigious Ivy League university ten years after college graduation, the men who had a strong need for power typically had wives who did not work.[8] The researchers' interpretation of this pattern was that since power-driven men are not happy with sharing power, they would be unlikely to "allow" their wives the independence that comes with a career and an income. The researchers concluded that for these men, who tended to wish to dominate those around them, "perhaps women are simply the easiest and most socially prescribed power target." In contrast, the men in this study who were shown to have a high need for "affiliation," for warm relationships with other people, often had employed wives.

But there may be hope even for hard-driving males. A study of recent college graduates by psychologists Abigail Stewart and Zick Rubin found today's young men with a high-power drive were more likely than others to encourage their girl friends to continue with their education or to be employed.[9] The researchers suggest two alternative explanations: perhaps we are seeing a real change and a working wife is becoming more acceptable—even a status symbol—for power-driven men, or else the students, in the rosy glow of dating relationships, are just fooling themselves about how they'll feel later.

If it is important in a marriage that a man encourage his wife's ventures, it seems equally crucial that he back her up with concrete support at home, cooperating with child care and housework. The cooperation cluster has a significant impact on Pleasure; as feminists have pointed out, who does the housework is not a trivial issue. Working these arrangements out often exposes the core issues of a marriage.

Reflecting on the aspects of day-to-day living that can enhance or destroy a two-career marriage, Peggy McIntosh of the Wellesley College Center for Research on Women notes that a husband's involvement and support for the routine chores of family life are crucial but specific arrangements are often ignored both by young men and women thinking about marriage.[10] She advises young women who are planning careers to look at the men they are planning to marry, and ask not "Does he want to share the housework?" but "Who picks up his socks?"

If there is any issue with potential for exploding into major conflict in a marriage, especially with more women working, it is the question of who is going to do the nitty-gritty work that must be done from day to day. Who will wash the dishes? Change the diapers? Toss the clothes in the washer? One of the major feminist critiques of marriage was that it functioned as a device to confine women to performing menial personal services for men. A noted economist agreed with this point of view.

John Kenneth Galbraith believes that when industrialization created new jobs, it also effectively wiped out the servant class that performed personal services for the elite. Modern society needed people who would both serve and manage consumption. Women were nominated for these tasks. "If consumption is to continue and expand, it is imperative that substitute administrative talent [for the old servant class] be found. This, in modern industrial societies—the nonsocialist societies—is the vital function that women have been persuaded to perform."[11] Menial labor was the way in which a woman expressed love for her family. "The family is both the justification and the disguise for the economic function of women. Their service in making possible the indefinite expansion, especially of affluent consumption and production, is justified, even sanctioned, as a service to the family."

But current economic trends dictate against the continued role of women simply as managers of consumption. With rising inflation and the growing need for two paychecks to keep a family afloat, women's incomes are becoming increasingly important to survival. Many women recognize the unfairness of being expected to work as hard as a man during the day and then come home to do all the housework as well. But for some women it may not be the specific details of who does what that are the major concern, but whether they get a sense of support from their husbands. *The Inner American* found women often dissatisfied not so much with the precise assignments of responsibility for child care and housework, but the feeling that they were not getting this support.

There is a message for both men and women about successful marriage in the caring husband and cooperation clusters. The qualities in a man that seem to enhance the marriage relationship for a woman are not the macho, sweep-her-off-her-feet bravado of the leading man in a swashbuckler. Women are supposed to sigh over the tough guys in movies, but such men usually prove disappointing as husbands. In contrast, a man who improves his wife's life with emotional support and practical sharing of tasks will benefit from the closeness and warmth that is likely to result.

The two clusters we have just described represent what women find rewarding about marriage. There is, of course, another side:

even the women in happy marriages have problems.* We found a willingness to be frank about marital problems that suggests that women feel less pressure today to present a perfect image of their marriages. The authors of *The Inner American* report that in the 1970s happily married couples were more willing to admit conflict or resentment in their marriages than were similar couples in the 1950s.

Just as the items about the rewards of marriage grouped into clusters, so too did the concerns. The first major cluster we call "emotional distance." Women with high scores on this cluster reported these marital concerns:

Lack of companionship
Not getting enough appreciation or attention
Poor communication
Not getting along
Not getting enough emotional support

The second concerns cluster is "husband's work problems" and it included these items:

Your husband's employment is unstable
Your husband has major job problems

The emotional distance cluster is the mirror image of the caring husband cluster: when good communication exists it's a big plus; its absence is a serious flaw. This may reflect what might be called a "revolution of rising expectations" toward marriage. When more seems possible, people are not likely to settle for less.

The emotional distance cluster had a very strong negative relationship to level of Pleasure and is perhaps the major stumbling block in marriage. When a wife reports concern over this cluster of problems, the marriage is in for trouble.

Renee Ames, forty-five, the mother of two children, found that her husband, Joe, was happy to pitch in and help with tasks when she went to law school, but he couldn't comprehend her emotional needs:

"He's always been very supportive about my being a lawyer.

---

* An important point to remember about our rewards and concerns items is that we didn't just ask a woman, for example, whether her husband sees her as someone special, or whether they argue about the children, but *to what extent* each is a rewarding or distressing aspect of her marriage. In this way, we found out what good and bad things really mattered to her. A woman may argue with her husband about the kids quite often, yet it may not bother her a bit; just knowing that they argue doesn't tell you how she feels about it.

He's a lawyer, and he always thought I'd be good at it and encouraged me. But he's not at all supportive when I feel rotten, and I want emotional support for my failures—or feelings of failure. I remember that in my first year, the night before moot court, we had this really big fight. He was just totally unconnected with the fact that I was scared to death. He kept trying to address it on the very rational basis of what my argument should be, and I was in tears, afraid. I had a very tough course and I was uptight about it . . . and he was very unsupportive. He just wasn't used to giving me emotional support. He had never been very supportive of my pain over trying to raise the children. I think, also, in the case of law school, he thought he'd lost something, which was my support of him. When we'd have these fights he'd ask me how I could accuse him of not supporting me when he was earning the money and fixing the dinners."

This issue might have destroyed the marriage, if Joe and Renee hadn't been willing to deal with the problems. Talking helped, Renee says. Although she still has not gotten the total emotional support she wants from Joe, she can be more objective: "I think I was awfully demanding of him, and it wasn't something he was able to give at the time, that feeling of support for me. He can't even ask for support for himself, and he couldn't give it to me, either. I learned how to get that kind of support from other places."

Therapy also helped Renee to understand the destructive pattern that Joe had fallen into and her reactions to it. When he had problems, he vented his emotions by getting angry at her and being critical. "You're a lousy housekeeper!" he would snap, or "What kind of mother are you!"

This is an easy pattern for men in high-stress jobs to fall into. Unable to let off steam at work, they are wound up so tightly that any minor irritation caused by a wife triggers an explosion. The wife's response may be to internalize the criticism with a destructive pattern of her own. While Joe brought his work problems home, Renee brought hers to work: "He used to just dump on me all the time and that was his way of getting rid of whatever problems he was having. He doesn't do it anymore, but at the time, my pattern was also always the same. The first thing I would do was wail in anger, and after that I'd just accept what he said as true and then I'd withdraw from him. And that's just what I'd do on the job."

Whenever she sensed any criticism—real or implied—from a

colleague, Renee would immediately blame herself, and disappear behind her office door. Once she realized why she was behaving as she was, she was able to change at work—and at home as well. "After I talked it out with the therapist, I went into the office and if anybody said anything critical of me, I said, 'That's not true!' I felt so different about the way I was responding. I wasn't just taking other people's opinions of me at face value."

Therapy helped to diffuse the tension in the marriage between two intense personalities, and to make them aware of each other's feelings. Neither Renee nor Joe made themselves over. Joe still gets tense and anxious, Renee can get too emotionally involved in problems at work, but they have learned how to avoid destructive behavior. Renee says: "We've been through a lot together, and we have a certain feeling of shelter in the marriage. It's a place of safe haven for me now, and for him too, I think." With effort and goodwill, emotional distance is a gap that can be bridged.

Most women never enter therapy but still learn how to get the understanding they need and can then take responsibility for enhancing their own well-being. Often the problem is lack of communication. It's a cliché, of course, to say that better communication makes a better marriage, but in a marriage already suffering from emotional distance, poor communication makes it even more unlikely that the couple can solve their problems.

An example of such a marriage is that of Eve and her husband Mac. Eve, now forty, is a high-school dropout who thought that she was "not very smart" until she enrolled in an adult education program and passed the high-school equivalency test. She discovered that not only was she bright, she could write well. Her success in that course led to continuing involvement in adult education; she eventually got a job teaching at an urban "skills" center. As her self-esteem improved, thanks to her success at work, she decided to get the rest of her life in order. She had suffered from a severe weight problem for years, and she tackled that first. She joined Overeaters Anonymous and lost one hundred pounds. Then she turned to her problems with Mac, who worked for a large freight express company and had a drinking problem. His drinking wasn't bad enough to get him fired from his job, but it made life at home miserable for Eve.

"Right around that time my husband had been drinking heavily. I put an ultimatum to him. He had to stop. The emotional calm was there and I was able to do it. I thought that was going to be the solution to my problems. He stopped drinking for a year and three months. But when I finally said to my husband that there were things we needed to discuss pertaining to our marriage and our communication, he couldn't handle that. He went back to drinking."

Eve was always brought up to support others, to put her own needs last. "I was the 'good girl'—I've always been—and what was happening in our marriage scared the hell out of me. The more I'd say to my husband that we needed to talk, the more he would say there was nothing to talk about. How does this 'good person'—me—stay in this marriage? It was insanity, that's what it was, and I went right back to my vicious cycle of overeating. I've always admired my husband's intelligence, but he has always sold himself short. He's a very well-rounded person who can converse about music and literature, he's no dummy by any means. Yet we can't talk, we can't communicate. Because he can't deal with what's going on with us right now, he brings out the history books, talks about the wars of the past, and I can't comprehend it. I'm in Alanon, I've run the gamut, and my husband will not go for any help at all. So it's gotten to the point where I've had to say we need to call it quits. That's where I am right now, I need a separation."

Clearly, for Eve the breaking point was not the fact that her husband had a drinking problem—but that he could not talk to her about that problem or the others in his life.

Why problems of emotional availability and communication arise between husbands and wives is a matter of disagreement among social scientists. Some put blame on the ways we treat boys and girls in our culture when they are very young. Young girls often spend a great deal of time talking to and being with adults. Studies have shown, for example, that girls spend more classroom time physically close to the teacher than the boys do. Some social scientists feel that boys' early experiences prepare them for a rough and ready competitive world at work, but that boys lag behind girls in the development of verbal skills that facilitate communication.[12]

Girls put interpersonal skills to work very early, according to psychologist Janet Lever, who studied play patterns of girls and boys.[13] She found that girls often form intimate groups of two or three and display a fine-tuned sensibility to the moods and emotions of their playmates. Girls often have a best friend with whom they play every day, and they get to know that person so well that they seem to understand the playmate's feelings through nonverbal clues alone. Lever says: "These relationships resemble nothing so much as miniature marriages, in which girls learn the kind of empathy they will use in later life as peacemaker, mediator, and glue of the nuclear family."

But ironically enough this empathy, which is often one of women's great strengths, can at times block communication between husbands and wives. When a woman can anticipate her husband's moods and needs, when she sees a certain look on his face, she knows that he is upset and needs to talk. But for just this reason, she can't understand why he doesn't give her the same kind of support without her having to ask. Resentment builds up—she is seething inside, and he hasn't the foggiest notion why she's angry.

The subject of power is also relevant to husband-wife communication. In any relationship between two people, the question of power arises. It may be held mostly by one or the other party, or it may be shared more or less equally. The fact that women have been totally dependent on men for their economic support has greatly influenced their behavior and their methods of communication, according to psychoanalyst Jean Baker Miller, author of *Toward a New Psychology of Women*.[14] She believes that there are two classes of people in society, the "dominants" and the "subordinates," who behave in clearly different ways. The dominants assign to themselves the jobs that are high in status and material rewards. The less-valued functions are assigned to the subordinates, who are encouraged to develop certain personality traits—dependency, docility, submissiveness, inability to think and make decisions. Subordinates are often thought of as childlike.

Subordinate groups, unable to make demands or reach for power, become experts at manipulation. They learn more about the dominants than vice versa. They *have* to, Miller points out, because their survival depends on it. "They become highly attuned to the dominants, able to predict reactions of pleasure and displeasure," says Miller. "Here, I think, is where the long story of 'feminine intuition' and 'feminine wiles' begins. It seems clear that these 'mysterious gifts' are in fact skills developed through long practice, in reading many signals both verbal and non-verbal."

Girls grow up learning to read and manipulate the emotions,

egos and libidos of men. They don't see it as a survival mechanism, but as a societal responsibility to take care of men. Psychologist Dorothy Ullian, in her study of girls' attitudes, finds that girls typically move from a phase she calls "Assertion" (ages six to ten) in which girls think highly of females and resent boys—to the stage of Ambivalence (ten to fourteen).[15] In this period, girls are moving toward support of males. By fourteen, she says, girls have accepted the need to support males and have entered the stage of Accommodation; a woman's job, they now believe, is to nurture the ego of men.

Jean Baker Miller points out that all subordinate groups learn to avoid expressing anger openly because it can have serious consequences. It's not surprising therefore that women have trouble expressing anger or making demands. They may be exaggerating the consequences of stating their wishes candidly and openly; in the long run, doing so will help communication in marriage. There is, however, a real risk of alienating men who can't accept a challenge to their authority.

Building better patterns of communication requires two steps. First, a woman has to believe that she has a right to "get" as well as give. Second, she will have to speak out about her needs. As Sue told us, "If I don't speak out, the issue dies."

It is not always easy for women to speak out. Lee Huston, a thirty-six-year-old mother of four who speaks glowingly of her marriage today, remembers that it wasn't always so rosy. Early in the marriage, she says, she went through a period of feeling invisible to her husband.

"I considered separation and divorce when my daughter was a year old. My husband is a very self-contained, very complete person without me and I didn't feel important to him. I felt loved, but not that romantic 'I love you!' sort of thing. I thought, To hell with this, I'm going to become somebody all by myself, I don't need him! I'm going to be busy in the evening and on weekends to show him I don't need him all the time! My husband is a busy, active person, and I went through that whole thing of 'I don't want to come last—after you've read *Time* magazine, after you've fixed the car, gone skiing!' "

Lee finally forced herself to work out her feelings by talking about them, not letting them fester inside. She learned to ask for what she needed:

"I had to learn to say to him, 'Look when you take off with

the car at nine to go to the store, saying you'll be back by ten, I wait to have breakfast with you. Then, when you don't show up until eleven, I'm really angry!' I've learned to say, 'When you came home late, this was how you made me feel.' Then he's able to see how it's affected me. That's better than what I used to do—not speak to him for two days and then blow up about something else. I guess at this point in our marriage I'm relaxing a little because I'm able to see what we've worked out, and I think we'll be able to work out problems that come up in the future."

The benefits of improving communication in a marriage are twofold. There's a good chance that talking about a problem and getting it out into the open will clear up the issue. But even when it does not, even when some residue remains unsolved, speaking up can make a woman feel better just because she no longer has feelings of resentment bottled up inside. Ruth Lake, fifty-three, who is married to a bricklayer, sees her marriage as far from perfect, although it meets most of her needs. One unresolved problem is that her husband gets uncomfortable whenever Ruth is angry or upset. She used to try to hide those feelings, but no longer does.

"I could never tell my husband when I was angry or upset. I always kept everything inside. It's not good to be like that. I've gotten out of it, but now and then I catch myself slipping back. I know my husband doesn't know how to handle it when I tell him I'm angry or upset. But I tell him I have to explain how I feel. You have to be pretty thick not to realize how you're hurting yourself when you keep everything inside. You become such a martyr, it's sickening. I didn't want to tell my husband anything that would bother him or make him angry. I understand now that you can't always cushion things for people. Whether a person's going to like what I say or not—that's their problem!"

Women often rein in their feelings of anger, as Ruth did, because they don't want to "hurt," or "bother" a husband. But this behavior can have an unexpected consequence, one that can be far more damaging to the relationship than getting angry. A common by-product of repressed anger in women is sexual dysfunction. One simply can't be loving and open with bottled-up anger inside. Ann Birk, director of a sex therapy program in the Boston area, finds that a major reason for sexual dysfunction in women is chronic and underexpressed anger.

Birk recalls one case that dramatically illustrated the link between bottled-up anger and frigidity. A young woman was very angry with her husband because he had a demanding job and spent too much time on the road or in the office, but she could not bring herself to confront him. She then developed a vaginal condition which prevented her from having intercourse. After entering therapy, she began to understand her problem, and summoned the courage to say to her husband, "I need you home more." The vaginal problem vanished almost overnight and she was able to function sexually once again.

Problems centering around rapport and communication are not the only troublesome ones for couples today. The second cluster of concerns, husband's work problems, we found, also has a strong depressing effect on Pleasure. When problems arise over a husband's job—when he is out of work or uncertain about his career goals or financial future—his wife's well-being is greatly diminished. Job problems can make a marriage go sour. This isn't hard to understand, given the powerful relationship between family income and psychological well-being. In most marriages today, the husband's income is the major part of the family's total income, and when that is threatened, tensions arise. Not only are there the immediate problems of not having enough money, but often a wife can't help feeling that her husband has "failed" as the breadwinner. Even when she means to be sympathetic, she will often find herself feeling resentful. Irene, fifty, is a homemaker who always wanted to be home, but in the early years her marriage was a struggle. "My husband didn't make much money and it was hard to get along. He got a second job in the Post Office at night. We didn't have furniture or anything."

When Irene's husband went into a small dry-cleaning business with a relative, their troubles seemed to be over. But because of the relative's incompetence in handling the finances, the company went into bankruptcy. Irene felt bitter and angry because she thought her husband didn't fight hard enough to keep the business afloat. She worried about herself, and about the two children. Her husband, Mel, was so distraught over the loss of the business that he started to drink.

"After the business was gone, he was drinking kind of bad. I had a car accident one day, when he was out drinking. It was Saturday and neither one of the kids was with me, fortunately. But he wasn't home from work when I left, and he should have

been. He never went out to barrooms, but he'd drink at a friend's
house. When I had the accident, nobody could get in touch with
him. My brother came right away to the hospital. He had seen
the car, and from the looks of it he thought I had been killed.
Finally, my husband showed up at the hospital at eleven o'clock
at night and he still wasn't quite sober. He stood there and said,
'Now I suppose you're going to blame me for this, too!'

"I told him to go home. So he left, and I turned against him.
I didn't want to, but I did. I didn't want anything to do with
him, and I kept telling myself I'd have to get over it. First, losing
the business had kind of turned me against him, sex-wise, because
I wanted to fight for what was ours and he's too easygoing and
wouldn't do it. Then I stopped talking about that, but the accident
made it worse. I did overcome it, but it took a long time. I could
live with him, talk with him, but it was 'just don't touch me!'
After he'd stopped drinking I used to feel so bad because he'd try
so hard. I finally got over it, but I could never say it was like it
was before. I always feel sorry for him. He's worked so hard all
his life and what's he got to show for it?"

Homemakers and employed women with low incomes may
be particularly vulnerable to concerns about their husbands' job
problems. When women don't have access to an adequate income
of their own, any disruption to a husband's income is a direct threat
to their livelihood. When you gamble on one partner in the marriage
to provide economic support, that gamble had better pay off. Many
times it does not, through no fault of the man who takes on that
role. Illness and accidents strike, firms shut down, inflation takes
its toll.

For women trapped in the vast "female ghetto" of jobs, who
are overworked and underpaid, such problems will be felt even
more intensely if economic conditions decline. It is critical that
girls get the best possible vocational and educational training they
can, and that they be encouraged to think of themselves as lifelong workers. Traditionally, women haven't seen work as a permanent part of their lives—even though for most it will be. It is also
hard for women to see that there could be a link between their
low pay and a possible crisis in their marriage, until their husband's
income is suddenly cut off.

The woman who can command an adequate income of her
own may not only protect herself from a sense of disaster when

her husband has job problems, she may lessen the burden for him as well. One of the worst difficulties for a man in financial trouble is the realization that his family is suffering along with him. Job problems are always rough going, but if a man knows that his family isn't going to be plunged into poverty while he struggles to get back on his feet, the situation will not be so devastating. Of course, given that our culture still equates the breadwinner role with masculinity, he may still suffer some loss of self-esteem if his wife is carrying the financial burden. But if she is not completely dependent on him, she will not be so obsessed with his "failure" to provide. She may well feel resentful at times but she won't feel the helplessness of the victim, which often is transmitted into fury against the person who is "to blame." And so she will probably be less vulnerable to the kind of repressed anger that turns so often into withdrawal and sexual dysfunction.

We've seen how important sexual satisfaction is to Pleasure for all women in our study, and married women as a group report that the sexual relationship is a very rewarding part of marriage. They describe themselves as highly satisfied; this means that they find their sexual relationships personally rewarding, not that they match some performance standard of frequency. And there's more good news on this topic. Many women reported that as they get older, sex gets better.

Irma Green, a thirty-eight-year-old therapist, was never able to come to grips with her sexual feelings in her unhappy first marriage. She married her college sweetheart, "because we didn't feel we had permission to live together. It was just so much against the ethic that we decided to get married. Even at the time, I felt inside myself that it wasn't going to last. I really didn't want to get married. It was kind of sad. I tried to put that feeling out of my mind, and tried to make the marriage work. I stayed for three years, and that feeling of not wanting to be married sort of numbed, but then it emerged again. I said to myself, 'I've got to get out of this!' "

Irma experienced a severe depression, feeling "fairly empty, not being in tune with my feelings, not crying or laughing, not feeling anything. Through therapy I learned to experience things as they were happening. I learned to live in the present and experience it."

The sexual part of life continued to be a problem for Irma

until her marriage to her second husband, George. "I didn't understand my body until very recently. Now, in my relationship with George, I've found more sexual satisfaction than I've ever had before."

Part of Irma's problem in finding sexual satisfaction was a misunderstanding of how women function sexually. "When I finally got information about how women achieve orgasm, the whole ball of wax turned around for me. When I was young, and when I was in therapy, I was convinced there was a difference between a vaginal orgasm and a clitoral orgasm, and not having a vaginal orgasm made me feel inadequate. Now that I know there is no such thing I feel much better and my sexual life is very satisfying. It's a major change in my life—major! To tell the truth, when I'm horny it's a very important part of my life. During the time when I was single there were periods of time when there weren't any men in my life and I was aware that I had to suppress sexual drives that couldn't be satisfied through masturbation. I knew it was taking some kind of toll on me. Now that my sex life is satisfying, it doesn't seem like such a major issue. The few times that George has been preoccupied or not interested in sex himself, I could see where it could become a problem. But one of the good things about our marriage is that we've been able to talk—he is able to understand my explanations to him about what I like, and he's very comfortable with my body. That's enormously important to me. I think our relationship has meant a change for him and his understanding of his sexuality. It's meant increased pleasure. His first wife was very critical of him sexually, but I think he's magnificent to look at, and in my estimation an absolutely terrific lover."

For Sue Ross the college administrator and her husband Bud, sex "gets better the longer we're married. When we were first married, we were both virgins, and it took us a number of years to learn. I think of sex as an indoor sport. It's something that gets better with practice and we've both found it more rewarding the older we get and the more comfortable we are with each other. I certainly wouldn't want to give it up. There have been times in our life when we didn't have intercourse—before and after the babies were born, for example. I was not climbing the walls, but sex fits into the context of our relationship. If for any reason we were unable to have intercourse we would still do a lot of cuddling. I love to cuddle and always have. I'm a very affectionate person and so is he."

Clearly, one advantage of getting older is that women stop comparing their sexual life with some ideal "norm." Judy Baker, a forty-four-year-old homemaker, says of her relationship with her husband Jim: "During the first ten years we were married I used to find myself wondering if we were really getting as much out of it as we should. It was as if I was testing myself against some kind of check list like they have in magazines. Are we having the right kind of orgasms? Often enough? But I don't think about it anymore. It's fine for us.

"From the time you're a girl, you're always measuring yourself against everybody else and you wonder if the boys notice you. Then you get married and you wonder if you're like everybody else. There were times I sat in the bathtub and thought about having affairs— particularly when Jim was in medical school. He'd come home and be very tired and I'd feel as though there wasn't much point in being up for him. I wondered if it wouldn't be fun to have an affair. Then I thought that if he had one I'd kill him. So I knew I wouldn't do it. I think it was one time that having fantasies paid off, because you could test out the idea without really having to act it out. I guess, at that particular time, I was so invested in ideal wifehood and motherhood that I thought he ought to be equally invested in being a husband. I thought that the fact that he was tired meant he wasn't interested. But then I realized that there's only so much energy that a person has. It helped that I had worked before getting married, because I remembered it wasn't so easy being out there. Now it's something that we're comfortable with and we don't have to prove anything. We don't really talk about it much. There are a lot of things that are fun to talk about, but this is one that's more fun to do."

CHAPTER FIVE

CHILDREN: AND BABY MAKES THREE

If I had to do it over again, I wouldn't have kids. I would say for the most part they have been the source of great sadness for me, so that I can't get a tremendous amount of joy from the good times.

Sherri Lane, 50

I think children give you a sense of what it is like to be a new being. They're discovering the world. Everything is new and I love to see that happening. To see my son grow from this funny-looking little baby to—well, he's as tall as I am now. I just look at him and I think, "It's magic!"

Judy Young, 44

THE QUESTION OF whether or not to have children may be the most emotion-laden one a woman faces. In the past, the issue rarely arose. A married woman who could have children did. Motherhood was a woman's duty, her destiny, her sacred trust.

In the 1950s, Americans who were surveyed about parenthood had what might be called a knee-jerk reaction of approval. When asked about people who chose not to have children, they used such words as "selfish" and "bad." Today the situation is quite different. By the late seventies, according to the authors of *The Inner American*, people's attitude toward parenthood had become less positive and they showed a stronger sense of the difficulties involved. The researchers found "no clearly dominant negative moral judgment" on nonparenthood. In other words, by the late seventies, it was "okay" not to have kids. The belief that a child could supply meaning and substance to life also seemed to have dimmed. "The parent role," the researchers said, was "only moderately relevant to most people's social selves." How satisfied people are in their role as parent, studies show, makes very little difference to their overall life satisfaction.[1]

For women, a decision that was once almost automatic has become a matter of choice. For many younger women, especially those seriously involved in careers, the age of thirty-five looms as an ominous marker on the biological time clock. Decisions must be made, and women have that now-or-never feeling, prompting them to reexamine their relationships, their careers, their priorities.

It doesn't help that in the past few years, the media have "rediscovered" motherhood. Newspaper headlines proclaim that the baby boom generation has a "boomlet" of its own in progress, and thirtyish career women adorn magazine covers in their chic on-the-job maternity fashions. In the seventies, women were advised to keep their eyes firmly fixed on career goals and not to settle for "just" marriage and children. Now, with motherhood back in vogue, women are feeling heightened anxiety about what they will miss if they don't have children. Should they forget about the M.B.A. and start looking for a man who likes children? Can they have both a child and a good job? If they have decided not to have children, should they reconsider their decision?

Too often they have very little information about what the consequences of decisions might be.[2] On the one hand, they have been told that if they don't have children, they are doomed to emotional emptiness because they have not fulfilled their most basic feminine need. On the other hand, the proponents of nonparenthood suggest that motherhood is nothing more than a life of indentured servitude. Young women may feel a bit wary about having babies when they note the response that advice columnist Ann Landers got when she asked her readers whether they would have children if they had it to do over again. Seventy percent responded with a resounding "No"!

Are children the sine qua non of a woman's happiness, or are they a millstone around her neck? What are the joys of parenthood; what are the problems? The women in our sample, for the most part, were looking back on the decision of whether or not to have children. We studied them at a time when most were beyond that stage of their lives, so our subjects gave us a look at the *outcome* of such decisions.

The experiences of women in our sample should be highly relevant to young women even though changing social conditions and social attitudes influence the experience of being a mother or being childless. How it feels to be childless, for example, can be affected by whether you have lots of company in that lifestyle or whether "everyone" you know is a mother. The percentages of American women remaining childless has varied throughout our history. For example, in 1975 20 percent of women ages forty to forty-four were childless, compared to only 7 percent in 1950. Demographers differ in their predictions about the future and in any case such predictions have often been wrong in the past—but we appear to be heading toward more, rather than fewer childless women compared to the 1970s.[3]

Perhaps the most critical finding in our study, one that should be of particular interest to those women now wrestling with decisions about having children, was that whether a woman did or did not have children had no significant impact on her well-being. A woman without children is just as likely to score high in Mastery and Pleasure as a woman who is a mother. It is very clear that having children is not the crucial element on which a woman's well-being depends.

This finding strongly contradicts the conventional wisdom about what makes for a happy and fulfilled life for women. The notion that children are *central* to well-being for women is so firmly rooted in our culture that to say the opposite seems almost like giving voice to an "unthinkable" idea. But our study shows that a great many supposed truths about women are based simply on myth and misinformation. The finding about children is just one reason we believe strongly that there is an urgent need to build a new vision about women's lives that is based on reality, not on stereotypes, assumptions, or wishful thinking.

Other major recent studies also find no evidence that having children makes a critical difference to the long-term well-being of women (or men).⁴ This finding is particularly striking in view of the fact that the women in our study grew up in an era that was strongly "pronatalist," and one might expect that motherhood would figure strongly in their lives. If these women can attain well-being with or without children, then young women today should be able to look forward to equally positive outcomes.

This is not to say that women who are in the throes of decisions about childbearing or who feel great distress over the possibility that they may not be mothers, aren't wrestling with a very painful problem. But while in the middle of that crisis, they may not be able to see it as a time of stress which will come to an end. So preoccupied are they with the present, they may be unable to realize that the future will be less turbulent than today. It should be encouraging to them to know that women who made a decision to remain childless, or those who simply didn't have children, most often find that the consequences of that decision have not been in any way catastrophic. Instead, many childless women find their lives full, rich, and rewarding—sometimes to their own surprise. "I thought at twenty-five that I'd be miserable at forty if I didn't have children," says one woman. "I'm happy to discover it isn't so at all."

Interestingly enough, while women are traditionally expected to be eager to have a child, and men to be somewhat hesitant, today these attitudes are changing. According to *The Inner American* researchers, women are less enthusiastic about the idea of parenting than men are. Women seem to recognize the difficulties of parenting, particularly if they plan to combine work and children, while men often don't think about it. We've noticed that when workshops on combining work and family roles are held on college campuses, a male face in the crowd is a rare sight. But men will find themselves faced with such issues in a direct and urgent way, as the two-career family becomes increasingly common. Male optimism may stem from unrealistic notions about the demands—or lack of them— that being a father will entail.

In this chapter we're going to look both at women with and without children, beginning with those who are mothers. We've seen that the mere fact of having children has not told us very much about a woman's well-being. For women who are mothers, however, the quality of the mother-child relationship does indeed have an impact. How things are going with your children can affect your life in important ways.

Since it's the quality of a relationship with children that's important, not just having them, it's easy to see why the old, simplistic notions about how being a mother makes your life wonderful just don't tell the story. Motherhood can be wonderful and fulfilling, but it also can be painful, stressful, and frustrating.

Interestingly, the negative impact when things are not going well is far stronger than the positive effect when they are. It may seem odd to think that children can be very bad for your psychological health when there are problems, yet don't do much for you when things are going fine, but this is the case. An analogy to one's health may explain the situation. When you're in good health, you tend to take it for granted. You don't go around saying to yourself, "How great that I'm healthy!" and you probably wouldn't think of listing health as one of your life's great rewards. But if you have serious health problems, they can overshadow everything else in your life.

Unfortunately, it's very hard to predict how things will turn out with children. Of all the choices, options, and life issues discussed in this book, having children is the one most like the turn of the roulette wheel: the outcome can't be known in advance. In contrast, when you marry, you have at least some idea of the character of the spouse you have chosen; in selecting a job, you can try to match your skills with the positions available. But a child is truly a surprise package, one that comes complete with qualities and characteristics you can't control or predict. A calm, relaxed woman can have a colicky baby who cries all night and frays her nerves, while the anxious woman who bites her nails to the quick can have an infant who smiles constantly and sleeps blissfully through the night. One child may be a rebel who has to test the rules all the time, while her brother or sister is a helpful, cooperative type who is easy to manage. There is simply no way to know in advance what, or, more precisely, whom, you're getting.

In fact, the authors of *The Inner American* argue that the major reason the women they studied were lower in well-being than the men in their study was that women have primary responsibility for the care of children. Therefore, they are at the mercy of others in a way that hasn't been true for men in our society. To feel, as women often do, that the problems of others—in this case, of children—are really *your* problems lessens the control you have over your life and leaves you vulnerable to feeling inadequate and incompetent.

While a woman doesn't have much control over what kind of child she is going to have, she may have a choice about what kind of a parent she is going to be. We found that the rewards of parenting were associated with two distinct styles of mothering, and fell into two clusters.

The first we call the "autonomous" cluster, and it included the following items:

Liking the kind of people your children are
Feeling proud of how they turned out
Enjoying doing things with them
Seeing them mature and change

The mothers who found these aspects of parenting the most rewarding focused on the children as separate people—on their individual qualities, rather than on their own connection to the children. They seemed to be able to see their children as different from themselves, and to get pleasure from them because of the kind of individuals they were. Often, the mother who fits this description has a firm sense of who she is, and is able to nurture her children without living through them.

Jacqueline Baker, forty-one, a recreation worker, says: "Right now I'm very proud of my kids. I really enjoy them. I enjoy talking to them, now that they're teen-agers. My two oldest used to kill each other when they were little but now they're very good friends. I try not to pretend to them that I'm a perfect person. Some parents set themselves up as little tin gods, and it's hard for a child to find out a parent isn't perfect. I've always tried to teach them that I make mistakes, and I've never been afraid to say I'm sorry if I made a mistake. I've learned to let them know, too, that I have to do things for myself, and I think it's for the benefit of the kids, too. I see a lot of women so wrapped up in their children in a negative way. They don't really communicate with the kids but they're wrapped up in their lives. It's like when they lose their kids they'll lose themselves."

And Sue Ross,* thirty-seven, the college administrator, finds in her children an opportunity for learning. "Children teach you a tremendous amount. The older they get, the more important are the questions that arise, and you have to think and rethink the issues you've grappled with before in childhood or adolescence. I look on it as a tremendous opportunity because it means I'm always growing. They're really just lovely people, each very different, and it's kind of neat for me to see how different three people can be who came out of the same gene pool."

A second cluster of rewards proved to be strikingly different from the autonomous grouping. This cluster, which we labeled the "coupled" cluster, reflected a style of mothering which makes the child an important element in the mother's sense of identity. Women with high scores on this cluster reported the following rewards of parenting:

> Children give meaning to your life
> Children provide a sense of being needed
> Being the best caretaker for a child gives you a sense of being
>   special and irreplaccable

The mothers in this category seem more focused on how important the children were to their own sense of identity than on the children themselves.

As one such mother says: "Children gave me something to do, something to focus on, that was my purpose in life and still is." Another says: "It's the kids that keep me going, really. This is how I feel. I don't see how people can be married and not have kids. The kids are my life, that's it in a nutshell, and I live for my kids and I do things for my kids. I'm in the car running here and there. I'm always running for everybody. I can't say no."

The "coupled" mode of mothering may sound like the classic description of the good mother, who lives for her children. On the other hand, the mother who is more autonomous, not so focused on her children, risks being seen as selfish. In fact, a group of psychologists at the Fels Institute in Ohio went even farther than that.[5]

When they studied mothers and children in the 1950s, they found a number of women who saw to it that their own needs

---

* Sue Ross was introduced in Chapter Four, page 62.

were met along with those of their children. These mothers didn't automatically drop whatever they were doing when a child asked for something; their own interests sometimes came before the whim of a child. But the idea of the twenty-four-hours-on-call mother was so firmly established as the model of the "good mother" that the researchers looked askance at these women and dubbed them "hostile" mothers.

The assumption was, of course, that these women were doing something wrong. But since the study was a long-term one that stretched over a span of twenty-five years, the researchers were able to follow up on what happened to these children. To their surprise, they found that the daughters of the "hostile" mothers turned out to be high achievers. Not only that, but these young women were less likely than the daughters of the "nonhostile" mothers to pull back from stressful situations. The researchers concluded that the mothers' early pressure on their daughters to be independent and to cope with something less than constant approval and coddling helped them grow up to be self-reliant adults. The mother who insists that her own needs and wishes are important is not harming her child—she is helping her on the path to mature adulthood.

But it's not only the child who is affected by a mother's style of parenting. What about the mother herself? Do different modes of mothering have different effects on the women involved? They do, and this finding has crucial implications for a woman's well-being.

The more a mother reports that she enjoys the autonomous rewards of being a parent, the higher she is in both Mastery and Pleasure. Conversely, the more coupled a woman feels to her child, the lower she is in sense of Mastery. This pattern is not hard to explain. As we've noted, if your self-esteem depends on your child, then you have a weak basis for your good feelings about yourself. When a child rebels, or goes through the typically adolescent process of devaluing a parent to make separation easier, a mother whose self-esteem is tied to the child is in for rocky times. The mother who is more autonomous, less intensely focused on her children, will not find herself so shaken if she doesn't have to have her child's constant adoration or approval.

The mother whose self-image is dependent on her children places on those children the responsibility for her own identity, and her involvement in the details of their lives can put great pressure on the children. A child suffers when everything he or she does is extremely important to a parent; this kind of overinvolvement can turn even a small problem into a crisis. One woman, for example, was obsessed about whether her daughter would get into a top-notch Ivy League school. The daughter had already been accepted by a good college, but it was not good enough for the mother. The mother's concern turned the issue into a major family crisis. The daughter, if she didn't get accepted into the right college, faced not only a sense of rejection from the school, but the weight of her mother's disappointment.

The coupled mother, one whose children are her "reason for living" also has a hard time letting go. How does a woman who had done what she thought society told her to do by living for her kids manage a quick about-face and cut the cord with grace and some degree of ease? Few of us could make such a superhuman effort. But if women are encouraged to ask the question "What about me?" even after they become mothers, they might avoid the trap of getting too focused on their children.

Women also could use reassurance that not everything they do every minute of the day is so crucial to their children. Child-rearing "experts" have placed a burden of guilt on women by giving the impression that specific techniques of child rearing make the difference in how their children turn out. Child rearing has too often been presented as an exact science, and mothers worry that if they aren't up on the latest theory or technique, their children are bound to suffer. Sometimes, often unwittingly, these "experts" force women into the coupled mode of mothering by being only concerned with the needs of the child. They don't understand that when a mother neglects her own needs, that neglect will boomerang to hurt both mother and child.

The idea that parenting should be as precise as a laboratory experiment—with careful attention to be paid to such details as the right-size blocks for the baby—tends to create anxiety in any parent. But do the details of child rearing really make a difference? Must one be obsessed with the exact age of toilet training or whether or not to breast-feed? That was the question Harvard researchers set out to answer in a followup study of children and their mothers.

In the 1950s, this group of researchers studied 379 mothers of kindergarten children in towns near Boston and charted 150 separate child-rearing techniques: Did the mother spank the child? Was she permissive or strict in dealing with sex play? and so on.

Then, in the late seventies, Harvard psychologist David McClelland and his colleagues interviewed the now-grown children and gave them a battery of psychological tests.[6] They found, surprisingly, that specific techniques used by the parents didn't seem to make much difference in how the children turned out. The researchers said: "We concluded that most of what people do and think and believe as adults is not determined by specific techniques of child-rearing in the first five years—we believe that parents should rest assured that what they do is not all that important. . . . Many other influences in later life serve to shape what adults think and do."

The important ingredient in the parent-child relationship, the researchers said, was how the parents *felt* about their children. When parents loved the children, and expressed that love so that the children were aware of it, the children grew up to achieve the highest levels of maturity. The only specific practice that seemed to harm the children was parental rigidity. When parents couldn't tolerate noise, roughhousing or spontaneous behavior, the child was not as likely to become an emotionally sensitive and independent adult.

Realizing that parents do not need to be overly obsessed with the specifics of child rearing may help mothers relax, and that in turn can lead to a more autonomous style of parenting, which will benefit both mother and child. The coupled mode, we believe, is another example of the "looking in the wrong place" syndrome. The woman who seeks the primary support for her identity in her children may in the end harm not only her own self-image but her children's ability to grow up as separate individuals.

Over-attachment to children is a zone of vulnerability for women who are mothers. Homemakers may be especially vulnerable to the trap of living for the kids, but working women are far from immune. In fact, some working mothers who feel guilty about being away from their children, overcompensate by throwing themselves headlong into their children's lives and catering to them.[7]

We should say here that we aren't blaming mothers for being overinvested in their children. This pattern is widespread largely because of social pressures, not just because women have wanted it. As we've said, the myth of motherhood as martyrdom has been bred into women, and behavioral scientists have helped embellish the myth with their ideas of correct "feminine" behavior. If women understand that they do not have to ignore their own needs and desires when they become mothers, that to be self-interested is not to be selfish, it will help them to avoid the trap of overattachment.

Women have not only been fed clichés about maternal bliss and "feeling like a real woman" as the rewards of motherhood, they have also lacked information about the problems, which have been glossed over, ignored, or, in some cases, exaggerated into horror stories. A child may not always be a bundle of joy, but neither is he or she a tyrant that will inevitably drain away all of a woman's energy and creativity. What are the real concerns that parenthood brings? What problems in the role of mother do women find most difficult to handle?

Looking at the concerns parents report, we found that there was one central cluster, the "conflict" cluster. The items that made up the cluster were:

> Not having enough control over your children
> Too many arguments and conflicts with them
> Children don't show love or appreciation

When a woman experiences high levels of conflict with her children, it has a significant negative effect on both Mastery and Pleasure. Women can experience conflict with children of any age, but studies show that the two times when problems seem most likely to occur are when the children are very young—preschoolers—and at adolescence.

While the myth persists that women should be happiest when at home with young children, in fact this is often a time of great stress. Sociologist Leonard Pearlin and his colleagues at the National Institute of Mental Health studied 2,300 persons aged eighteen to sixty-five in 1977, and found that women at home with children under six were extremely vulnerable to depression.[8] And psychologist Marcia Guttentag, who analyzed mental health data from all over the United States in the mid-seventies wrote, "There's nothing more depressing than a houseful of young children."[9] Looking back, Judy Young, a forty-four-year-old homemaker, would probably agree.

Judy had two of her children very close together. "We had them the way we wanted to but I'd never do it that way again," she says. "We had seventeen months between the first two and that was a mistake, too close. My daughter, my first child, was such a little terror, I thought, that first month, 'My God, what have I done?' My son was very good, not hard to take care of, but I couldn't really savor it because I was running from one to the other changing diapers. I was compulsive about doing all the work myself because Jim was an intern and I didn't want to spend any money. I remember, when they got a little older, disliking the chaos, everyone fighting with one another, the unreasonableness that children can display. There I was, trying to talk to them like a reasonable adult and ending up giving them a whack and feeling like a louse afterward."

One of the problems of having very young children is their unending demands. Battered by this assault, a woman can feel out of control. "They want what they want when they want it!" Judy says. "There is no sense of fairness—no sense that you have to have a little peace and quiet. You're there to dispense what they want and sometimes you feel like a nothing because you're just there for everyone. I think in these darker periods you start wondering if there's any point to it. But fortunately, these feelings are more prevalent when the children are small, and looking back, I think other mothers took steps to prevent that overburdened feeling—which I didn't do."

In many cases the conflict eases when the children reach school age, but when it does not, the continued upheaval can take a huge toll on a family. A child with a special problem, for example, can nearly bankrupt a family's emotional resources. Tobi, forty-five, was the owner of a small restaurant, but had to give it up because of emotional problems caused by trying to cope with her son.

"The day he was born they brought him to me in the hospital—in a straitjacket! He had turned completely over. I didn't have the capacity to raise a child like that. By the time he was a year old, he was talking, walking, all his faculties were going full blast. He outsmarted me at every turn. You have no idea what it was like! I never taught him to read, he taught himself. The public schools, forget it, they couldn't handle him. The first day in school, the nurse called, he'd climbed to the top of the jungle gym and fallen off. We rushed him to the hospital. I was always anxious about what was going to happen to this boy. He looked like an angel, but he was into everything. He took a lot of my strength, and at the same time I resented him and he resented me."

When there is intense conflict with one child in the family, problems may arise with other children as well. Tobi reported: "It was difficult for my daughter, because she was born into this situation. She was a good child and no problem. But she became a problem because she resented her brother for taking everyone's time. I went to clinics, I went to doctors, everything! I was suffering, I tell you! There was such a strain on our marriage and on this family! I still have bad feelings toward my son now that he's grown, believe it or not. I've tried to realize that it wasn't his fault, but he still blames us and we blame him."

Tobi realizes now that she was struggling with a problem that was nobody's fault. "I know what I would do if it were happening now. I would continue to search for someone who could tell us what Rudy is—hyperactive. But they knew so little about it then. Maybe I had a genius on my hands and didn't realize it and neither did the schools. They only came to me with complaints about his being disruptive in the classroom. He was mishandled from the very first day. Thank God, after years of searching and torment he's finally found himself. He married a girl who is completely the opposite of him and that's good for him. I wish we had been able to get close to him. He couldn't get close to us because of all that conflict over the years. We tried, but we couldn't."

In families where relationships with the children have been flowing smoothly, the problems of adolescence often hit with the impact of a bombshell. Dorothy, fifty-one, the wife of a policeman and mother of six, says: "Nothing is a preparation for teen-agers. When it hits, you just react. I remember when my son, a good, self-disciplined kid who was into sports, was brought home drunk by the police. He went to his first dance, and in order to get enough nerve to ask a girl to dance he had a bottle of wine and just zonked out and never got to the dance. The police found him asleep under a tree in the park. Well, I just went crazy. My husband said to me, 'Please, let's just go in and sit down.' He went and took care of our son. I know I was overreacting, but you don't know what having five teen-agers can do to you! Even small things, one after the other—their fights with each other, bickering—wear you down. One would argue, another would stomp out, another would slam the door. I think that might be why I overreacted, because when you multiply small things by five, there was always a crisis going on."

At the time of our study Dorothy's family was in the midst of a crisis that was no "small thing." Her seventeen-year-old unmarried daughter was pregnant. "When she was about a month and a half along the boy was killed in an accident. The first couple of months were really bad. We didn't know if she was going to make it. She had no will to live and we had to be sure that someone was with her all the time. I had not approved of the boy for the whole year and a half she was dating him, and to have this come up, it was awful! She's a little scared at this point, but I think she's going to be all right. She's talking about going to school next September, and there will be somebody here to take care of the baby. She's gone through counseling—I really forced her into it. At one point when she was about four months along they couldn't detect a heartbeat and she went hysterical in the office. That was when I said, 'You are going for counseling!' I myself do not believe in abortion, but I told her I would support her in whatever she decided to do. She decided she wanted to have that baby."

It's easy for parents to blame themselves when problems set in with adolescents who are testing the rules and trying to find a sense of identity—and often making bad mistakes. "I figured it must be my fault," Dorothy says. "I must be doing something wrong. Why are these children acting like this? Then you talk to other people and you find that other children are doing the same things."

Dorothy was sure that the family would make it through this crisis, as they have others in the past. "My husband and I have a good relationship, and my relationship with my daughter is much better. Her experience, as bad as it was, has had a positive reaction from the family. We've all pulled together. My daughter was the one who was defiant and always stood toe-to-toe. But now we can sit down and talk and discuss our feelings, whereas before we couldn't. All my children are good people. I can look at the almost finished products and be proud, knowing what they are. I have added something good to this world."

It is important to note here that adolescence doesn't automatically bring major problems, and major problems aren't confined to adolescence. When a child's actions come into conflict with the moral or social values of the parents, that's when problems arise, and that can happen long after adolescence.

The parent-child bond, for good or ill, is one of the constants in life. You can't divorce a child or send him or her back. And while stress may be greatest while children are living at home, problems can arise in later years as well. Most women in our study whose children were grown described good relations with their children; but for some women, like Irene Harris, fifty-four, the problem times come later. "Since my children have been married, they've caused me more worry than I've ever had in my life," she says.

Conflict with one's children—at any age—is always distressing, but it may often be more distressing to women than it has to be. The nuturant imperative that makes women sensitive to others' needs can also leave them hypersensitive to their own role in any conflict. Their first reaction to a problem—like Dorothy's—may well be "What am I doing wrong?"

But conflict between parents and children is a natural part of the growing-up process. As psychiatrist Jean Baker Miller points out, there is good conflict and bad conflict.[10] Good conflict is constructive, because people learn from it and grow. From parent-child struggles, the child learns values, discipline, and inner controls. Bad conflict leads to violence or self-destructive acts. But women often see all conflict as negative. This isn't surprising, given the saccharine image society offers us of the ideal family, with the ever-smiling mother always talking to her children in honeyed tones. Does the mother on "The Brady Bunch" every yell at her kids? Do the mothers in the TV commercials ever get upset because little Janie just got a grease spot on her brand-new playclothes? As they dump in the detergent, these women smile as if they have just won the sweepstakes. Such images may seem trivial, but they can easily get lodged inside the heads of women, making them think that it's only at their house that arguments occur.

A woman who feels that something is wrong because she can't run a tranquil household may blame herself. Too often, women refuse to take credit for their successes, writing them off to luck. But with failures, it's another story. Women, more than men, tend to see failures as due to some flaw in themselves, rather than as a product of outside forces. So it's easy to see why conflict with children can be a "double whammy" for women. First, they feel upset because conflict exists at all, and then they compound their bad feelings by blaming themselves. Although there are no simple answers to such problems, recent research does suggest some helpful steps.

Behavioral scientists have long known that social supports—sympathetic friends, relatives, professionals—are important to people in crisis. But recent studies have shed light on just how this support operates. It seems that a social network bolsters the self-esteem of the person in crisis, enabling her to get that "I'm a good person" feeling so essential to well-being. But a woman enmeshed in conflicts with children might be tempted to withdraw from social contacts and friends, feeling she ought to concentrate all her energies on the children or feeling ashamed of her situation. Such a decision, we now know, would be damaging to her own self-esteem, and this could make the conflicts worse. A woman needs to feel good about herself to deal effectively with the problems of others.

In this situation a married woman might expect to rely mainly on her husband for the support and ego-soothing she needs. But he's caught in the problem himself, often suffering from feelings of inadequacy because he can't fix everything up the way a man should be able to do. At this point, she may have to look elsewhere for support. She needs others who are not involved in the problem and who can focus on *her* feelings.

Conflict with children has a greater negative impact on employed women than on women at home; for them, conflict with children diminished the sense of Mastery more than it did for homemakers. This may be another example of out-of-step anxiety at work. The woman at home may find it difficult to cope with problems with children, but just because she is at home, she may see herself as doing all she can to resolve the problems and may therefore be less vulnerable to automatic self-blame than is the employed woman. After all, she is in the role that society classically prescribes as "best" for her children. The working woman may be quick to see any problems with children as her fault because she isn't as available to them. However, the fact that she is employed is rarely central to the conflict. And overall, studies show, being employed doesn't have negative effects on children; carefully done research consistently makes this clear.[11]

One concern item, separate from the conflict cluster, that was difficult for many women—was "not being sure that I am doing the right thing." And when women felt this way, their Mastery was impaired. There are few ways for women to get reliable and realistic feedback about how well they are actually doing in the job of being a mother. At work, one gets promotions or praise from a boss and co-workers, but no one stamps a gold star on your head for being a good mother.

While the rewards and concerns of parenting offer a good picture of the experience of motherhood, we also used another "barometer" in the study we made. Our measure of the balance between how positive and how negative a woman felt about being a mother—child balance—gave us some intriguing insights. We didn't find any differences between employed and nonemployed mothers in child balance, but the effects on their lives of the quality of their experience with children were different.

Homemakers, as we've seen, suffer less in terms of Mastery when there is conflict with children than do working women. They cope well, in terms of self-esteem, with this specific problem. They are more affected than employed women, however, by a less favorable balance of rewards over concerns; their sense of Mastery suffers more. It may be that conflict is a specific issue they can wrestle with and resolve, or at least live with, but if, in the broader sense, being a parent is not highly rewarding, the whole purpose of their life is called into question. When you begin to doubt the value of your major role in life, it's not hard to understand how that can lower your self-esteem.

On the other hand, if the experience of being a parent is a satisfying one, the well-being of homemakers is greatly increased. But this isn't true for working women! The homemaker's life, it seems to us, is focused on a narrower base. The analogy of a porch that is built on poles is useful here. If a structure is supported by only two poles, each must bear a large share of the weight. But, if a porch is supported by half a dozen poles, each one bears a smaller percentage of the weight of the whole. Although a favorable child balance may contribute to the well-being of a working woman, this contribution is smaller because she has more sources of support in her life.

Surprisingly, the amount of money a working woman earns is related to the quality of parenthood—child balance. We think earning her own money makes a woman feel competent and in charge of her life, and this, in turn, can make it easier to tolerate daily ups and downs with children.

The quality of a woman's relationships with her children affects her relationship with her husband as well. When things are going well with the kids, her satisfaction with her marriage is also high. On the other hand, when there are problems, not only the quality of the marital relationship but also a woman's sexual satisfaction declines. A woman's relationship with her kids, it seems, spills over into the marital arena. It's very difficult to keep the husband-wife relationship satisfying when there are problems with the children. No wonder researchers find that marital satisfaction increases as children begin to leave home. As Michigan psychologist Angus Campbell wrote, " 'the empty nest' appears to have a reputation it does not deserve."[12]

Having children is a decision which can lead both to deep joys and to severe problems, but the decision to remain childless also has its pros and cons. One encouraging result to come out of our study, in addition to finding no differences in well-being between mothers and childless women, is that for childless women, the more satisfying life was without children—that is, the higher a woman's childless balance score—the higher her well-being. This was true not only of women who made a decision to remain childless, but also of those who wanted to have children but couldn't, or who just "drifted" past the childbearing years. Many of the women who now feel very good told of going through a difficult period in which they wondered if their chances for happiness were being lost, or if they would regret not having children in later years.

However, some women do suffer diminished well-being because of being childless—those who have not come to terms with it. The woman who feels that she is not a "real woman" because she hasn't borne children, or who deeply longs to be a mother years after the time is past, is the one whose well-being is diminished. It is not so much the fact of childlessness that's important, but how a woman *feels* about it that makes the difference.

That's particularly important information for younger women today who decide to be childless. It's less likely now than in the past that society will brand them as selfish or unfeminine because they don't have children, so it should be easier for them to feel positive about their decision than it was for women twenty years ago, or even ten years ago. Often we feel the way we do about certain issues because of repeated messages from people around us that we *ought* to feel that way. As the messages about what women should be and how they must behave become more varied and less intensely focused on home and family, the more likely it will be that women in nontraditional roles will feel good about their choices.

We've noted that women who are conflicted about having children may think that the issue will never be resolved. When you're involved in this kind of struggle, it can overshadow everything else. There seem to be so many arguments pro and con. Lorraine, thirty-five, a writer, is in that position, and describes her dilemma; she wonders if she will have the energy to combine work and motherhood.

"I think I may try to have a child after I get this novel finished. I want to feel that I'm really moving and the momentum is there, and then maybe have a child. I somehow feel that the writing comes first, and that seems peculiar to me. My husband and I have talked about it a lot. He's older—late forties—and he seems really worn out by this whole issue. I think, ideally, for my own sake I'd like to wait a year or two. But if I'm this tired now with my work, what am I going to be like in two or three years? Everybody tells you that after thirty-five you do have to be careful, and I worry about it. I also worry about the fact that my mother had breast cancer, and suppose it hits me before it hit her, and suppose it hits when I have a child? I also had a real struggle to free myself from the psychological clutches of my folks. There's been a lot I had to work out and I feel pretty good about having worked some of it out up to now. The writing has begun to flow because I'm free of the other stuff. I feel I should take this process further before I have a child. Part of me wonders whether I really want to have one. But I feel so sad about not having a child. I really would feel incomplete without a child, I think I really would like to raise one. But I worry what I would be like if I had two hours of sleep: would I be patient enough to be a half-decent mother? I'm used to quieter things, and if a baby were screaming in the background all the time I'd go crazy!"

Once the decision period is behind them, however, most women who are voluntarily childless get on with their lives and find they are in lifestyles that suit them. When childless women talked about any regrets, there was often a wistful tone of "It might have been nice, but . . ." Rarely did women express the kind of deep, wrenching sorrow that childless women are expected to experience, and many expressed no regret at all. When Charlene Depner analyzed data on parents and nonparents from a major national survey at the University of Michigan, she concluded that "there is little evidence that the childless are yearning for a role which they do not have.[13]

Jodi, fifty-one, and an only child, remembers that a relative said her decision not to have children was unfair, because "your mother would like a lot of grandchildren." Jodi snapped back, "Then my mother should have had a lot of children!" She recalls another relative who "used to say there was no reason to get married if you weren't going to have children. She got married when she was in her forties and insisted on having a baby. She was sick to start with—had diabetes and colitis—had a lot of trouble with the pregnancy and was never right afterward. She died at forty-four. Her husband died soon after, leaving the child an orphan. He had never wanted the child. He had told her, 'Katie, what do we need a baby for? You have a job you like, so do I, let's buy an automobile instead.' But no, she had to have that baby—poor little thing."

Some advocates of nonparenthood present a rosy picture of the childless life: travel to exotic places; exciting trysts on Caribbean isles; days and nights unfettered by diapers, baby-sitters, or the need to scrape up college tuition. This one-dimensional portrait of the childfree life was probably a natural reaction to the doom promised by those who preached the child-centered life as the only virtuous—and happy—one. But romanticizing childlessness is as unrealistic as mythologizing motherhood. The picture of the childless woman that emerged from our study had both its bright spots and its shadows.

So childlessness is like parenthood—a mixed blessing, offering both rewards and concerns. What are the good things about not being a mother? In looking at how the rewards of childlessness clustered, we found one major grouping that we call the "freedom" cluster. It includes these rewards:

Being able to do things spontaneously
Being free to follow your own interests
Not having children is financially easier
Lack of heavy emotional demands from children

The virtues of freedom have long been praised in song and story—but only for men. Men are thought to be footloose and restless, while women are only happy in the security of the nest. The woman who wants to pursue her own interests is often viewed as peculiar. But freedom and spontaneity may be just as important to many women as it is to men. Many of the childless women in our sample find this to be the case. It's clear from both the tone and content of their remarks that they do not see this reward of childlessness as minor, nor are they putting up a "brave front" to cover up hidden longings for a more traditional life. Instead, they find that freedom from child-rearing responsibilities makes it possible to invest more of themselves in other responsibilities.

Marian Williamson, thirty-seven, a high school principal, finds that work fills much of her life and that of her husband, Charles, also an educator. "We both go to bed very late and put in too many hours—but we're both very similar in that we need to put in many hours at work. We both need to have the sense that we're doing a good job. I think we're both hook, line, and sinker into the Protestant work ethic and won't ever get out of it."

Both Marian and Charles spent many years getting advanced degrees. "We kept saying, 'Well, we won't have children now.' It wasn't until a few years ago that it became clear that neither of us had a strong urge to reproduce ourselves. I had sort of expected that a time would come where this little cloud would come over my head and say 'Do it!' and I'd get all enthusiastic. But it never happened. And as we look around and see our friends with children and those without, we like the lives being led by those without children. It's not that we don't like children—I think we'd be good parents. I am quite sure that if either of us had a strong desire to have children, we would have had them. We're happy with our marriage and with our work."

Jo, forty-eight, a social worker, assumed that she would have children, but after she was married her husband discovered that he was sterile. Jo and her husband opted against artificial insemination and talked about adoption. "This discussion went on for years—should we or shouldn't we? I think it got to the point where my life was so comfortable, where we were both so happy that we didn't see what having a child would do for us. I felt that I was satisfied through my marriage and work. I'm very involved in my work and I like it very much. We come and go as we please, we like to travel together. I thought that a child wouldn't add anything to my life—if anything it would interfere."

Like many childless women we interviewed, Jo finds that not having her own children doesn't mean that she is isolated from them. "Between my husband and myself we have twenty-one nieces and nephews that we see every weekend, and the nice part is that you can leave them behind once the weekend is over. I love them and they love me, but I'll tell you, when I have them around more than just a few hours at a time in a day, I have to lock myself in my room. I think if I had kids I'd go loony.

"When people ask if I have children, and I tell them no, they sort of look at me as if to say, 'Poor thing.' They ask what will happen when I get old. Well, I've thought about that and I've decided that worry about old age is no reason to have children. Especially not in this day and age when kids get married and move to California—or Egypt. I could be ninety years old with ten kids and not have one anywhere near me."

Jo's attitude about her old age is supported by recent studies of just what difference having children or not actually makes to the elderly. The answer, put bluntly, is hardly any. Researchers detect no difference in well-being associated with parenthood, even when they look at the group we'd expect to be most affected— widows over sixty.[14] What does make a real difference is whether the older person has strong social ties to friends, siblings, and so on—what social scientist call "same-age peers." The authors of a study called "The Effect of Offspring on the Psychological Well-Being of Older Adults," conclude after a very rigorous search for the impact of children: "The best evidence now available indicates that the present young adults should not decide to have children on the basis of expectations that parenthood will lead to psychological rewards in the later stages of life. The prospects for such rewards seem rather dim at best."[15]

Researchers also consistently find an association between childlessness and marital satisfaction.[16] Although our study found that there was no difference in the quality of marriage—the marriage balance score—between women with children and those who were childless, childless married women believed that one of the rewards of their lifestyle was that it made their marriage special to them.

Lena Barnes,* the forty-four-year-old teacher, met Paul when she was in college but broke up with him to marry her first husband. As the first marriage was unraveling, she ran into her old boyfriend by accident. This time the relationship worked. Lena married Paul expecting that she would have children. She was thirty-two then,

---

* Lena Barnes was introduced in Chapter Four, page 55.

and the children didn't come. They discussed adoption, but Paul didn't seem too eager, and Lena says: "I didn't push it very much. It would have made me happy, but it was no longer something I needed in my life. I thought, when I was very young, that I'd have deep regrets if I didn't have children, but I don't. I can go to my brother's house, hold the baby, bring the present—and then go home. I do make an effort to be with my brother's kids, because I do like children. But I enjoy being able to leave. I like my privacy. I guess I've become a very private person, which surprises me."

Lena thinks her marriage is different, and special, because she doesn't have children. "I see a lot more of my husband—there's no interference. I'm not taking the kids off to piano lessons and he's not taking kids off to football games, so that when we're free at the same times, we're always together. I would rather do things with him than with anyone else I know, which is nice. I think what a loss it would be for each of us if anything happened to the other. We go out for coffee together every morning—every single morning—and that half hour is a very important part of our life. And the same thing again at night, no matter how late we've worked. When I laugh he laughs with me. When I complain, he complains with me. He is the nicest man I know."

If freedom and the sense of specialness in marriage are the major benefits of childlessness, what do women see as the costs? The major concern we found, is a feeling of missing out. The items in the "missing out" cluster include feeling deprived of a special experience and of a "real" family. As one woman puts it: "I believe very much in the family and in the idea of a family. I love children, and I wonder how I would have fared with a child."

These concerns may be heightened by an exaggerated notion of how wonderful things are in a "real" family. Just as women who are not married have a rosier picture of the wedded state than do married women, childless women can easily fall prey to unrealistic ideas about the joy of the nuclear family lifestyle.

The impact of the missing-out cluster is different for women at home and women at work; it depresses Mastery for homemakers—but not for employed women.

Why is this so? It may be harder for the nonworking woman to feel comfortable about her childless state. She has no job to "justify" it, and she is likely to be surrounded by other homemakers who do have children. And the woman at home may have a more traditional concept of what a family ought to be, so she is more bothered by childlessness. Working women may find it easier to build a network of friendships that enrich their lives. The woman at home, who, as we've seen, is often very husband-centered, may expend so much of her energy on that relationship that she has little left to build networks outside the marriage.

Not surprisingly, women who have not chosen to be childless— involuntarily childless women—are more concerned about not having a family than are women who are voluntarily childless. But there was no significant difference between the well-being of childless women who could have children and those who could not. No matter what the reason for not having children, if a woman comes to terms with childlessness, she will be able to get on with her life.

The question of whether or not to become a parent, as we've seen, is a perplexing one for many women today. Every woman must answer that question for herself, but our research suggests that some ways of making that decision are better than others. It might be helpful to look at some ways that seem problematic. We've compiled a list of what might be called "Wrong Reasons for Having Children":

• *Children will give my life meaning.* This belief is an example of "looking in the wrong place" for a sense of Mastery. A woman who has children for this reason may be drawn into the coupled mode of mothering, in which she puts the burden of her own self-worth on her children. This can be harmful to both herself and them.

• *I will be miserable in my later years if I don't have children.* As we've seen, this fear is unrealistic for most women; our data and those of other researchers show that whether or not a woman has children has no significant long-term impact on her well-being. Women without children can lead rich and satisfying lives.

• *I will be a good daughter if I have children.* While women don't usually express it quite this way, they often feel this pressure. Rosalind Barnett finds that many of her clients who are struggling with decisions about having a child are very much involved in issues centering around pleasing their own parents, or being like their mothers. But the woman who decides to have a child for reasons other than her own preferences can be in for serious trouble. As we've seen, being in the lifestyle you prefer has a strong positive impact on well-being. Being in the lifestyle your mother prefers for you is asking for grief, and being where you really don't want to be can make you miserable.

• *I can't be a real woman without having a baby.* Social mythology suggests that motherhood and femininity are synonymous, and that childless women are something less than completely "womanly." Some psychologists have even suggested that women who choose not to have children are in fact abnormal. But when psychologist Judith G. Teicholz compared a group of women who were planning to remain childless with another group similar in age and social class who planned to have children, she found there were no significant differences between the groups in "feminine identification" or neurotic symptoms.[17] Being feminine has nothing to do with whether or not a woman chooses to be a mother.

• *A baby will patch up my marriage.* A risky proposition, at best. Children bring to a troubled marriage the possibility of even more conflict. And our data show that conflict between husband and wife over children has a major depressing effect on both Mastery and Pleasure.

In making a decision about whether or not to have children, a woman would do best to examine her own life and feelings, rather than relying on mystical social pronouncements about what babies do for women's lives. Most of all, she should ask herself whether she is thinking about children simply because she is afraid of society's warnings about what great deprivation she will suffer if she is childless. If so, she could wind up constantly resenting the things she gave up to have children—hardly the best conditions for happy motherhood.

A woman might ask herself whether she in fact likes being with children; whether the idea of being part of a family that includes children appeals to her; whether she would feel comfortable juggling the demands of a job, if that's important to her, with the demands of children—a not-impossible task, but one that calls for a degree of flexibility and tolerance for something less than perfection in all things. She might ask herself whether she thinks she would be a reasonably good mother—not a perfect one.

Most of all she should understand what a child can't do for her. Children can add richness and variety to life, but the woman who expects that having a child will insure happiness in her life is being unrealistic . . . looking in the wrong place.

FINDING THE CHALLENGE

The group I have working for me consists of forty people, all skilled. I get a tremendous satisfaction out of solving a problem. I feel very good about myself. If you'd asked me how I felt at twenty-five, I'd have said, "I don't feel so hot." My ability to work is a good part of the way I feel today. I've developed confidence in my technical competence, and social competence as well, and I have been able to get my act together.

Diane Wright, 40, middle manager
In a computer firm

DIANE, IN SPEAKING ABOUT her own experience, describes the sentiments of many other women. We're paying a great deal of attention to work in this book, not only because it's been overlooked too often in the study of women's lives but because of the findings about the positive impact of work on women's sense of well-being.

This is perhaps the most important finding of our study. In the past, a woman's love life, her age, and whether she was or was not a mother were considered more central to her life than her work. Our study shows that these aren't very useful in predicting a woman's sense of pride and power—her Mastery, in our terms. But the relationship between paid work and Mastery, particularly among women in high-prestige occupations, shows just how vital a role work plays.

This doesn't mean, of course, that you won't find individual differences within the groups. Some nonworking women are higher in Mastery than some women in paid jobs. But with the interesting exception of never-married women, even women in low-prestige jobs—jobs you might think would offer more misery than satisfaction—are higher in sense of Mastery than nonworking women. The authors of *The Inner American* argue, based on similar findings, that for many women "merely assuming the role of paid worker contributes to a sense of resourcefulness that compensates for problems experienced on the job." So, work—having a paid job—accounts for a substantial "chunk" of the sense of Mastery in women. Knowing this can be very useful to women who are deciding whether to enter the workforce, to stay in it, or to reenter it.

Sometimes when we mention these positive findings about work to women, their first reaction is one of skepticism. We hear this sort of comment: "But I know so many women who have good jobs and they're asking, 'Is this all there is?'"

We may be seeing a reaction to unrealistic expectations about work that are related to the job-oriented rhetoric of the seventies. We've pointed out that women have traditionally been encouraged to think that one life role—marriage—would be the source of all their feelings of well-being. The danger now may be that women still seek a simple solution—and merely substitute the letters M.B.A., M.D. or LL.B. for the old "Mrs."

If you think that even the most exciting job will automatically provide everything you need in your life, forever, you are just as vulnerable to the looking-in-the-wrong-place syndrome as is the woman who makes the same assumption about marriage. Work does play a strong role in enhancing Mastery, and, as we'll see, the quality of one's work experience can have an impact on Pleasure as well. But work alone can rarely provide all the feelings of satisfaction and delight that are the components of Pleasure.

Careers may have been oversold in recent years as a simple cure-all for women. But that doesn't mean, as the pendulum swings back, that we should now make the even more critical mistake of underestimating its importance. What we should do is begin to look at work in a more complex way, trying to sort out the nature of its impact on women.

There is another element involved in the skepticism about

women and work. People find the idea of woman as "economic provider" to be strange and disconcerting, as though it were something new. They ask, in effect, "Hasn't woman's place always been in the home, supported by a man so she can raise her children and be happy?"

In fact, the idea that man is naturally the sole breadwinner is really the new idea, in historical terms. As sociologist Michael Gordon of the University of Connecticut puts it, "The housewife, as we understand that term today, is largely a middle-class phenomenon created by industrialization."[1] Women's place may have been in the home, but the home was in fact a work place—whether it was the medieval manor house or the tribal hut. Both men and women performed tasks that were necessary to survival and were highly interdependent. No one would have imagined that women were not part of the "workforce."

Anthropologists teach us that women have traditionally held central roles as income providers. Marjorie Shostak, in her study of the !Kung tribe of the Kalahari desert, says that in this gatherer-hunter society the !Kung women are the mainstay of the economy.

> Vegetable foods constitute about 80 percent of the !Kung diet. . . . Groups of about three to five women leave the village, usually early in the morning, and head for an agreed-upon area. They proceed at a leisurely pace, filling their leather sacks with a variety of foods as they travel, and return to camp by mid-afternoon. After a brief rest, they sort their piles of food, setting some aside for gifts. Most of the food is distributed and consumed within 48 hours. !Kung women also care for children, repair tools, build huts, keep fires, prepare food, and fetch water. The men spend about three hours a day mending tools and doing domestic work. Devoted and loving fathers, they also participate in some child care.[2]

The !Kung women hardly resemble the stereotype of primitive women as downtrodden serfs. Shostak writes:

> !Kung women maintain a status that is higher than that of women in many agricultural and industrial societies throughout the world. They exercise a striking degree of autonomy and influence over their own and their children's lives. Brought up

to respect their own importance in community life, !Kung women become multifaceted adults and are likely to be competent and assertive as well as nurturant and co-operative.

Some anthropologists believe that women lost stature when tribes ended a nomadic way of life and settled into an agricultural society. Property became important, and often, the patriarchal system replaced a more cooperative one.

As women's economic provider role diminished, their status declined, and so did their independence. In our culture, we see the results of economic dependence in the welfare statistics of our own day. The problem of poverty in this country is largely one of women and children—women who cannot earn enough money to support themselves, much less their children.

Women, of course, "work" at home, but there is a profound difference between the impact of paid work and that of homemaking on well-being.

Why do the two kinds of work that women perform have such different consequences? Some theorists think it is due to the nature of the job of homemaking. First of all, homemaking is a socially devalued role. In one official Labor Department ranking of jobs according to the complexity of skills required, homemaker got the same ranking as parking lot attendant—and was ranked below marine mammal handler!

Secondly, homemaking does not generate income. As critic Elizabeth Janeway writes, "Women working at home are in an archaic situation in the sense that what they do stands outside the money economy and the values related to it."[3] And this, of course, is a fairly recent development. "It used to be quite usual for them to earn by work at home, even if their earnings were less than men's." Not earning money, we found, was among the major concerns of homemakers. And the economic value of what they do has been ignored by traditional economists. Perhaps most important, for homemakers there are no standards, no objective ways of measuring performance. As Janeway says, "Now that women at home have lost their old tie with the production of economically valuable goods, they lost, too, the chance of being judged by the objective standards of an outside community, no matter how small." In the words of sociologist Helena Lopata, the author of a major study on American housewives: "homemaking has no organized social circle which judges performance and has the right to fire for incompetence, no pay scale, no measurement against performers in the same role. It is vague, open to any woman who gets married, regardless of ability."[4]

The woman at home may be protected from the risks of a competitive world in which performance is consistently judged and rated—but she is also out of the running for its prizes.

Given all this, it is not hard to see why being a homemaker is hazardous to Mastery for most women. It's hard to derive self-esteem from a role that society doesn't think much of; it's hard to feel in control of a job where the standards are so unclear. It's hard to give yourself a good grade on how well you are doing when it's not clear what "good" really is. This isn't to say, of course, that every woman should run right out and get a job. Homemakers reading these findings could say to themselves, "Just another attack on my way of life!" But that is the opposite of our intent. Understanding that homemaking cuts a woman off from an important source of nourishment for her well-being can help her avoid the pitfalls of that job. A woman who knows that the role of homemaker involves risk to her sense of Mastery can take care to get involved in other activities that offer the sort of feedback, standards, and rewards that are so vital. In the long run, such knowledge will make the role of homemaker more viable for women, better suited to individual needs.

Our findings, we believe, added to those of other recent studies, should help sweep many of the old notions about women and work right into the trash can. Work is not peripheral to women's sense of Mastery, it is central. Women do not fully develop their capacities if they function primarily in the sphere of feelings and emotion; the idea that a man is what he does and a woman is what she feels is archaic. If work per se is important to a woman's well-being, so too is the quality of her work life. The balance of rewards over concerns at work turned out to be important to both Mastery and Pleasure.

To measure the balance in the area of work, we asked women to indicate how rewarding or distressing certain features of their current jobs were. Items such as "the job fits your skills" or "the job is insecure" were scored on a four-point scale. Each working woman thus had a numerical score that measured the rewards and concerns of her job; the more the rewards outweighed the concerns, the more favorable her work balance, and the higher her scores on Mastery and Pleasure. The more a woman likes her job, the better her self-image and the more she enjoys her life.

This is important for women to know, because in the past, young women have not been encouraged to think seriously about work, or to put much energy into the task of matching their skills with possible careers. Research on girls' career choices shows that girls choose a more restricted, less varied range of occupations than do boys; girls' career choices are highly stereotyped at an early age, with about one-half to two-thirds of girls aspiring to be a teacher, a nurse, or a secretary.[5] Regardless of age, intelligence, or social class, girls have shied away from choosing high-prestige careers.[6] But among employed women in our study, we found, the higher the prestige of the woman's occupation, the higher her scores on Mastery.

So the young woman who doesn't think much about work—or who thinks only in terms of stereotypes of what women should do, not what she likes to do—is being set up for problems later in life. It's disturbing to see that these young women are hesitant to consider demanding careers. Given the relationship between well-being and an occupation that commands respect (and often a good income), young women who settle for any job are unwittingly helping to sabotage their own chances for heightened well-being.

Irma Green,* the therapist in her late thirties, is now seeing the consequences of not considering a high-prestige career when she was younger. "Because of not being a psychiatrist, I can't be as independent as I'd like to be. I feel as though I made a mistake in my very early education and I'm hindered because of the variety of restrictions that are placed on nonphysician mental health people. I don't necessarily reject those, but they do restrict me and that's a drawback. I can't be as independent as I'd like to be."

An important part of our study was finding out just what it was about women's jobs that gave them the major rewards and problems, and how these affected well-being. We found that many old beliefs were false.

---

* Irma Green was introduced first in Chapter Four, page 75.

The things women find rewarding about work are, by and large, the same things that men find rewarding and include both the inherent nature of the work and the social relationships. It has been believed that when women *did* work, what mattered most to them were the social aspects of the job. Women worked, it was said, to get out of the house and make friends, to enjoy warm relationships with co-workers and bosses, to be in a congenial atmosphere. What women workers actually did on the job was decreed to be of only passing importance to them. Not so! The items that make up the most important reward cluster of work form what we call the "challenge" cluster:

> The job offers challenge and stimulation
> There is a variety of tasks
> There is an opportunity for learning
> The job fits your skills
> You get a chance to make decisions

We also found a second cluster of rewards that had more to do with the social side of working; the "social relationships" cluster:

> Liking the people you work with
> Liking the boss
> Being able to help people and interrelate with them

What women found most rewarding about their jobs were the challenge items, and these had a strong positive relationship to Mastery and Pleasure. So challenge on the job is a very important contributor to well-being for employed women. Social relationships were less rewarding; this cluster had no effect on Mastery and only a slight effect on Pleasure.

These findings show a serious commitment to work among women today, one that is corroborated in the book *The Inner American*. There has been a profound change in women's attitudes toward their work in recent years. The Michigan researchers found a "remarkable increase" in commitment to work among women between 1957 and 1976. Women don't work merely "to get out of the house," and it's not just to help the family either, the researchers say. "This finding is of great significance because many people have argued that women have entered the workforce increasingly over this generation primarily to provide the necessary income to maintain an adequate style of family living. This is clearly not the entire story. Most employed women today are similar to men in their commitment to work."

Diane Wright, the middle manager, is typical of many working women who value the challenge in a job: "I guess I'm just ambitious enough that I'm ready for the next job at this point—not that I'm looking or anything like that, but I feel I've had this particular job for close to two years and I've done it fairly successfully, and so I'm ready for another promotion. I like being in a little bit over my head and I find that after about two years of doing some things, you're no longer in over your head. The challenge isn't quite there."

Diane's competence at work has not only helped her develop the good feelings about herself she didn't have at twenty-five, but it has also nurtured an important ingredient of Mastery—a feeling of control over her life: "I'm at the point now where I can say that if I want to, I can make things happen. I think in a business environment there are always things beyond your control—the economy can go wrong, for example. But in general I think I can make things happen if I want to."

For Marian Williamson,* the high school principal, the best parts of working are the variety and getting to make decisions, important ingredients of the challenge factor. "There are lots of rewards in my work," she says. "You see students grow, you see creativity; I can be creative developing programs, that sort of thing. There is also the administrative side, which I rather enjoy, which is keeping things organized and developing policies. I find I like that more and more. Then there is the range of difficult responsibilities that are part and parcel of the job—a student becomes emotionally upset, the parents have to be called—things like that."

Marian also feels a sense of control in her life from seeking even greater challenges: "I think I have much more sense of control over what I do than I ever did. I think my decision to get a doctorate is part of that. Once it dawned on me that I wanted to do it, I did it, and I've rather enjoyed it. It will give me a sense of accomplishment, that 'worthless' degree. Yes, I do have a feeling that I have some control over what's going to happen next. If I want to be in X place in five years, I had better do what it takes to get

---

* Marian Williamson was introduced in Chapter Five, page 98.

there. I no longer believe that if you just go along and do a good job, things will happen."

For Carolyn Stone,* the director of women's programs for a small foundation, the most important fact about her job is that it fits her skills and values. "It is a marvelous job. I think of all the things I have ever done in terms of work, I have enjoyed this job more than any other. The reason for my liking this job so much is that I have never had a job so completely in tune with my own value structure. While from a professional point of view, the scale of this project has not been large, the scope of the issues we've been dealing with and the opportunities for learning that I have personally had have been enormous. I'm unlikely to find this kind of opportunity for professional growth in very many things. I've been working with ten of the major organizations in the city in terms of developing new instruments for job analysis and along with that have developed some training workshops for employees, so it's a very rich opportunity."

It is not only women in high-prestige jobs who find challenge an important part of their work. Esther, forty-two, has been a typist for thirteen years, and while some might think of her work as tedious, for Esther it's a source of self-esteem and a chance to grow. "I love it. It's very interesting. I'm getting an education. I type all kinds of journals; I typed a whole study on economic conditions in India. And then I type all these other books and doctoral theses and it's very gratifying because, when I looked at the list of graduate student [theses] at the university, there were thirty-six, and I typed twelve. That's a third. I do resumés and these hard statistical tables with numbers and it's very challenging. Out of everything I do in my whole life—I always say I can do very little—but I know I do one thing very well, and that's type. They can very rarely find a typing error in my work. The more papers I type the less they can find a typing error."

The main thing Esther likes about her job is the pride it gives her. "It sends me on ego trips. I don't get ego trips from anything else I do, so I really do devote my entire body to getting ego trips from my typing. I know a lot of people at the university—they all come back and forth to my house and they make so much of me and my typing and that's wonderful."

* Carolyn Stone was introduced in Chapter Two, page 23.

Esther says: "I have a goal now and eventually I will do it because I am very determined. And that is to teach typing at the high school. I can honestly say that I am a professional who knows how to do things. When I type, I look for all the different things—the content—and absorb it in my mind and get smarter. I look for grammar as I type and edit, and every change I make I note it on their copy. I spell very well but still I always have a dictionary where I can check out hyphenations. Someday I'm going to teach at the high school and I'm also going to write a book with my own ideas about typing."

She adds: "If someone calls me up and says they have a 500-page thesis—well, that would floor a lot of people, not me. This kind of project drives some people crazy because they don't know how to deal with big things. I approach it from a completely different angle. I break it down into chapters and then it doesn't seem like 500 pages. I can visualize it. I take it in chunks rather than in a big mess, and I do it very easily."

Although some women in our study were negative about their work, we were surprised to find that most women valued their jobs and were very attached to them, even when the jobs seemed downright dreary.[7] This phenomenon, we think, reflects the low self-esteem and isolation that characterizes the situation of so many homemakers. The authors of *The Inner American* comment, "The reason women do care about social contact at work and mention it more than men is that men aren't so conscious of an alternative role of housewife with its isolation and loneliness."

For women who have been in the workforce for a long time, there is sometimes nostalgia or longing for the life of a housewife, particularly if their job has lost any excitement it might have had. But often they have forgotten the realities of life at home and again are looking in the wrong place. If they do go back to the role of housewife, it is often only for a brief period.

Sometimes what women who are feeling burned out really need is a better or more congenial job. Elise Martin, forty-one, does clerical work at a small museum. "I used to think when I was first going to work that just being able to get a job would be an accomplishment. I didn't think enough of myself to realize I had any other value. I would have been thankful had anyone hired me for anything, at one point, because I felt like, what did I know? Nothing! What kind of an education did I have? None! But now, it's very different. I don't want to do just anything. I couldn't be stuck just sitting at an adding machine. I really want to do something I like."

So any old job may do for a while, but eventually something more is needed. And women are becoming more vocal in saying so. Not only do more women complain today about their work problems, but they are much more likely to cite a work issue as one of the major concerns in their lives.

Noting a rising level of complaints, some people are quick to conclude that women are unhappier than they were in the past because the workplace is an "unnatural" place for them. We agree with the authors of *The Inner American,* who see the situation quite differently: women are voicing more complaints because work is now so important to them. When women didn't see work as central to their lives, they were less likely to complain about it. The findings of the Michigan researchers support this point of view. They found that complaints about unhappiness at work had increased most among professional women. These women, they say, are likely to be the most politically aware group, and the least likely to ignore such issues as inadequate pay and sex discrimination on the job. "The change observed in reports of job-focused unhappiness among professional women might reflect this political sensitization rather than an increased and deep-rooted demoralization about work among this group." In other words, as women's perceptions of inequality—and their own expectations of what they deserve—increase, the level of their complaints rises as well.

We can probably expect that women will complain more, not less, about job issues in the future. There has been a striking change in the attitudes of young women between 1957 and the present. In the fifties, younger women were quite different from other groups in the workforce in that they were much less dissatisfied. But undoubtedly many of those women saw their jobs as an interim step between leaving home and getting married, or, if they were married, as a way to earn extra income before the birth of their first child. Since their expectations of work were so limited, it's not surprising that they seemed content with their jobs.

Today the situation is reversed. Job dissatisfaction among younger, more educated women has grown tremendously. *The Inner American* researchers found increased job dissatisfaction most dramatic among high school- and college-educated young women. And when psychologist Kay Deaux of Purdue studied women managers, she found the younger executives much more dissatisfied with their salaries and rate of promotion than were the older managers.[8]

But if women are becoming more vocal about problems at work, they are also quicker to understand that work has a positive effect on their well-being. At least, this is so for women in good jobs. More professional women spontaneously mentioned work to the Michigan researchers as a source of happiness than did any other group—male or female.

If the rewards that seem most important to women on the job are those that deal with challenge, the concerns seem to be a mirror image. We found two major groups of concerns. The first one we call the "dull job" cluster:

> There is little challenge
> The work is dull and monotonous
> The job doesn't fit your skills

The second group was the "dead-end" cluster; it includes these items:

> Little chance for advancement in the organization
> Lack of recognition
> Poor opportunities for professional development
> Inadequate pay

Both the dull job and dead-end clusters were strongly associated with diminished well-being. Women who had high scores on these clusters tended to be low in Mastery and Pleasure.

The dead-end and dull job clusters create a trap that women are especially likely to fall into when they are forced into the workplace unexpectedly. For Ellen Dudley, a forty-year-old divorcee with three children, her work as a secretary in medical sales is often tedious. "If I really start to think about what I would like to be doing, I could make myself miserable sitting here. If I think about the conditions of the job, I consider myself very lucky because it's a young company, tremendous flexibility, no clock-punching, totally flexible. There's minimal politics, minimal sexism. I only wish the work had something to do with things I'm interested in. When I start to examine that, I get very unhappy. But then I think about my goal of being able to be financially independent, and if things work out, this is the right path to choose, and then I can do what I like at home and outside the job. It's the compromise I've had to make."

Just as dull, repetitive work is a big problem for many women, so too is the lack of recognition. Ego rewards in the outside world are not supposed to be important to women. But when they don't come, a woman's well-being can be diminished. Brenda Flint, forty-nine, is single and works in an insurance company, where she rarely gets praise or any other positive feedback. "In my old job, my boss used to come back and say, 'When I go to the West Coast, they're singing your praises up and down.' He used to call me his right arm because I really was vital to his job and made the whole thing run. But in my job now, they don't even know you're there. Even though I'm making more money now, I still think you need to have somebody say something about what you're doing—even if they say you're doing a terrible job. In this job, they don't say anything."

Lack of recognition may be much more painful for women than previously believed. Men were traditionally thought to derive great ego rewards from work, while women did not. But when the Michigan researchers asked their subjects whether they would rather be regarded as excellent in their work roles or family roles, more employed women than men opted for work, and even when the researchers omitted single women from the analysis, the pattern persisted. Trying to figure out this response, the researchers speculated that perhaps women, more than men, may take it for granted that they are good spouses or parents. "Consequently, a social reputation for being excellent at work provides a much more distinctive ego boost for a woman."

For Brenda, the absence of this "ego boost" is clearly painful, as it is for many women. Lack of recognition is not the only problem Brenda faces at work. "I work a seven-and-a-half-hour day, the regular desk-chained job, which I hate. I have been working here twenty-three years. Isn't that terrible, to work in a place that you really can't stand for twenty-three years? It's just that I wasn't able to go to college; I would have liked to but we just didn't have the resources and one brother was going to dental school and another was going to be an engineer, and in our day, no one encouraged you. I'm a people-oriented person and in this job you're strictly stuck with policies and applications, so you don't have any contact with people. The first two hours are good, but to sit for eight hours and read and sign gets to be too much because I like more creative things, even though I'm not trained in anything."

Brenda didn't always feel this way about work. "I started out years ago in a job in personnel and I really loved that job. I worked in the training division. My boss was the training director and I was a secretary. Then I went from there into sort of being an assistant. That was a very good job; it was people-oriented. He was the sort of person who was always thinking of new ways to attract people to the company and he recruited at the college level. It involved working with agents all over the country and we had to set up schedules with hundreds of agents at thousands of places. You could set your own schedules and he didn't care how you did it as long as it got done.

"I liked that because that kind of challenge makes you feel good. Sometimes the wives of applicants would be coming in, and I'd take them around the city. In the summer there were training programs—all the time there were people coming in for interviews and the office was an active place. But finally, I went as far as I could go there. I applied to be an interviewer in personnel but at that time they only wanted college people. I went into this job because I was told I would keep getting promotions, but I don't know, I always seem to stay the same and my boss says he always puts in for me but I don't get promotions."

Despite all the negative aspects of Brenda's job, she doesn't feel she would be better off at home. For nonmarried women, and for many married women as well, even work that isn't satisfying fills many needs. What women in bad job situations usually want is to find a way to get a better job, not to be at home. Among older women, of course, the priorities may be different; by fifty-five or sixty, and earlier for some, the option of retirement may be desirable.

Our findings, we believe, offer important guidelines to women who are deciding what kind of work best suits them. Since the challenge cluster is so closely tied to well-being, and the lack of challenge is so distressing, it's clear that women should look at the work itself, at the stimulation and variety it offers, and not just at the nice folks in the office. Though liking the people can be a reward of work, the fact that it has no relation to well-being tells us that this aspect can be a bonus for women but should not be the crucial element in one's decision. The boss may be wonderful, the co-workers terrific, but if the job is dull and dead-ended, a woman is vulnerable as far as her well-being is concerned.

The importance of challenge to well-being is connected to the relevance of occupational prestige—that is, of a job's social standing. Our study shows, not surprisingly, that the higher the prestige of a woman's job, the greater the challenge. And the higher the prestige of the job, the greater the sense of Mastery—the two rise together.

Some people—including women—worry that if women become increasingly concerned with advancement and prestige, they will become just like men, or more accurately, just like the male stereotype. Some envision an armada of hard-eyed, hard-boiled, competitive females set loose in the world, and what, they wonder, will become of nurturing and caring?

What really does happen, it seems, is that women take the nurturant imperative into the workplace with them. As we've seen, the nurturant imperative is so strong in women that they make moral decisions in accord with it. They also incorporate it into the way in which they function at work. One intriguing theme to emerge from our study is that even in jobs which require a fair amount of assertiveness and leadership, women find ways to fit their wish to "care for others" into the job description.

For example, Susan Gardener, a forty-one-year-old cardiac surgeon, finds her ability to relate to people an integral part of a profession that is often thought of as the domain of men with muted emotions. "Coming away from seeing a juvenile patient and knowing that I've had a terrific time with a mother, the patient, and the other children this mother may bring along, is important to me. In other words, the children like the experience of coming to see the doctor, even if they're only visiting and a sister or a brother is the patient. They've had a good relationship with somebody in a white coat and the mother is happy with the visit and I get a chance to do some 'well-baby' care in addition to cardiac care."

Susan feels her actions are atypical for a surgeon. "Very often I will, for instance, pick up on a one-year-old child who has no immunizations, something like that. Or I'll see a three-month-old baby who has a diaper rash, who's dirty underneath the diaper area and a mother doesn't really know how to care for the child. I'll go and get one of the nurses who is in charge that day, send her in, and we start helping the family and teaching the mother how to take better care of the baby than she is doing. So, it's not just taking care of a valve or whatever, it's a relationship with the whole family. These are the rewards. Of course, it's always nice when you make a great discovery, when you find something in an X ray that no one else has, or you get a feeling that all the training you've had and the experience are being put to use. You've found something that is going to help cure the symptoms of the patient or at least you've gotten down to what's caused them. That's always nice, but it happens much less often."

Of all physicians, surgeons are the ones who most often have the reputation of being technicians, of being detached from patients. Susan senses that she is somewhat different from the men she works with. "I know my strengths and I know my weaknesses in comparison to the men in this department. I have no ego. Well, I guess there isn't any such thing as having no ego, but there are incredible differences between them and me. I think some of them don't have any close contact with patients at all and I think it's easier for a woman. They're surgeons and they may wield the knife, but beyond that, while they may have a pleasant relationship with a patient, they don't quite have that nurturing side to their personality that a woman has—like when you watch the nurses with the patients. So when I say I know what my strengths are, that's one of them. I'm able to relate well with them—patients and children. I have always done that well. Nurses will bring difficult patients to me."

In managerial jobs, women often find that their concern for people under their direction can make them extremely effective managers in organizations. Edith Wheeler, fifty-five, chairman of a biology department at a large, prestigious university, finds that in setting her priorities, she displays a strong concern for the quality of experience of both faculty and students. "I was very concerned about faculty salary kinds of things and interested in seeing about increases. I was interested in sabbatical leave pay, which at the time was quite minimal—so minimal that people weren't taking leaves because they couldn't afford to. I was concerned about teaching loads, because I felt that faculty couldn't be very effective if they had to spend too much time in the classroom. There was not energy left to teach well or do any research and the obvious problem was one of money. I presented costs to the president and then went to the different departments to plead for changes, and by cooperation from the faculty and the president and the board of trustees, we were able to institute a new teaching load."

For some women, the idea that possessing power and the nurturant imperative can go hand in hand comes as a surprise. Amy Faulkner, thirty-six, an editor at a national magazine, finds that she brings the caring she developed from her days as a Peace Corps worker and teacher to her present job. "In journalism, you do have a lot more power than you do being a teacher. The humanism thing didn't go by the board—the subjects I write about are various compassionate things, but from a position of much more power than I had before. It started to dawn on me when I first started working at a small paper that I was probably doing more and with more power than when I was a teacher. That was a surprise. I thought I'd have to give up the whole liberal, hairshirt, nurturing stuff."

As Amy discovered, "nice people" can have power; the resources and income that come with a good job do not make women less nurturant or unfeminine.

Entering the workforce or climbing a career ladder is not such an all-encompassing change that it will transform women's lives beyond recognition. Becoming life-long workers will certainly not make them imitation men. It will not provide a cornucopia from which all the good things in life will pour. But the role of worker can greatly enhance a woman's sense of Mastery. If she finds herself stuck in a low-paying, dead-end job, of course, the quality of her life will suffer. On the other hand, in a job that offers challenge, variety, and recognition, her sense of Pleasure as well as of Mastery will be nourished. In our modern, urban, technological society, the workplace is one of the major areas from which people draw their good feelings about themselves and their lives. The power to earn one's own way in the world has a profound impact on the inner landscape. Often, when women discover this power for the first time, they experience a sense of exhilaration. Feminist Charlotte Perkins Gilman, in a story first published in 1914, describes this sensation.[9]

In a fantasy titled "If I Were a Man," Gilman tells the story of Mollie, a devoted wife who has just been reprimanded by her husband because she had neglected to give him a bill for an item she purchased until the bill became overdue. As he strides angrily away from her down the walk, Mollie weeps and wishes with all her heart that she was a man, free to stomp off in a huff into the world beyond the front walk. Suddenly, she becomes a man—her husband—striding down the street, and her first realization is that her feet, in flat, practical shoes, are comfortable for the first time. She is amazed by how free and strong she feels. She slips her hand into the suit pocket and is flooded all at once by a powerful new sensation:

> The pockets came as a revelation. Of course she had known they were there, had counted them, made fun of them, mended them, even envied them; but she never dreamed of how it felt to have pockets . . . it was full—the firmly held fountain pen, safe unless she stood on her head, the keys, pencils, letters, documents, notebook, checkbook, bill folder—all at once, with a deep rushing sense of power and pride, she felt what she had never felt before in her life—the possession of money, of her own earned money—hers to give or to withhold, not to beg for, tease for, wheedle for—Hers.

CHAPTER SEVEN

RISKS AND DREAMS

I've thought of changing jobs, but I can't see how I could walk into something new, without the seniority that I have here. How could I just walk in some place and get as much money without being able to say to someone, "Look, I can do this or that'?

Brenda Flint,* office worker in
an insurance office

A CRUCIAL WORD that should be in the consciousness of every woman who is thinking about getting ahead in her career is RISK. Risk has a clear connection to the challenge cluster of rewards. To find a job situation where you get to make decisions, where you find variety and an opportunity for learning, where you can stretch your capabilities to the utmost, you may have to take a few chances. And taking chances is sometimes very hard.

A disturbing picture has emerged from studies of employed women: typically they don't get into positions where they will get on-the-job training, yet often they don't feel comfortable venturing into unfamiliar territory. Too few are like Diane Wright, the middle manager we met in the last chapter who said, "I like to be in a little bit over my head, and I find that after two years of doing things, you're no longer in over your head."

---

* Brenda Flint was introduced in Chapter Six, page 115.

In the job market, too often women's progress is like a crab's—sideways. Barriers to advancement within the workplace are a big part of the problem, but there is also a tendency to look for jobs that women know they can already do—ones that offer minimal risk. One executive, looking for a female assistant sales manager, put an ad in the paper specifying that the salary range was $22,000 to $25,000. She had only a few women applicants. She ran the same ad dropping the salary range to $18,000 and was bombarded with hundreds of applications. Clearly, the higher salary had frightened away women who thought that since the salary was above their expectations, the job would be too tough for their capacities.

Why is it that women too often don't move as fast or as far as their talents could take them? In the early seventies, as a "new wave" of social scientists began to examine issues concerning women in the workplace, they tended to focus on early socialization. What was it about the way girls were raised in our society that created problems for them at work? Did the fact that they didn't play football or other competitive sports put them far behind in the race for the corporate boardroom? Did they dread success because they thought it to be "unfeminine"? Did they fall prey to the "Cinderella Complex"[1] of dependency on Prince Charming? This intense concentration on inner dynamics and socialization, critics such as Rosabeth Kanter argue, tended to deemphasize the real barriers to women in the labor force. It tended to "blame the victim" and create in women the misguided belief that the only barriers are inside their heads.[2] We should concentrate instead, Kanter argues, on women's experiences in the workplace.

We would suggest that both areas should be tackled. While socialization can be overemphasized, there are often deeply engrained, long-lasting habits of thinking and feeling that create real difficulties for women. One of these is the way in which women explain their behavior to themselves—their "attribution patterns," as social scientists say. Research shows that compared to men, women more often write their success off to luck and see themselves as less talented than they actually are. Men fall prey to these problems too, but not as consistently as women. For example, in a study of 7,700 college seniors, women with B-plus averages said they didn't think they could do graduate work, while men with C-plus averages said they thought they could. And, in another study of male and female junior executives, the women saw themselves as less competent than did the men—even though their supervisors reported little difference between them.[3]

In her clinical practice Rosalind Barnett often finds this tendency to underrate one's own ability or to misread signals at work about the quality of one's performance. One woman, for example, was applying for an extremely competitive advanced degree program. She had returned to school later in life, thought of herself as a marginal student, and had real questions about whether she should go on to get the final degree. She needed a reference from one of her professors, but was unsure about whom to ask. She had taken a course from a nationally known expert in the field, but was hesitant to approach him. Rosalind asked the woman how she had done in the professor's course, and was astonished to discover she had received an A plus. The woman's low self-image of herself as a student had not allowed her to see and accept a real badge of achievement—or to act on that success.

Another woman had been with a large firm for twenty years, and had just moved to a new division where she was mastering a different set of skills. The company announced an early retirement plan for twenty-year employees, with generous pension and benefits. The only catch was that those employees who didn't take such an offer would then be subject to being fired if their work wasn't up to par—with no such benefits. The woman loved her work, and didn't want to retire since she was only in her early fifties, but was convinced that she would be one of the employees who would be fired. Rosalind encouraged her to have a frank talk with her supervisors about her performance. In the interview she discovered that the company had no intention of firing her if she didn't take early retirement—in fact, they talked of her value to the company in glowing terms.

Knowing that you might be underrating your work should encourage you to take positive steps to combat this tendency. It's important to seek feedback from supervisors and co-workers about the quality of your performance so you will have a realistic picture of how you are doing. It's also important not to dismiss or explain away cues that point to success—like the A plus Rosalind's client received. Fortunately, recent studies show women are becoming less quick to see failures as their fault, and are quicker to claim their successes.[4]

Being able to assesss your talents realistically is essential to building the courage to take risks in the job market. And one theme that emerged with particular strength in the intensive interview phase of our study was the important role risk had played for women in good jobs. Very often these women made a difficult choice in their careers. They went back to school even though it was hard to find the time and money; they opted for a less secure but more challenging job instead of staying in a settled one; they jumped at an opportunity when it came along. Usually, the results were very good.

Fran Crane, for example, who at fifty-five is the administrative director of the pathology department in a large hospital, felt "stuck" in a job that had become routine. She had been working as a personnel director at a small college for twenty years. "I had gotten to the point where it wasn't fun anymore and I really wanted to make a change." So at age fifty, she left her secure job to get a management degree. "I'm probably the oldest person who ever went full time. At first I wanted to go into business, but when I saw what openings there were, a lot of it seemed very phony and I guess I liked the feeling of a nonprofit institution. Now I'm in a hospital, and while it's quite different from a college, we're still nonprofit and dealing with the serving of people. You can feel that what you're doing has some impact, and I like that."

At the university Fran found she had some problems adapting to being a full-time student again. "I hadn't been doing that type of reading for a long time. I had worked with older women at the college when I was there, in the continuing education program. I encouraged them when the going got tough. I told them, 'Go on, you can do it!' then I found myself having all the problems they had, and that surprised me. But it shouldn't have. The issue of age cropped up. It had never bothered me or been a factor before, and all of a sudden it was hitting me over the head. In the middle of the year I seriously considered dropping out. I thought it was really dumb of me to think that I could do it, and why was I here? But somehow, having paid the tuition, I decided I might as well stumble along." Despite the difficulty, Fran stuck with it, and "wound up doing relatively well. They put us into study groups which turned out to be very effective for me. There was a thirty-year-old, a forty-year-old, and me, a fifty-year-old. We became very close and worked very well together."

In her new job, Fran had to take on a major challenge. Her

predecessor had been fired, and his assistant had only been on the job for a month. "I walked into an office where there was absolutely no one who knew anything, so I had to dig it out bit by bit, which was terrible, but was a good learning process. I think another good thing is that I can work independently. I can define the job as I see fit, and once I decide what we need in the way of personnel help, I can hire those people."

Her experiences on the job and at the university have convinced Fran that women don't do as well as they should in the job market because they don't take risks when they should. "Women wait to be chosen, instead of presenting themselves for the job. Women will not take on a job unless they have mastered it and know how to do it. A man takes it on and learns on the job. A lot of people have asked me how I thought I could even go in and run that department of pathology when I didn't know what was going on. I wasn't afraid of what I didn't know and I think this has happened as a result of my change of thinking in recent years. I find that I'm encouraging a lot of the young females that I supervise or have something to do with."

Sometimes encouragement from a senior person gives a woman the courage she needs to make the career leap that will make the difference for her. Pat Spaulding, a psychologist, now forty-seven, had been working as a nurse and was in the process of getting her master's degree in nursing. She found herself getting very interested in psychology and the psychological aspects of patient care. One professor she worked with was both a nurse and a psychologist, and the professor urged Pat to get her Ph.D. in psychology.

"When I went into nursing," Pat says, "working in hospitals was hard work, low pay, lots of rotating of shifts—something that I couldn't see doing for many years." Now Pat works at a large hospital, helping nurses cope with the psychological problems of patients. But at first she wasn't sure she had made the right decision. "I wondered if I should have just switched and gone into psychiatric nursing and tried to stay within nursing. But a psychologist teacher of mine told me, 'if you do that you're not going to feel like either a nurse or a psychologist,' and that was a big turning point. I'm now feeling good about my choice. I like my co-workers, I think there is an opportunity here to try out new kinds of things. I don't feel the frustration here that things can't be done. It's just a question of trying to figure out new ways of doing things."

For some women, a complete career change involves a great deal of risk and difficulty. Amy Faulkner,* the editor for a national magazine, had held a series of jobs that were "basically female, nurturing—doing things that I thought required a more passive personality than I had. I was a Peace Corps volunteer, I worked with juvenile delinquents, I was a teacher. And it finally sunk in to me that I wanted a job that had power, that there are nice people with power." Amy acted on that insight. She left a $12,000-a-year teaching job for an $89-a-week reporting job at a small newspaper. When her marriage broke up, leaving her with a young son to support, she still didn't regret having made the job switch, but she says: "It kind of changed my view of politics. My first inclination was that everyone was getting paid as poorly there as I was and we should all clamor for more money, together, and that didn't work. Finally, I realized I'd have to ask for a raise myself, and I did. It was just ten dollars a week, but it was a moral victory. I did take other jobs to help out, like teaching at an adult education center. Gradually there were step raises which helped, but it took a good year or more. I liked journalism so much better than teaching that I didn't even consider going back."

When an opportunity came for Amy to take a part-time position with a large magazine, she left the security of the small paper. In the new job she was paid only for what she produced, which meant she was working long hours, with very little financial security. But the gamble eventually paid off with a full-time staff job, giving her a better salary than she'd ever had before and more freedom to deal with subjects she liked. But she is still not content to stop there; she is interested in doing some television work on the side that wouldn't compete with her work at the magazine. "If I could do that without jeopardizing my staff job, I would. It's important to get enough clout within the system so they don't treat me as just another employee, so I can earn and get special privileges."

Amy is still learning and growing with the job, getting more sophisticated on the issue of politics in the workplace. She says she is surprised to find herself where she is. "I had the most traditional family imaginable. I'm really a black sheep in the family, emotionally, politically, psychologically. My mother only worked as a secretary before she got married; she won't work now. The

---

* Amy Faulkner was introduced in Chapter Six, page 119.

women's movement has engendered absolutely nothing in her and my father except hostility. To be doing all this—doing it and liking it—really surprises me."

The way women like Amy go about changing jobs or entering new fields can be important in shaping not only their careers but their self-concepts, according to psychologist Patricia Gurin of the University of Michigan's Institute for Social Research.[5] Women's initial experiences in the labor market, Gurin argues, may be the key to their later job patterns, rather than what happened to them in their childhood.

Gurin analyzed 1977 national survey data on black and white men and women in the workforce who attempted to improve their work status during the past year. She found significant sex differences in the ways in which workers tried to advance. The men tended to either change jobs or find on-the-job training. The women more often left the workforce to go back to school or find some other method of improving their skills outside the job market. When these workers were asked to rate their own abilities, the men had more favorable self-ratings than the women, and the men also tended to feel more in control of their lives.

But when Gurin looked separately at women who stayed in the job market—who either changed jobs or got into on-the-job programs—the results were strikingly different. These women had higher estimates of their own performances and expected more in terms of advancement. They were more similar to the men in the study.

Women, it seems, often feel they are not ready to take risks in the job market, so they decide to improve themselves rather than try to forge ahead. But sometimes women can spend too much time "getting ready to get ready" for a job. Sometimes the decision to go back to school is a good one; at times women are correct in believing they need more skills in order to advance. Sometimes, however, a woman can decide to go back to school because it is safe, a way of putting off risk, avoiding rejection. Gurin's analysis indicates that there can be real benefits to a woman's remaining in the job environment, at least in terms of her self-evaluation. It may be that success on the job provides a stronger underpinning for one's self-confidence than does course work—it may seem more "real," in terms of achievement, than what happens at school. Certainly it's important for women to seek out the advantages of opportunities for on-the-job training, which, according to Gurin, may be the real key to what happens to women's careers.

Diane, the middle manager we quoted in the last chapter, was able to learn about her field after she got her job. For her, answering a newspaper ad for a position in the computer field was a critical event: "I didn't know much about it. I didn't even know what a computer was, to be honest. But I had put myself through college and when I graduated I owed about $500 and decided I'd better get a job, fast. After I answered the ad I went through a series of interviews and tests, and in retrospect I'll be honest and say I didn't know what these people were talking about."

But unlike many women, Diane didn't wait to be sure she understood all the nuts and bolts of the job before she decided she could do it. "They offered me a job and I took it. I had the option to go into teaching that September and I guess one of the reasons I was brave enough not to, was that I figured that in my computer job it would take until at least August for them to figure out I didn't know what I was talking about. If they fired me then I would have some money and I'd go and teach. I found that I started to understand it after two months and then it all came together. I also found it was something I enjoyed."

Sometimes, a step that at first seems impossibly hard turns out to be "do-able." Risk may seem more threatening than it really is.

Sharon, a forty-seven-year-old lawyer, grew up in a home where both parents were professionals; her mother taught at a midwestern university. Sharon says: "I always knew I would do something. I didn't know what I wanted and it certainly wasn't law, I never thought of that. I don't know what I thought I would do—maybe teach." But after she had been teaching for four years, she decided to take a giant step and go to law school. "I wasn't very happy with teaching. Then I had a baby and I was home for a year. I just knew I was not cut out to be home; I wanted to do something. I debated whether to go back and get a Ph.D. in history and teach some more or do something else. And something else—when it got to be law school—just seemed like too much to undertake.

"But one day I discovered that a law school near where we lived had a part-time law program you could go to at night. It suddenly seemed to me it might be possible to do this, so I started very tentatively with just a few toes in the water. I thought I'd try it and I'd drop out if it were too hard or took up too much time. Well, I loved it. I just loved it. The same courses were taught in the morning and then in the evening, and the dean was very nice and let me float in and out of courses as I needed them. But I didn't have any role models. Looking back, I realized that I sort of stumbled along with all these problems of trying to raise a family and go to school and feeling very inadequate, like there was something wrong with me . . . because nobody was in front of me. I'm that role model now for a lot of people. People call me up—people I don't even know—and say, 'How do you do it?' "

Sharon sees in her friends, and in her clients, an ambivalence about taking the risk of getting into the job market. "One woman was in here, and I identified with her a lot. She was in her forties, married to a doctor, the whole shtick. She is trying to decide 'Who am I?' and she's facing the whole professional decision, which is so hard for a woman that age to make: putting yourself on the line and facing the possibility of failure. I've been encouraging her to work full time and she is petrified. It's like putting both feet in the water, terribly frightening. I keep saying to her, 'You'll never get any real satisfaction out of committing yourself until you're there. You might fail, you might not make it and get fired, but you might make it. And you're never going to know unless you try.' But it's scary and I'm really sympathetic with her."

Failing to take risks can leave women with a sense of powerlessness and of being left behind. The feeling that one's life just happened rather than was chosen can diminish well-being. Pamela Daniels of the Wellesley College Center for Research on Women writes:

> To change and grow as adults—to be able to transform or transcend the recurrent moments of stagnation, confinement and aborted promise . . . depends upon a sense of purpose, the feeling of being in control of our lives, in a position to make choices that will work out over a lifetime in such a way that identity is extended, elaborated and renewed in patterns of love and work and care that are both fruitful and feasible.[6]

This sense of aliveness and purpose is connected with early images of one's life's work, according to Yale psychologist Daniel Levinson and his colleagues.[7] Reporting on an intensive study of forty adult men, they argue that having what they call "the Dream" was critical to the well-being of these men. As they define it, the

Dream is a young man's conception of what he might be in the adult world, a vision that creates excitement and the sense of possibility. A man without a dream of his own, or a man whose life strayed too far from his dream, could lose the sense of vitality that makes the adult years a time of growth.

This intriguing concept struck a responsive cord in many readers. However, critics of Levinson's work point out that while the idea of the dream has a lovely ring to it, most men, including many of the men he studied, don't have one.[8] And when applied to women, the idea of a youthful dream that shapes one's life course has a particularly hollow ring. Most women who are now adults had little sense as young people of a future in the world of work.

How the majority of women in our study thought about their future is shown in the words of a married woman with children, now in her mid-forties, who teaches and practices physical therapy: "I thought Prince Charming would come and take care of me for the rest of my life. . . . I thought, as I'm sure every little girl has, that when I grew up I'd be married and wouldn't work . . . even in professional school I thought it was a sort of temporary thing and I didn't value the profession."

A married childless woman in her forties, who does secretarial work in an upholstery shop, recalled that she had very few goals: "I must have been semiconscious as a youngster. I hoped I would be richer . . . that's not a goal, I just thought it would happen. . . . I would marry a rich man, which I didn't. . . . I don't know how all this was going to happen. I don't know what I thought, how my life would turn out. I don't think I thought much about it."

And a never-married woman of fifty, now struggling to support herself as a bookkeeper, said when asked how she had thought she would make her way in the world: "I didn't sort of think I was going to have to do it. . . . I think that's why my thinking was kind of unrealistic in the sense that I didn't realize that the work was out there for me to have to conquer or do. . . . I just sort of grew up and got here by day-to-day living. There was no planning, nothing, so it just sort of went on."

If adult well-being is tied to youthful goals, what does that mean for women? If they have had no dream to sustain them, will they forever lack a "sense of possibility" in the world of work? Not at all. As opportunities increase and ideas about women's role change, women do find such goals and dreams, often in midlife, that energize and renew the sense of possibility.

The employed women in our sample were a "mixed bag" in terms of whether or not they'd had youthful ambitions. Some knew very early in life what their career goals were. Others didn't decide on a career until much later—often after they were mothers of school-age children. These women all developed a goal, but it certainly wasn't inextricably tied to early youth.

Some women in high-prestige jobs did have an early sense of their place in the world of work. Sometimes this idea was definite and well articulated; at other times it was less specific—a sense of a personal destiny to do and be something important.

Lucille Frost, fifty-two, an architect well-known in her field whose business is thriving, remembers this sense from an early age: "I wanted to be an artist when I was young, a painter. I drew and I painted. I still draw cartoons. . . . I went to a life class for a bit but I don't think I'm really interested anymore. I never anticipated not working, or not being some kind of professional. I always thought of myself as a practitioner of something. I trained in architecture and I had a professor at school who was very supportive of women in architecture."

But even with such strong ambition, Lucille had learned negative messages about women's proper role, and for a time they overpowered her own needs and desires. "After I had my first child I went into analysis because I didn't want to stay home all day and didn't see why I should, yet I was convinced it was evil and wicked for me to want to practice my profession. I was having extraordinary anxiety attacks and the only thing my doctor could do for me was to say reluctantly that if staying home was going to make me very unhappy, then it would make my child very unhappy, so I'd better go back to work."

Edith Wheeler,* the biology chairperson, knew when she was very young that she wanted to be a scientist, even though it was very unusual for someone of her background to dream of such a career. "I come from a small farming community in Minnesota. I was the first person from my college to get my Ph.D.—notice I didn't preface that statement by saying 'woman.' During summers in college I would work for my father in the drugstore he ran,

---

* Edith Wheeler was introduced in Chapter Six, page 118.

and [once] when I went into the local bank and the teller wanted to be pleasant, he said, 'Now that you're going to graduate from college, what do you want to do?' And I said, 'I want to study biology.' And he said, 'Oh, you'll be able to help your father out in the drugstore.' " Edith of course had other ideas.

Another woman knew even earlier exactly what her life's work was, and she never wavered. Susan Gardener, the cardiac surgeon,* remembers that her future plans were set when she was fifteen. "I can remember my mother, when I was about ten, asking me about being a doctor, and I absolutely decided then against it. She had suggested this might be something that I would like to do and so I said, 'Well, that's what I'm *not* going to be!' I guess I was being a teen-ager at ten. She had been a research assistant for a famous surgeon down at the university hospital when she graduated from college."

Her mother's work in the lab intrigued Susan. "It was the only interesting career I had heard anything about, but I had no real contact with it until I went to a surgeon for a minor problem and he was just great. The whole thing just sort of went together and I said to myself, Well, if I think I do want to go into medicine, I'd better find out whether or not I enjoy it." She went to a local hospital and started volunteering, "and then I found out where the operating rooms were. One floor had twelve amphitheaters above the operating room. I went up there and peeked around the corner and saw a secretary, and knew she wouldn't let a fifteen-year-old girl get by, so I waited for her coffee break and went flying by. Once you got in you could stay all day, no one would throw you out. I used to go in there all the time. I'd go in at 9:00 in the morning and watch the surgery until 5:00 in the evening. I knew not only that I wanted to go to medical school but that I wanted to be a surgeon. Absolutely no question in my mind! The question about my being a girl never entered my mind, whether that would make a difference. I guess I was hopefully naïve. I just had blinders on."

So some women have vague but intense career ambitions as adolescents, others have very specific goals, and many have none until adulthood. But all of them can achieve well-being. We found repeated evidence that even a woman who hasn't the slightest glim-

---

* Susan Gardener was introduced in Chapter Six, page 117.

mer of a "dream" as a young girl can be successful and fulfilled
at midlife. Sherri Lane, fifty, a partner in a thriving design firm,
never expected she would work as an adult. "I expected that you
got your teaching certificate in case, God forbid, your husband
died, and you had to take care of yourself. I got a teaching certificate.
But I never thought of myself as someone who would have a career.
I just thought I'd be married and have kids, and maybe keep busy
on the side."

She was married at nineteen and had three children. The marriage began to deteriorate, and Sherri felt powerless. She stayed
at home, caring for the children, trying to cope with a husband
who would not speak to her for days, thinking of herself as useless
and passive. The turning point for Sherri was when she got involved
in the campaign of a man who was running for Congress. "It was
a major break for me. I met people I'd never known before and
they thought I was perfectly acceptable. My husband was off working, my son was thumbing his way across the country. So I signed
up for a two-week trip to France with a local political group."

Sherri remembers one event with particular clarity: "One night
I had supper and went for a walk alone in Paris, and there was a
sign in French that there was going to be a concert and I figured,
what the hell, I'll go. And if I don't like it, I'll leave. It was the
first time in my life, ever, that I didn't turn to somebody and say,
'Would you like to go? If you don't it's all right with me.' It was
amazing. I could go or stay all on my own. And it was after that
that I joined the campaign and met my [future business] partner,
who was doing fund-raising."

Starting a career in midlife worked out well for Sherri. Sometimes this pattern has the advantage that work is new and exciting
at an age when many men—and increasing numbers of women—
begin to feel stale or even "burned out."

But the problem, of course, in coming late to career goals is
that one might not have the time or the resources to fully realize
them. And there is a sense of lost years. Fran Crane, the hospital
administrator, regrets the years in which she just drifted along,
never making any plans. She calls herself "a classic underachiever."
"I was the oldest daughter and very bright. I thought I would go
to college, get through, maybe work at something dilettantish or
something not very important for two or three years and then get
married—and then I didn't. In the management program I attended,

they made much of the fact that women didn't plan careers and that things would just happen to them, and they were not in control of their situations. That's just what happened to me. I got through college and I had no idea of what I wanted to do or be. I wanted to go to New York and share an apartment with friends and I got a job as a secretary in a little advertising agency that went bankrupt, but it wasn't terribly important to me—what was important was that I was in New York with friends. I was a bridesmaid at a lot of weddings and at that point thought vaguely that marriage was going to happen to me, but I didn't take any steps to make certain that it did. All of a sudden I got to an age where I decided it wasn't very troublesome, as I remember it. It was just that my life seemed to be taking a direction that I hadn't planned. I never planned my life and that's the sad part of it. Things just happened."

Many of the women we interviewed reported, like Fran, that as young women they had an almost magical view of the future. Things would somehow turn out fine, though exactly how was almost mystically vague. If women are to be spared the consequences of an "accidental" life, a vision of themselves as part of the world beyond home and hearth is critical. We must recognize that such goals are not important only to men, that women also have need of them.

Many of the internal "brakes" holding women back will probably affect younger women less, as they mature in a society with increasing numbers of women following diverse careers. But the psychological freedom and energy to pursue one's goals won't take one very far in a social context where women still face formidable obstacles to achievement in the world of work. A central obstacle is persistent sexism. The data from the random-sample survey part of our study showed that women did not rate sex discrimination as a major concern at work. Perhaps this is because other issues such as low pay, the threat of unemployment, or the dreariness of a dead-end job seemed more immediate and compelling. But we also suspect that women are reluctant to allow themselves fully to recognize and react to sexism at work, just as so many women claim never to have been discriminated against and to see no reason for "all those angry women's libbers." There is a tendency for oppressed groups to deny their oppression, as we've noted, and women who live and work so closely with men, the dominant group, seem particularly eager to avoid conflict.

But clearly, a pervasive sexism in the marketplace can prevent women from getting out of dead-end jobs and can also block advancement to the jobs that offer women the challenge and variety so vital to their sense of well-being. Often, what women reported encountering was not blatant or overt prejudice, but subtle attitudes that are perhaps harder to deal with, particularly when male colleagues were not aware of their attitudes and the impact they had.

Janet Blake, a senior staff member in a high-powered consulting firm, finds that she has to invent her own solutions to get through the maze of corporate politics. "My goal is to be president of the company, and I really don't know how to do that. I am convinced that the way a woman gets there is different from the way a man gets there. I remember an article in *Fortune* about the man who just took over at Georgia-Pacific Corporation; they described him as a really tough guy and the right man; he goes around talking to the managers and says to them, 'One of your balls is on deposit with this company.' This is given in the article as evidence of what a strong leader he is. Well, I go into a plant and make a crack like that and I'd be laughed off the floor. And of course, not too many men do that. But I think men basically choose their successors, and they choose someone who's basically like them. Very few men can make the abstraction that a woman is like them. She starts with one strike against her. The man is looking for someone like him, and I don't think administrative changes or the law can really change that."

This wasn't so much of a factor, Janet feels "when I was first hired as a bright young thing. But as I move up and I'm in competition for fewer and fewer jobs, I experience it very strongly. One of the things I notice now repeatedly is that I'm ignored."

This happens most often at meetings. "The last incident involved a very large commercial case. There were four of us from the firm—the man who was heading it up, and then me and two men. The man who was heading it up was at the blackboard saying, 'Now, here are the data we will need so that Sam and Gene can do their calculations.' Now, in the first set of calculations that Gene had done, I had found some inconsistencies, and Sam had done nothing on it. It's hard to handle a situation like that. And it was repeated not once, but twice. But I think the way to handle that is confrontation."

So Janet spoke up, rather than keeping her feelings hidden:

"In this case, Gene was being very aggressive and taking on all the work. Finally, I went in to Gene and told him how I felt, and what the effect of it was on me. He didn't even realize he was doing it. I was just astounded—I'd been ascribing all kinds of motivations to him that he wasn't even aware of, and I'd been silently seething. So in that case it [speaking up] worked out very well. But it was difficult and exhausting for me."

Fran Crane, the director of the hospital pathology department, says: "I'm running into sexism for the first time in my professional life and it's maddening and fascinating. I think the job I hold at one time, when departments were smaller, probably was handled by the secretary of the chief pathologist. When they needed something more, they took a secretary and upgraded her to administrative assistant. My title is administrative director and a lot of people think of it as being secretarial, but I haven't done secretarial work in twenty years. I'm a manager. If a male were occupying this job they wouldn't think about it the same way. Some eyebrows were raised when I said I needed an assistant and a secretary. But I'm bringing them along."

Instead of just accepting all the work handed to her, Fran speaks out. "People expect me to handle some things that were handled by a clerical person way back. I think my predecessor did them and I'm just refusing to do them. I realize it would be easier for me to redefine this job if I were male because people would not be expecting certain things, but I try to do it with a grin, and after they get over the shock of realizing that I have a couple of assistants, we manage to get things done."

Lucille Frost, the architect, sees her field as fraught with risk for women. "The stakes are very high in this business, both ways. You can make a lot of money and you can lose a lot. You're vulnerable every step of the way to all of the people that you deal with. It's almost like being in war. It's a more intense war because it's a game of matching vulnerabilities, or escaping the risks of vulnerability. I think men perceive women as more vulnerable and architects are very vulnerable. So because I am a woman, it is more risky— more of a war. I've had bad things happen where I'm sure that it was because I am a woman. People try to take advantage of me. Sometimes it works to my advantage, because women can say and do things and get away with it when men can't. But many men are predatory and women are their prey—and business is predatory, this business especially so."

It seems to be more effective for women to confront the situation than to ignore it. Most women decided to take a firm stance, but not do it in a way that would make it seem an attack or a feminist crusade. Nancy, forty-two, who develops health-care programs for a major hospital, says: "When I first became a senior staff person at the hospital, I was the only woman in management, and whenever the president wanted to send anyone to meetings as a representative from our center, he would always send me, to show them he had a woman in management. So I got sent to all kinds of places because I was it. However, I was always treated as a second-class citizen by him because he was from the old-boy network and women were always second-class citizens; and he never related to women, nor to me. He tolerated me, and I think sort of respected me for the contributions that I made, but he really never put me on the same level with the guys. So I really appreciate the women's movement in that I think I was able to assert myself more in this position and I got to the point of being able to say, 'No, I'm not going to this place to be your representative; get yourself some more women so I don't have to be everywhere.' "

Sometimes, tact doesn't get results. Jacqueline Baker,* the recreation worker, found she had to take direct action: "My boss is the most chauvinistic man I've ever known and I have had to put him in his place. He got a very substantial raise this year for work I did, and I said, 'Hey, buster, I want a raise. I did the work!' But he has this idea of a woman's role—not taking any credit. I got the raise. But God forbid if his wife should try that."

Before she went to work for the neighborhood group, Jacqueline was on its board of directors. "I was the only female on the board. We used to have luncheon meetings and they would leave the seat next to me empty, they were so against having a woman on the board. Finally, one member of the board, a senator from the western part of the state, said, 'We have a very attractive woman on our board and she's always sitting there alone; I'm going to sit with her,' and he moved over. Maybe 50 percent would talk to me and the rest would ignore me. And since I left they haven't had a woman on the board. I wouldn't give in to their pressure, I went to every damn meeting just to be stubborn, and when there was something coming up I would sit there and put my two cents in. That kind

---

* Jacqueline Baker was introduced in Chapter Five, page 83.

of thinking still goes on there and in business, where only an exceptional woman will get ahead, a really exceptional one."

Clearly, women differ in their attitudes toward sexism in the workplace, and in the strategies they use to cope with it. But cope with it they must. Young women may be surprised to find that such issues will confront them at times in their own careers. Old attitudes die hard; often they sink below the surface, reappearing not as blatant statements or practices, but in subtle forms. Younger women who think that the issues the women in our sample face will be ancient history by the time they get into good jobs may be in for a rude awakening.

In any event, the many ways in which work entwines with women's lives must be an important focus for those concerned with the well-being of women in our society today. We neglect them at our risk. Love and Work, Freud's two pillars of a healthy life, are as vital to women as they are to men. Women can no longer afford to worry about only one of them.

CHAPTER EIGHT

OVERLOAD AND UNDERLOAD: WHO HAS MULTIPLE ROLE STRAIN?

I'm the type that likes to keep going. It bothers me less that I'm rushed than it would if I had too much time. When the children were small, I was going bananas looking for something to do. I don't know how people manage to stay home all day. I guess you could fill the time polishing the furniture for long periods. I just couldn't picture myself having to do that. But I do have to manage my time so I'm not pulled too many ways.

Elise Martin, 40, a clerical worker
and mother of three

IS ELISE HAPPY and healthy, invigorated by the excitement and rewards of a busy life, or is she a potential candidate for an ulcer, heart attack, or other ailment caused by stress? Is her well-being heightened or impaired by the fact that she is combining so many roles—wife, mother, worker?

This is an important question for women, because the conventional wisdom has been that women who try to do "too much" are bound to face serious consequences. A woman like Elise was expected to be in bad shape, stressed, harried, feeling pulled apart. But one of the most positive findings of our study is that involvement in multiple roles has a strengthening effect on well-being—for both Mastery and Pleasure—for women. This contradicts the conventional wisdom so directly that it made us ask why. Where did those old notions come from?

First of all, in the mental health field, concern about the effect of multiple roles on women was due partly to the rapid movement of women into the labor force. The immediate assumption was that when women "went to work," this added role was the major—in fact, the only—source of strain. Strain was something like a virus that you could catch in the workplace but not at home. Nobody bothered to ask whether women at home were harried and felt they had too much to do. Perhaps this was because the woman at home was not thought to be "working" in any real sense.

Second, the notion of how one "measured" roles was fairly simplistic. If a woman was a wife, she had one role; if she was also a mother, she had two roles; if she was also a paid worker, she had three roles. Entirely overlooked were less obvious but equally demanding roles that can affect women at home as well as women in the workplace. The role of daughter, for example, can cause overload, pressure, and the need to juggle responsibilities.

Another problem arises from using too simple arithmetic— the erroneous assumption that the person with one role is under less stress than the person with two roles, who is under less stress than the person with three roles. This assumption was based on what might be called a "limited model" of resources. This model pictures energy as a pool of a fixed size. Anything drained off by one activity must therefore leave less energy for others. This model concentrates on "outgo," but doesn't take into account that a person might be recharged by certain activities, and so that activity might actually increase the size of the energy pool. For instance, many people know that when they come home drained and exhausted from work, they feel much more energetic if they go out and jog or play tennis than if they just collapse on the couch. Similarly, the energy a woman "uses" in selling a home to a client may replenish itself when she closes the sale successfully, while the effort that goes into coping with a parent's illness is more likely to be draining or exhausting.

The limited resource model seems to have been applied more often to women, particularly in eras in which women were seen as weak, frail creatures. The medical literature of the nineteenth century cautioned against strenuous mental activity for young women, because it was believed that the brain and the ovaries couldn't develop at the same time. The female body only has so much capacity, it was thought, and the ovaries were much more important than the female brain.[1] (One example of the way the limited resource idea was applied to men was the notion that sexual intercourse depleted "precious bodily fluids" and that too much sexual activity drained a man's creativity and vitality.)

To find out if the number of roles a woman occupied did in fact increase her sense of strain and diminish her well-being, we asked each subject two questions: How often do the things you do add up to being just too much? and, How often do you have to juggle different obligations that conflict with one another and give you a pulled-apart feeling? Her score on these two items was our index of role strain.

If the old theories were correct, role strain would be higher among employed women than among women "at home," and would be related to how long—the number of hours—a woman worked. This did not turn out to be the case. What did make a significant difference was whether a woman was a mother: role strain was higher among women who had children. So it's being a mother, rather than having a job, that is most likely to make a woman feel pulled apart and overloaded. The workplace can sometimes seem like a health spa compared to life at home.

Emily, forty-one, has four children, lives in an affluent suburb, does not have a paid job, but hardly leads a life of leisure, or even of one demand at a time. "My day is fairly frantic. There are a couple of hours a day where there are household things I do—folding laundry and such. I spend a tremendous amount of time in children's activities, which is to say, driving them. I think that's the suburban life. I spend a lot of time in a station wagon driving children to activities of all kinds and to Camp Fire girls— when I'm not a troop leader—and violin lessons and swimming, and it's endless. I drop them and do shopping errands, dry cleaning.

I'm very involved in activities of the college I attended, and go to numbers of meetings. I'm active in town politics, and we go out socially once or twice a week. It's such a busy life.

"There are always a million chores. I never do get things finished, there's never a sense of completion about anything. I was thinking today of this friend of mine who had a meeting at her house one night and she'd gotten the downstairs cleaned and the goodies baked, but one of the women at the meeting came up to her and said, 'Barbara, would you mind if I go and lie with my head on the top stair—I've wrenched my neck and I have to get in a certain position to get it back.' Barbara didn't know what to say because her whole upstairs hall was filled with laundry that she had thrown up there, thinking no one would ever know."

This kind of strain often occurs when the wife is totally responsible for the home and family. This arrangement is often justified on the grounds that her husband has a job and she does not, but for nonemployed as well as employed women, the extent to which the husband was involved in child care and home chores greatly influenced the amount of role strain on women. The less he did, the greater her strain.

Emily clearly is feeling the effects of this "traditional" arrangement. "It's the way life is: you put together the parts that need putting together and the priorities, and it's really crisis management. Men have this notion that women are so lucky, they kind of lie around all day and eat chocolates and talk on the phone and stuff like that. I remember one day when the furniture movers were here, trying to bring a couch into the living room, and then the phone rang and it was a call from Kentucky, and meanwhile my daughter, who was just a baby, threw up all over the front hall. Women are expected to be such incredible jugglers. And you have to be a sensible, bright person to some stranger on the phone while your child is throwing up in the hall. My husband doesn't understand this. He has a secretary at his elbow and he can just say, 'Mary, take this call,' or 'Mary, take this letter.'

"I have felt very often that it would be much simpler to have a paid job. Simpler only because it's structured and I would know what to expect and my plans would be made in such a way that I would be ready for the contingencies. I guess there's constant juggling, whether you work or don't work. I would like to be paid. That's one of the problems about doing what I do. I am constantly feeling that many of the things I do are at a cost to our household, whether it's driving the car constantly to go where I go or having the appropriate wardrobe to go certain places. There's psychic income in what I do and I think that's very important. I don't feel what I do has no worth because it has no monetary value to it. But there is a little guilt there."

We also found that the number of roles a woman occupied told us very little about her level of role strain. Women with three roles had only slightly higher role strain scores than women with only one role. The real issue turns out to be how a woman manages the roles and the resources she commands.[2] A working woman who feels she has to be "superwife" and whip up three-course dinners after work or keep the kitchen floor gleaming with a new coat of wax may feel role strain, while a more relaxed woman may not. A wife and mother who decides to take on an outside job need not fear that this is going to pull her apart. She can decide whether or not to enter the labor force on the basis of specific situations in her own life. (Obviously, we're talking here about women who have a choice. A divorced woman with children who is the main breadwinner in the family is just one example of the many groups of women who haven't the luxury of worrying about whether they are going to feel strain or not.)

A key finding of our study, that we've referred to before, is that the women who scored highest on all the indices of well-being were married women with children who have high-prestige jobs. This is the group one would expect to be the most harried, rushed, and conflicted—and yet they seem to come through with flying colors. This finding dovetails with that of a major study of psychiatric disorder reported in 1977 by Frederick W. Ilfeld, a professor of psychiatry at the University of California Medical School (Davis).[3] The researchers surveyed 2,299 Chicago households, and found that the percentage of women with "high symptomatology"— a lot of problems—was twice that of men's. The only group of women who had symptom rates as low as men were employed women whose occupational status was high. In other words, they had good jobs.

A similar finding emerges from the research of Boston University psychologist Abigail Stewart.[4] When she studied the relationship between life stress, depression, and illness in 133 adult women, it was the married career women with children who reported feeling the least depressed or ill in response to stress. Stewart says, "I hope this means that being able to balance the stresses of one role against the benefits of another is an inherently more healthy way to live." Based on national survey data on physical health, Lois Verbrugge indeed found that employed women are healthier than homemakers.[5]

The nature of the job a woman has may have more impact on her well-being, and on her physical health, than the simple fact that she is working. One hears a great deal these days about how women in demanding jobs will start having heart attacks at an early age just as men do. This is not happening, according to the federally sponsored Framingham Heart Study.[6] This major study found no evidence of increased coronary risk to working women— with one very significant exception. Women in clerical jobs, which are usually low in both prestige and salary and high in frustration and insecurity, showed higher rates of such problems. Among these workers, the women who were at highest risk were those who had husbands in blue-collar jobs and several children. The inference is that these women had a heavy load at home on top of a dead-end job. For women, it's not having a job that's bad for your health, it's having a lousy job with inadequate support for at-home responsibilities.

Why is it that married mothers in high-pressure jobs seem to be so well off? Certainly it's not that they don't have strains in their life, or that they never feel that they have too much to do. But the notion of balance applies here: the rewards far outweigh the problems. What might be called the "recharge your batteries" model of energy is probably operating rather than the "limited" model. The variety and richness of these women's jobs gives them a sense of vitality, rather than draining them.

There is another likely explanation. Some theorists believe that adding roles to one's life is only a process of addition; you simply add on extra tasks to all the ones you already have.[7] But a "revisionist" view of this process is emerging,[8] and our study further confirms the new idea. What actually seems to happen is that when they take a paid job, women drop off many of the things they did before. They cook less elaborate meals, they say no to a request to chair a fund drive. They don't have to accompany a mother-in-law on a shopping trip. Often, a paid job is a great excuse for a woman not to do the things she didn't want to do in the first place. And the more prestigious the job, the easier it is to shed the unwanted aspects of other roles.

In fact, an exciting new concept of work as a buffer against stress, an escape from tension, is emerging among researchers in many different fields, as they look at how employment affects women and at how employed women compare with homemakers in terms of stress. A major English study of psychiatric symptomatology[9] found that homemakers whose life situations were stressful were more likely to develop symptoms than were employed women with the same degree of stress in their lives. Having a job seemed to protect the women against the worst effects of difficulties in other areas of their lives. And a review of major surveys of sex differences in psychiatric symptomatology[10] showed that the gap between male and female rates of symptoms— men have consistently lower rates— is getting smaller over time. The authors attribute this to an improvement in women's mental health associated with their increased presence in the labor force.

Many women in our study told us that going to work made it easier, not harder, for them to cope with family responsibilities and problems. Not that they found themselves doing more for their families— rather, they felt more comfortable about doing less, and even more important, they were able to worry less. They could be more objective about minor problems children had when their minds were also occupied with work issues. They also found it easier to reject unreasonable demands of others. Often, they reported, it took time to arrive at this more relaxed state; it didn't set in immediately after getting a job. Perhaps that explains the new results reported by psychologist Joseph Pleck of the Wellesley College Center for Research on Women.[11] For years he has found evidence of "role overload" among employed women whose home and job responsibilities gave them a "work week" longer than either nonemployed women or men. But recently that differential has been decreasing, and the reason seems to be that employed women are doing less at home, rather than that their husbands are taking over. Perhaps we are finally seeing the effects of women's "settling down" into long-term employment; they are beginning to give up dispensable household tasks and even think about building some leisure time into their lives.

Since how well a woman manages the different roles in her life seems to be the key to avoiding strain, rather than the number of roles per se, the woman in the high-prestige job has obvious advantages over the woman in the low-level job.[12] She can usually afford to pay well for child care and other household help, so she is spared the desperate search for affordable support systems. She can afford to take the family out to eat on a night when things are hectic at work, or plan a vacation. For such women, despite the burdens of managing both a family life and a challenging job, the middle adult years are filled with rewards.

So, work provides a sense of self-esteem that seems to character-ize women in good jobs. As one woman says: "It is quite nice to feel—how do I describe it?—a sense of personal accomplishment, the satisfaction of doing something that's good, competing with people that are supposedly very good, doing well. I think it's very satisfying, and I find it stimulating."

The knowledge that for women in middle adulthood, multiple roles can tie in with well-being should help younger women who are struggling with the pressures of small children and a job, and who may be tempted to abandon or severely curtail their career goals. The women who did just that regret it. When the women in our random sample were asked about major regrets in their lives, the most common regret was abandoning their education or not pursuing career goals more seriously. The woman who manages to hang onto her career may be in for some stress in her younger years when the pulls and tugs of family and career can be intense, but if she can persist, her chances for much smoother sailing in her mature years seem very good.

For Renee Ames,* forty-five, who finished law school in 1974 and now is employed full time at a law firm, life seems a good deal better than it did in the past. Renee's career goals developed fairly late in life, after her children were in school and she had spent a number of years at home. She was married at twenty-three and had her first child at twenty-five. She says, "I think I was a fairly typical young woman, I wasn't really very heavily involved in anything." Renee's second child was born a year after her first, and she found herself coping with two toddlers at the same time. "My second son was conceived while I was wearing a diaphragm and that was upsetting. I was very unhappy to be pregnant again and I found it hard having two boys so close together."

---

* Renee Ames was introduced in Chapter Four, page 66.

Remembering those years, she says: "When I'm feeling bad or depressed now, I remember when the kids were very little and would act in certain ways and I had no control and I was sure this was going to go on for the rest of my life: Tom was going to be pushing Bill down and Bill was going to be throwing catsup at Tom, and you know, you get this feeling of desperation."

When Renee decided to go to law school, her husband Joe, also a lawyer, supported her decision. He found himself with more responsibilities for the children and the running of the house. "He never was really that involved with the kids before I went to school," Renee says. "Then he got involved in more of the decision-making, more with the kids, more cooking. I think it's been good for all of us."

Now that she is working, she says, the family has become closer. She thinks her job has had a good impact on her children, especially her older boys. "Ever since I started working there's been quite a change in those two boys. Before, they were never into family things. We all seem to have a better time together now. When I was home, I was always busy organizing things, and there was never sort of a relaxed time to just do whatever we wanted. I think when the kids were little I spent too much time trying to direct them. I'd tell them to go to the swings, to do this or do that. Or, I would go in and say, 'Is there anything you want to talk about?' and put them on the spot instead of being able to respond freely to whatever it was that was on their minds. Now, work takes up a lot of my time and energy; before, I was probably devoting too much of it to the kids."

Renee says she can now relax and enjoy her children because they are not the sole focus of her life. "I'm proud of them as people. They're going to be gone before long and I do think about that. Where will they be? Will they be a thousand miles away and will I see them or have any connection with them? I'm so glad I have this profession to take up some of my time."

It has sometimes been said of women in high-prestige jobs that they are there because they are running away from bad marriages or they don't like parenting. That is not so, according to our findings. Women in such jobs derive as much enjoyment from their marriages and from their children as other groups do. And for most women in high-level jobs, the future seems bright. Renee says: "Looking ahead five years, I think I'll be practicing law and

I'll be happy with what I'm doing. I feel myself going in a couple of different directions. People say to me there are all kinds of possibilities—I can be a judge or whatever. But I don't know yet. It's all very new to me and I like it, the lawyering."

Renee would probably never have considered a career as a lawyer when she was much younger. As we've seen, young girls have tended to shy away from high-prestige careers when making vocational choices, cutting themselves off very early in life from a path which has a good chance of leading to well-being in adulthood. Young women may react this way because the only model they see of a high-prestige career is the "typically" male one—a straight line upward, going full-steam ahead day and night. They don't see that high-prestige careers can follow a more varied pattern, allowing some slack time when family demands are great, accelerating at other times. As one woman says: "I think you do make some sacrifices in your professional life to have a family, but it's not that you have to abandon your career ambitions, you just slow the pace down at certain times. I think the idea that you have to be going full-tilt all the time in your work is crazy. That's how a lot of men burn out in their forties and fifties. It's not an either-or situation, unless you're the kind of driven person who can't be happy except at the top of the heap."

It is interesting to note that the high-prestige women in our study did not follow any one path in their career development. Some, like Renee, made a career choice late in life and went through some difficult times trying to go to school while children were young. Others, like Susan Gardener, the cardiac surgeon, walked a straight line and never deviated. In the future, however, it may be harder for women to follow Renee's course, to start a whole new career close to midlife. Women now in their forties who made their career move a decade ago were able to benefit from the early momentum of the women's movement, which offered them a great deal of support. The economic picture then was better, and a whole range of programs and services were created to help women reenter the job market. If the economy is weak, women may have little support in the future if they try to reenter a tight job market.

Family planning issues also have an impact on the timing of women's careers. M.I.T. economist Lester Thurow, writing about women and why they don't get as far as men in management, notes that the years between twenty-five and thirty-five are the prime years for establishing a successful career.[13] These are the years when hard work has the maximum payoff. They are also the prime years for launching a family. Women who leave the job market completely during those years may find they never catch up, he says.

Few of the women in our study were still raising very young children; 80 percent of the mothers had no children younger than second graders. If we had interviewed them at an earlier time, perhaps those with full-time careers would have shown greater signs of role strain. It would be naïve to suggest that building a career at the same time that you have pre-school children doesn't involve stress. The way to think about different life patterns, though, is not to expect to find one with no stress and no problems, but rather to understand that in different lifeprints, the stress will be felt intensely at different times. The woman who is trying to juggle young children and a demanding job may feel the most pressure in her late twenties and early thirties, but by her forties her investment in the job will be paying off and the demands of the family will be lessening. The woman who has been a homemaker in a very traditional pattern may experience a great deal of stress around the issue of redefining her life as the active role of mothering comes to an end.

One of the major themes of this book is that no one lifeprint fits all women, that women must, as much as possible, design combinations of roles that fit them. This freedom can be both exhilarating and frightening. We have noticed that many women want to be told what "the right way" is for them to work out their lives, asking, "What can I do, specifically, to make things work out for me?" Just as many women are uncomfortable with taking a job that they don't already know they can do, they seem uncomfortable with the idea that no one can give them one-two-three answers. It's risky, but essential, for a woman to look at her own life and make her own choices. Just because there are so many choices, today's women probably face more conflict than women did in past generations. But the old way was hardly problem-free. There was only one acceptable life pattern for women, and for the many women whose talents and personalities were an imperfect fit with that pattern, the cost was depression and lack of self-esteem. The new cost may be periods of struggle and conflict.

But even when a woman does experience role strain, the result is not nearly as devastating as was once believed. For our sample as a whole, role strain did not affect Mastery at all; it did have a somewhat negative effect on Pleasure. A woman can be feeling a fair amount of strain and yet feel very good about herself. Overall, moderate amounts of role strain cannot be viewed as a major mental health problem. Although there is certainly a threshold where the benefits derived from a variety of roles can be outweighed by the problems, the sense of "juggling" that a woman sometimes gets from involvement in multiple roles is more a nuisance to be managed than a cause of psychiatric symptoms.

As we've seen, multiple roles turn out to have a favorable impact on well-being for women. What about the reverse? Is there such a thing as too little role involvement, or "underload"? Are too few serious commitments negatively related to well-being? The answer is yes. Our study shows that the women who scored lowest on Mastery were those with the fewest roles—married women at home without children.

The scenario that seems to be operating with these women might be called the "eggs-in-one-basket" syndrome. We know that the more roles one has, the more potential sources one has for experiencing Mastery and Pleasure in one's life. With fewer roles, one has fewer supports for the psyche, and a weakness in any one can be devastating. Married, childless women at home are in this situation. We saw earlier that for these women, well-being is closely tied to particular attitudes of their husbands and to qualities of their marriages. His approval (or disapproval), his income, sexual satisfaction, marriage balance, and the way decisions are made in the marriage all have a major impact on her well-being.

So, this is a group of women whose self-esteem is very closely tied to their husbands' lives, to the condition of their marriages. If something goes wrong with their marriage, or with their husband's job, these women could be "wiped out" emotionally.

Some women in this group—those married to affluent men— have a style of life many women would envy. They are free to travel with their husbands, and they are not battered by the ever-present demands of children. But even for them, this lifestyle seems risky.

Charlene, for example, at thirty-six is married to a highly paid corporate executive a decade older than she, and spends a great deal of time traveling with her husband and entertaining with him. It is a life that sounds wonderful, but Charlene has very real problems with self-esteem. "I don't feel that I've really accomplished anything. Everyone I know has at least a master's or a doctorate and I don't know anyone who isn't doing something terrific. That makes me self-conscious. I feel guilty that I don't have a self-supporting job. I think it's important that people be able to support themselves if they have to. Financially I don't have to, and I just feel guilty about it."

Charlene was an administrative assistant in a government agency before she was married but says that that kind of work would not be compatible with her marriage; she believes her husband wants her to be free to travel and entertain for him. For Charlene, this is certainly less than sheer joy.

There is something of a generation gap, she finds, between herself and the friends they have as a couple. "That's a big problem for me because most of my friends are my husband's contemporaries. Their lifestyles are pretty well set. Many of our associates are very liberal, very upper class, who can intellectualize a lot in the right way, but basically, when you come right down to it, they're as arrogant and snobbish as anybody else. I guess I'm bored with my lifestyle a bit."

Charlene says her relationship with her husband is close and good, but she has few other sources of support. She does not have close friends; the friendships she has are on a superficial level. "I don't tell people the really deep things. I don't trust people. I do trust myself to keep confidences, but I don't trust other people. And I can't be friends with people I don't respect intellectually. I guess that's a fault. I have lots of acquaintances, but no friends."

Charlene in no way feels overloaded or pulled in different directions; role strain is not a factor in her life. But she pays a heavy price. Charlene finds that she has "too much time to do the things I don't want to do," and she has a nagging sense that she has not lived up to her potential. "I don't like myself now, but I think that since college I've had a chance to reinforce all kinds of negative images of myself. Probably when I was in high school, I did like myself but I didn't think of it in those terms. Regardless of what I do, I don't think it will ever be meaningful. I think that's just the way I perceive myself. I dismiss anything I'm capable of doing.

What I have to do is try to understand my strengths a little better and develop my potential, which everyone tells me is untapped. I don't have any confidence in myself. I have a feeling that if I did, nothing would stop me from doing what I wanted to do. I was brought up not to have any professional goals, but to find a man who would be good to me, and I did it. But I realized there was a lot missing in terms of orientation, professional orientation."

Charlene blames not having her own work for her problems, yet characteristically she is not able to use this insight to fight off her negative feelings. It is very difficult for a woman to provide her own positive feedback in the absence of a structured, objective environment like that of the workplace. Charlene has decided not to have a child, and she derives some self-respect from that decision. "I'd be a good mother, I think, and it would be nice to have that relationship. But I would not have a child because I think there are too many children in the world already; if I were going to have one it wouldn't be a biological one. I couldn't permit myself to be a biological mother, which is my way of contributing in a constructive way to society, a way that's not valued by 99.9 percent of the people so I don't get any credit for it. I feel very good about the fact that I have not had a child, have resisted all the pressures to have one."

Charlene is understandably ambivalent about the women's movement, which embodies how the "rules of the game" seem to have changed in the middle: "I support it, every little bit of it. But it has made me feel guilty. See, my one dream was to marry a man who would take care of me, with whom I'd be happy and at peace, and I've achieved that. I thought I'd take courses, dabble in volunteer work, but it just doesn't give me satisfaction. When I was growing up I found that women were supposed to realize themselves and not be dependent on a man, and not even necessarily to marry, so part of my dilemma is that I'm self-conscious about not being at least a Ph.D. in something. There has been support for childlessness, but it is always accompanied by a career. You become childless to pursue a career.

"I've got to think about what I'm going to do with myself so I can stop wallowing in this low self-image. I've always been waiting for things to happen and they always have—that's the old female conditioning and I recognize that about myself. I'm afraid to do anything, precipitate anything. Maybe this is simplistic, but

I relate it to wanting to take a boat out on my own when I was young and never being permitted to. It was always my brother's right, not mine. Every time I would take it the pin would shear and inevitably I'd have to be towed. After a while I said, 'To hell with it.' "

Homemakers often feel affronted—and rightly so—when people say to them, "Oh, you're not working!" The unstructured nature of the job often leaves the homemaker feeling she has to respond constantly to demands. It's not only the physical demands that can be draining to a homemaker, but the emotional ones as well. Carole, fifty-one, an actor's wife and a homemaker with two children, says: "I think probably the most difficult part of being at home is having enough time and being around so you have to deal with all the downs in the family. I'm not sure having a job would change that. The hardest part of my life is having to deal with two college-age kids and a husband who has professional needs and an eighty-year-old mother who is going through great difficulties. I don't know if having more focus—a more focused life of my own—would throw off some of that. I don't know. I'm very dependent on the feelings of the people around me and I don't know whether it's because I have the time and not that strong a commitment to something else on my own. I sometimes feel put upon by all the demands made on me by others, that's all. And I think that's a difficulty, but being a concerned mother, that may not change."

Many women at home find it harder to justify time spent in activities away from their children than do women at work, who have the paycheck to show for it. Emily, despite her intense focus on her children that we saw earlier, is not certain that she's giving them enough attention. "A huge chunk of the time goes to the children and I feel that's appropriate. I feel guilty that I don't do enough for them, although I don't see how humanly I could do more because I don't think I have the patience to devote more time to them than I do. I need some time for me—I guess it's that there isn't enough time for me that's not structured, and isn't doing what others wish I would do."

A homemaker often finds that her job description involves not only coping with her own husband and children, but with other relatives as well. One thirty-eight-year-old woman who went back to work remembers that her husband's extended family seemed omnipresent: "I've never seen such a close family. Somebody gets a hangnail and it's the topic of conversation for nineteen people for the day. Really . . . they're on the phone every hour, every day. John's mother talks to every one of her daughters on the phone every day. If they don't come over, she's on the phone three times a day. My mother and I talk once a week: hello, what's going on, that's it. I don't feel the need and neither does she. That's just how you're brought up."

Her job permits her to have control over her relationships with her in-laws. "This is the way I handle it: we go out there two days a week and sometimes I get overwhelmed with the whole process but then if I have this place [the office] to come to five days and have my silence and my work—no one bugs me." Here's an example of how work serves as a buffer and an escape.

As we've seen, for many women, having a paid job provides a legitimate excuse to refuse demands, while the job of homemaking does not. Homemakers find it hard to feel justified in setting limits on what they are supposed to do. Perhaps this is because society doesn't define this role as a job, but rather as a state of being in which "goodness" is equated with continually being available for everyone else. But the homemaker who can't say no runs risks to her own well-being. A therapist who runs a workshop for women who deserted their families says: "A good mother is supposed to take care of everyone's needs. When a woman finds she does not or cannot fit that mode, it seems like the worst thing that can happen. Many of the women attending my workshops were super-moms. They talk of devoting, devoting, devoting until they just burned out. They had no time to develop a separate identity."

Difficulty in feeling allowed to set limits may explain a finding that emerged from our study: homemakers were the only group of women for whom role strain was associated with a diminished sense of Mastery. While working women suffer some diminution of Pleasure when they feel role strain, homemakers suffer in Mastery as well. Why is this so?

The issue of control may be the key here. When you can't set limits, when you must always be on call, you can easily fall prey to the sense that other people are determining what's happening in your life, and you may feel powerless to do anything about it. Moreover, a homemaker may feel that if she can't manage everything calmly, that's a reflection on her since she can't blame it on having a job. So for her, to feel overloaded and pulled apart is to perceive herself as inadequate. For an employed woman it's easier to see such feelings as caused by external demands, not internal weakness.

A strong sense of identity and a conviction that homemaking is a job that fits her skills and desires are needed by homemakers today more than ever. One intriguing finding from our study was that even if an employed woman preferred to be home, that conflict didn't have a significant impact on her well-being. But a homemaker who was at home when she wanted to be at work suffered serious consequences to well-being. The woman who is at home out of a sense of feminine "duty" is in trouble. The woman who is there because she wants to be is apt to be pleased with her life.

We saw in Chapter Seven that homemakers scored lower than employed women in Mastery. The self-esteem problem was echoed in our interviews with homemakers. Judy Young* expressed it well when she said: "I think my idea of myself is adequate—but it's not super. I don't feel as if I'm everything I would like to be or would have wanted earlier. I haven't done as much with what I have as I would have liked. It's sort of mixed—C plus, maybe. I guess I'd like to be involved in something more exciting, that I'm doing myself, I guess I'd feel more successful. I find that when I'm painting I get that very selfish enjoyment, but it would be nice to be financially successful at it. If I could make some kind of financial contribution doing that, I guess that would be it. Something of my own that's successful."

Ruth Lake,** fifty-three, comments: "Maybe this is just an immature part of me, but I thought I was going to do something more than just be a homemaker. . . . When I was growing up, I think my mother encouraged me to be quiet. She used to say, 'Just give Ruth a piece of paper and pencil and let her draw.' I think she liked it when I was quiet. I always admired people who were vivacious because I think I always thought of myself as being, you know, Miss Milquetoast. I think a strong part of me is still self-critical. I'm not critical of other people, but I'm terribly critical of myself. I make allowances for others, but not for myself."

But if self-esteem can be a problem, the same is not true of Pleasure. Homemakers did not score lower than working women

* Judy Young was introduced in Chapter Five, page 78.
** Ruth Lake was introduced in Chapter Four, page 72.

on those indices of well-being. So clearly the woman who chooses the role of homemaker should be aware of the risk to her sense of Mastery. She should plan to get involved in activities that will allow her to accomplish things in which she can take pride. The nature of these activities is critical; some volunteer activities involve only caring for others with no opportunities for feedback from peers or objective standards—they're too much an extension of home responsibilities.

When homemakers take on important volunteer or community commitments, they often feel guilty about the time and effort involved. At one national convention of volunteers, a group of women who were planning an enormously important educational program worried out loud about the fact that they were away from home for a few days, and that there were expenses involved. Despite the significance of their work, they found it hard to justify spending even a short time away from the family. They had no feeling that they were entitled to the time, feelings that are vital to volunteer workers if they are to gain the sense of Mastery that is so important to well-being. It is certainly possible to engage in nonpaid work that provides all this. As Emily says: "A friend of mine who works with alumnae from our college [finds] a tremendous guilt that they haven't measured up to all that the college made them capable of doing. And I've not felt that, because I've had some meaningful volunteer jobs and have been able to contribute enough through them that I've felt I've managed to keep my head above water in that sense."

But what about the nature of the homemaker role per se— what proved to be the most important positives and negatives? There were several major clusters of rewards of homemaking.

The first cluster is "freedom," and includes the following items:

Being free to make your own schedule
Being able to pursue your interests

As Emily put it: "I love the freedom of not having a regular job because on most days if I really feel that I don't want to do X job, I wouldn't have to. There are commitments that really have to be taken care of, but there are days when I can say, 'Gee, I'd really like to make a long skirt today,' and I can let other things go. I like that, I like the freedom of it. I love to do gardening, to do entertaining, cooking, love to sew, and lots of things I enjoy at home when I'm here. I had worked for five years before I was married and I had gotten out of my system a certain amount of desire to 'find myself' in a working atmosphere. I know life wasn't all a bed of roses out there. I would not want to be here without having outside activities that mean a lot to me; I would find that lonely and nonconstructive. I need to be involved with other people and I love to go. I'm going with a friend to the Antiquarian Society to the house that has been decorated authentically as eighteenth-century rooms, and I really do look forward to that. Because I don't work and have other commitments, I'm able to do that and I like it. I would miss that very much."

Carla, a forty-six-year-old homemaker who has four children, appreciates the freedom in contrast to her former job: "I worked for a long time—ten years—and punched a card from 8:00 to 5:00 and I enjoy the feeling that if I want to do something I can do it. If I feel like doing housework, I do it. If I don't, it really doesn't matter that much; and if I visit a friend, or if somebody's sick and I have to help out at school or at the church, I have the freedom to do that."

Carole, the actor's wife, has used her freedom to take on major projects that provide social ties as well as ego satisfaction. "I don't have weeks that are all the same all the time. Most of my time is spent at the art institute, I lecture there two mornings a week, and I take a course two afternoons a week. I play tennis once a week; I've been doing it for four or five years and can see myself continuing for another ten years, five anyway. I like the teaching part at the institute and there is a nice sociability about it; the gals who do this work with me are the most interesting, stimulating people. We're from varying backgrounds and socioeconomic areas, and it's very nice."

She likes a flexible schedule because of her husband's career. "There's all sorts of flexibility for me because there are times I want to go on tour with Tim. He has an abnormal schedule. We have a summer home in Provincetown and I'd resent not having my summers there. I'm at a point in my life where the kids aren't so demanding and I want to be able to spend time with my husband. The flexibility is very important and somehow I don't feel the need for the paycheck. I know there are some women who don't need it financially who do have the need. I don't feel this at all. I feel as though I'm socially committed and I'm worthwhile and I'm doing something for society and myself. I don't feel the need for the paycheck to feel my worth at all."

So for some women who are not paid workers, it isn't homemaking per se but the time they have available that shapes their lives and allows them to work at a craft or art. We were intrigued to find that this kind of activity had a particularly strong impact on well-being, for both women at home and employed women. Those who reported they had rewarding interests or hobbies, such as music, tennis, needlepoint, cooking, were higher in both Mastery and Pleasure. It may be, of course, that when you are feeling good, you tend to have more energy for varied activities, but we think that for homemakers these activities may function like a kind of nonpaid work in promoting well-being. After all, involvement in an activity you have chosen, in which presumably you have developed skills, and get feedback about your accomplishments, is in a way the best kind of work. It can also help a woman find friends. This finding can be important to homemakers, encouraging them to get involved in such activities and to benefit from the enjoyment and competence that they gain. Writing functions this way for Karen, who finds that her role as a homemaker meshes well with her avocation as a poet. "If I had to write for a living, then I would probably be writing things I didn't like. As it is, I have enough time for everything because I make time for everything. I have to read a certain amount a day, so I do. I don't have enough time to clean my house, so I don't clean my house. I don't feel the pressure of time."

The second reward cluster is "emotional availability"; it includes:

> Being there for your husband (and children)
> The appreciation you get from your family
> Having enough time and energy to enjoy your husband (and children)

Carla says: "My children are small and I think that it's important for me to be home. I want to be here if something happens or if they get sick. I wanted children and that's what I want to do now, take care of them. When they grow up, maybe that will change."

For other women, the skills homemaking requires are precisely those they enjoy exercising; homemaking is truly their occupation.

"Liking the work" emerged as the third reward cluster of homemaking, and includes:

A sense of competence, of being good at what you do
Having other people enjoy your home
Having the amount of responsibility you can handle
Keeping the house looking nice and cared for
Doing creative things around the house

Irene Harris,* fifty-four, who is married to a construction worker, finds that homemaking fits her skills well and makes her feel competent: "I love being home. I love being *in* my home. I don't have a lot of neighbors running in and out, and I like that. I like baking, cooking, getting meals ready. I love this kind of work. I like wallpapering, painting. I have worked part time, but I'd still rather be home. You know, today is the day for career women to go out and work, but to tell you the truth, they don't do half the work I do, but I would still rather do this. I just finished wallpapering and painting the house. I love that kind of thing."

A finding that intrigued us was that of the three "reward" clusters, freedom, emotional availability, and liking the work, only the last had an effect on Mastery. The more a woman found that homemaking involved the kind of work she liked and was good at, the higher her sense of Mastery. For her, homemaking functions as paid jobs do for employed women—engaging one's skills, providing pride and a sense of worth.

Pleasure, on the other hand, was affected only by how rewarding a woman found being emotionally available. The more she felt rewarded by being there for others, the higher her level of Pleasure. This connection suggests once again that Pleasure is tied to investment in intimate relationships.

What about the concerns we found among homemakers? There were two major ones: boredom and isolation from adults, and distress about not earning money or contributing to the family income.

The boredom-and-isolation cluster includes the following:

Boredom and monotony
Having too much free time
The lack of adult company

---

* Irene Harris was introduced in Chapter Five, page 92.

This concern is common among women who are at home with very young children. Most of the mothers in our sample had children who were at least school age, but they too experienced distress over the long days at home. Lee Huston,* forty-two, the mother of four, says: "I think once the children go to school you have that block of time from 8:30 to 3:00. Last year my youngest two were in first grade, so it was the first year I was free from 8:30 to 3:00. Before that I always had somebody in kindergarten or something, which is more confining even than when they're toddlers. When they're toddlers you can pack them in the car and go; when they're in nursery school or kindergarten you're driving them at 8:30, you go home, get yourself together to do errands, and by that time it's time to go back and pick them up. Now I have a difficult time having free time. I looked forward to it for so long. I have a lot of hobbies and interests—and I didn't expect to have this; I really did not expect to have that empty-nest feeling. The very first day the kids were in school all day I was walking back and forth in the house suddenly feeling I had the whole day and what was I going to do with it? I had listened to other friends who said that it was going to seem like a lot of time and don't fill it up with a lot of committee meetings because you're going to over-extend yourself. I have had several friends who have had nervous breakdowns feeling that they had to fill that time, so I think listening to them helped me. But I still didn't expect it to be so strong a feeling."

The second concern cluster, "not earning money," includes the following:

> Not having your own money
> Not contributing to the family income by earning money
> Having to justify not having a job

This concern was strong among homemakers, perhaps reflecting recent social changes. As more women are providing income, it becomes an issue for those who are not. Emily says: "Sometimes I feel I'm not being productive, not making any money, and my husband has the whole burden of that, which is not a light one. That's what I mainly feel guilty about. I never wanted to be a helpless person economically—and I'm probably about as helpless

---

* Lee Huston was introduced in Chapter Four, page 71.

now as I could be in that respect, because I'm not making anything and don't really have many ideas about a lucrative job that I could go and get. If anything happened to my husband I'd be very worried with the kids at this point, because it would be very hard to do anything about getting them through. I feel as if I could support myself adequately; it's the kids I worry about. I find it's terribly expensive to give them the things you want them to have—not what other people are giving their kids, but the things you feel they need and would give freely without agonizing about it. We just couldn't live this way on any income I could have. The family is completely dependent on him."

We were somewhat surprised to find that neither concern about not earning money nor feeling bored and isolated had a significant impact on well-being. These may be the "known risks," the conditions one expects in choosing to be at home, and as we know, it is unanticipated problems that are the most upsetting. The home-maker who finds that the work suits her and that she enjoys her central emotional place in the life of her family clearly can withstand the negatives. The balance between positives and negatives in the domain of homemaking, in fact, had the strongest relationship to well-being of any balance scores. This means that in homemaking more than in any other area of life, the degree to which the gratifica-tions outweigh the problems will profoundly affect both Mastery and Pleasure. The implication is that this pattern can be associated with a variety of outcomes, from best to worst.

For homemakers, "home" can be a base of operations for an involved, active life, or it can be hideaway from a world that seems too overpowering. When the latter is the case, a woman can exagger-ate in her mind the risks of the outside world so that she burrows even further into shelter and inactivity. The price of such a retreat often is anxiety. Ruth Lake, the bricklayer's wife, for example, says: "I don't do much outside my home. Two or three times a week I go to visit my mother. She is in a nursing home in Boston. I don't drive, so I have to depend on my husband. I have a lot of plants so that takes up part of my time, and housework and cooking and reading. Maybe I'm using the nursing home as an excuse not to do things, I don't know. I think about taking some courses and learning how to drive; my husband has a truck and the car is right there. So I keep saying, I'm going to learn how to drive and get out more, but why don't I do it? It's boring at home, but at least there's no tension. About ten years ago I used to get a lot of head-aches from tension, so maybe that's why I don't attempt to do more things. I feel there has to be more to life than just staying home and taking care of the house. I mean, I think it's good, but not very exciting or fulfilling."

And another homemaker says, "I wish I didn't have this sense of life always being on the brink of disaster, so many terrible things could happen, but so far they haven't."

This sort of anxiety, in extreme cases, can lead to a malady that has sometimes been called "the housewife's disease"—*agorapho-bia*. Literally, it means "fear of the marketplace" and typically takes the form of fear of venturing out of the home. Among the clinical signs are panic and faintness in public, sometimes accompa-nied by pounding of the heart and a racing pulse. Janice, a fifty-year-old homemaker who has four children and is married to a successful businessman, suffered from this problem: "After I had my second baby, I became very ill, very lethargic, had no appetite. I know I weighed in the eighties, but had nothing wrong with me. I just didn't want to eat. I took care of this child whom I loved, but I took care of her because I had to. Then I decided I'd get pregnant again, but I wasn't very enthusiastic. My life was very routine; my husband was in business and he was out three nights a week. I was totally in the house every day, other than an occasional trip to a supermarket. We would go out Saturday nights and I couldn't eat. Once I went shopping in town with my next-door neighbor and we went into a restaurant and we sat down. I picked up a menu and said, 'Oh my God, I'm going to be sick!' They had a nurse's station and I went in and lay down and felt better. I went back to the restaurant, but the same thing happened, so we left. From then on it got gradually worse. I couldn't go out of the house. I panicked at the thought of getting on any kind of public transportation. My husband took me to the theater one day and we had to go on a train and I got panicky. When I got to the theater and started to go in, I became totally ill. It got worse and worse and finally we decided I should go to a psychiatrist. But she just left me nowhere. I was very bad, I just stayed home all the time."

Finally, Janice had a series of shock treatments, which made her feel ill and impaired her memory. But gradually, she began to get better. "I mean, I didn't get up one morning and say, 'I really love the world,' or 'I'm going for a ride on the subway,' but I began to feel better and I haven't had a setback since then."

Janice still worries about her ability to cope and worries excessively about her children. "I worry terribly and have terrible fears for my children and I always will. People say, 'Oh, your children are grown and you don't have to worry about them anymore,' and I know I worry about them every night when I go to bed. Where are they? Are they in an automobile? And I will transfer that worry to my grandchildren, and I'll be doubly miserable for my children if they have problems."

To Janice, the everyday activities of the outside world—eating in a restaurant, for example—seemed more heavily laden with risk than they could realistically be. The more she stayed away from the outside world, the more exaggerated the risk became in her mind.

The role of homemaker seems to work out best for women who have made a conscious decision that at least for the time being, they best meet their own needs as well as those of others by remaining out of the paid labor force. Typically, it is responsibilities for young children that shape their decision, but as we've seen, there can be other reasons too: the special requirements of a husband's career, the need for a break from the constraints of employment, the goodness of fit between oneself and the tasks of homemaking.

Staying home out of a sense of duty, fear of one's capacity to cope with the work world, overattention to the desires or opinions of others, sets women up for growing unhappiness and discontent. To prevent these consequences, women must consider the role of homemaker as carefully as they would any other occupation and way of life rather than as their "natural" state and fate.

DIVORCE: COMING APART, GETTING IT TOGETHER

I was unhappy most of the time in my marriage, but it never occurred to me that not being married was an option. I was married! My vision was that the kids were going to grow up and leave and that I was going to sit on the couch with this man with our arms around each other's shoulders and say, "Oh boy, thank God that's over, now we'll have the golden years!" That was my fantasy, that something wonderful was about to happen. Divorce was not something I thought about.

Sherri Lane, 50, the divorced mother of three children

EVEN THOUGH HER MARRIAGE was admittedly unhappy, Sherri* couldn't let go of her fantasy of a happy, romantic ending to a love story. But divorce is a reality for millions of American women today, including Sherri, and will continue to be so in the foreseeable future. It is estimated that some 40 percent of new marriages will end up on the rocks, yet the role of divorced woman is one few anticipate and almost none choose, except as relief from an intolerable situation.

* Sherri Lane was introduced in Chapter Five, page 78.

There was a time when the average American woman had few, if any, divorced people among her circle of friends. The word "divorcee" had an exotic and somewhat disreputable ring to it, and a woman whose marriage had failed suffered from a distinct social stigma.

In the past, the goal of many divorced women was to remarry as soon as possible. Being divorced was thought of as a temporary state, an interim period in which a woman's major task was to search for another husband.

Today, the picture is quite different. The stigma of divorce has faded; a more educated, psychologically aware populace looks to marriage as an opportunity for intimacy and growth, not as a badge of adulthood or an economic necessity.[1] Marriages that don't serve personal needs tend to be dissolved. More women are working, so divorce, although it creates financial problems, less often destroys the entire economic foundation of a woman's life. Divorce as a life role is in a major period of transition. It is becoming a "stable" role, and because of this, many findings about the well-being of divorced people based on past studies may no longer be valid. Many divorced women will make a conscious choice not to remarry; thus many American women will spend the greatest portion of their adult lives as divorced persons.

Despite this forecast, we know too little about what divorce is really like for most women, especially after the crisis of the marital breakup subsides. We have all heard stories, many of the who-did-what-to-whom variety, and we probably share the general assumption that divorce must be terrible for women because marriage is supposed to be central to a woman's happiness. Most people would probably guess, if asked, that divorced women have negative feelings about themselves and their lives. And indeed, at least until recently, large-scale studies of various segments of the population have shown divorced women to be significantly less satisfied with their lives than other women.[2]

This negative picture, we think, has a lot to do with *which* divorced women you are talking about. As we'll see, the months right after a marriage breaks up are a very difficult time for almost everyone involved. So most women, if interviewed shortly after the divorce, would show great distress and anxiety. And when a divorced woman must rely mostly on alimony or child support for her income, the dependency and the uncertainty, not to mention the financial strain, can give her a very gloomy sense of her situation. Of course, loneliness is a central problem when one has been in an intimate relationship, however unhappy it was. Divorced women who do not have children may suffer particularly from this lack of connection, although, of course, children in no way replace the intimacy with another adult.

In contrast to other studies, the way we chose to study divorced women was to treat this pattern as a stable way of life, as it is for increasing numbers of women. We included only women who had been divorced for at least a year, to avoid confusing divorce as a crisis with divorce as a way of life. We chose divorced women with children, because it is the ongoing parenting of children that makes these women most different from never-married women. And all the divorced women were employed. The large majority of divorced women now thirty-five to fifty-five do work, and this proportion is increasing. For most divorced women, then, divorce is a long-term state that includes being a mother and worker, and this is the group we studied.

In this way, we leave out important groups of divorced women—those who are solely dependent on ex-husbands economically, or who are on welfare, or who are students.[3] But we believe that those we studied are most relevant to how life will be for younger women; those who are divorced are likely to be paid workers who are committed to their work. There is increasing evidence that among older divorced women those who see themselves as career women are more satisfied with their lives than those who are homemakers or see their work as just a job.

The women we studied showed a different picture from the gloomy one of the past. Divorced women, it seems, are sharing in the enhanced well-being that characterizes women today. This doesn't mean, of course, that life is always rosy. As we saw in Chapter Three, for example, divorced women are lower in Pleasure than are married women, although the gulf is not a huge one. But as we reported earlier, divorced women score higher, as a group, than do any other women in the study on Mastery.

The self-confidence and zest for life of many divorced women came as a surprise to our interviewers. They set out expecting to find these women depressed and gloomy, and braced themselves for listening to many a tale of woe. Instead, they came back with renewed enthusiasm, saying, "We met some real people in this group!" They found that the divorced women had not only been able to rebuild their lives, often under difficult circumstances, but had also thought deeply about their lives and were articulate in discussing what had happened to them. These were women who had faced a difficult crisis, and in many cases, not only survived but thrived.[4] It is said that adversity strengthens character, and that old adage certainly proved true here.

While the divorced women in our sample were high in terms of Mastery, we've noted that if we had looked at them closer to the time of their divorce, our findings might have been different. From our study and from other research, a "pattern" of divorce for women can be discerned. In the first year after a marriage breaks up, life is often very difficult. When psychologist Dorothy Burlage[5] studied the effects of separation and divorce on women, she found that they experienced severe financial setbacks. After the divorce, family income for women and their children dropped by roughly two-thirds. In addition, the women went through a period that can best be described as floundering: trying to get back into the job market, trying to adjust to being single again, trying to deal with the confusion—and sometimes hostility—of their children. But because we were interested in how divorce affected women over the long term, after this initial crisis period had passed, we deliberately chose women for our study who were past the first year and on the way to getting their lives back on track again. The average length of time divorced for the women in the sample was seven years.

When you look at women who are in the crisis period, you rarely find them glowing with emotional health. But as the situation stabilizes, particularly if a woman has a job to ease the financial strain and enhance her often damaged sense of competence, a different picture takes shape. Freed from the tension of what has been an intolerable, or at least a problematic, marriage, the divorced woman often finds she is beginning to feel better about herself than she has in years. Even women who thought that their marriages were fairly stable before the breakup in retrospect could see the cracks and fissures that they had ignored before. For many of the divorced women in our study, marriage had been a source of anxiety, tension, and loss of self-esteem. When we talked with women who were happily married, a specific positive part of marriage they frequently mentioned was "my husband brings out the best in me."

For divorced women, the experience within marriage they described was often the opposite. Their ex-husbands had brought out the worst in them.

Perhaps this is the reason for one of our most striking findings: these women experience, in the aftermath of the divorce, a strong sense of personal growth and competence. Often their situation was somewhat akin to that of the child who is tossed off the end of the pier and learns to swim in that traumatic fashion—but swim she does. Divorced women speak of having "grown up," of having become a whole person, of taking charge of their own destinies at last. This sense of growth and competence was far and away the most positive aspect of divorce for women, and two clusters of rewards of being divorced that we found illustrate this.

The first rewards cluster was one we called "being in charge" and it was composed of the following items:

Having privacy and independence
Feeling able to manage
Not having to answer to anyone

The high value divorced women placed on these newfound freedoms gives us an insight into what was wrong with so many of their marriages. Often, they were not able to grow, to develop self-confidence, or to feel in control of their lives. Perhaps too many women had been willing as young women to give up the struggle for autonomy and accept the identity of "Mrs. Somebody." Are things different today? Perhaps. It's true that young women today hear much about developing their own identity. But rhetoric changes more quickly than behavior. The temptation for young women to set aside the search for self and to seek all the answers in marriage is still strong, and those who are lowest in self-esteem are too often the most tempted. But low self-esteem can get even lower in a bad marriage. That was the case with Sherri. Growing up, she never expected to support herself or to be independent. "I never thought of myself as someone who was going to have a career. I just thought I'd be married and have kids. That's what I'd do."

Sherri says she was "the first kid on the block to get married" and she had very little sense of herself or of what kind of a person she was marrying. "I'd seen a pretty bad marriage between my parents and I never spoke much to Fred, my husband, before we got married. I think I was crazy. I expected to be put down and looked down upon, and for the most part I was. The marriage gave me a lot of pain and I figured there must be something wrong with me."

Sherri found her husband very uncommunicative, and she never felt he approved of her. "I married a man who never valued me at all. I was never accepted, confirmed, or acknowledged in the marriage. He often told me I was impossible, and I guess I thought I was. I was told I made him sick [he was often depressed] and I thought I had. He was in law school when we married, but I was never expected to share his career. I was supposed to take care of the house, take care of him, take care of the kids, and not ask questions. I was expected to wait at home while he worked, while he played tennis, squash, bridge. So that's what I did."

The picture Sherri presents of herself as a wife is one of a person who thought she was invisible. "I strongly disagreed with my husband about what it meant to be a human being, what it meant to be a child, so I let him behave toward the children [two boys and a girl] in ways that I found very unacceptable, even including hurting them physically. I can't explain that now, but that's how it was. So I feel I didn't protect them in ways that I should have. Once I took my son to the hospital to see if my husband had broken his nose."

The marriage finally unraveled when Sherri's oldest child was a teen-ager and her youngest was nine. But by that time Sherri had discovered some talents of her own. She'd started working in local politics and had discovered, to her surprise, that people thought she was bright, talented, and fun to be around. Sherri's husband was the one who initiated the separation, but she says, "months before I had stopped wearing my wedding ring and was just busy living my own life in that house."

After they had separated, Sherri remembers hearing that her husband was dating a model, "one of those things a lot of guys fantasize about. I had a dream, and in it I met her and—I remember this so clearly—I shook her hand and I said, 'I'm so glad there's somebody to take care of him.' I felt I had shed such a responsibility."

The divorce removed Sherri from an atmosphere where she could never get approval, where her self-esteem was constantly being undermined. One of her first steps was to become her own boss. She went into the interior design business with a woman she had met in her political work. She is now co-owner, and is still a bit dazzled about what she has been able to accomplish. Sherri thinks the divorce is partly responsible for her new sense of being in charge: "I never really felt good about what kind of a person I was until after I was divorced. Today, I'm very pleased with being a woman, which I never was when I was younger. I thought being a woman was an 'entry level job.'"

Being pleased with who you are is closely tied in to "personal growth," the second group of rewards for divorced women. These were the items in the cluster:

> Feeling you have grown as a person
> Feeling you have developed skills
> Having the freedom to pay attention to your own development

Such growth is far from painless, however; many women go through a period of grieving immediately after the breakup of the marriage. But the person who emerges from that difficult process can be stronger and more confident. One fifty-four-year-old woman exemplifies how the trauma of divorce can strengthen the sense of self. For Marge, the sudden crumbling of what she believed to be a happy marriage threw her life into a turmoil.

Marge and her husband Tom were the parents of three children, born very close together. Tom had quit college in his senior year because of emotional problems and went to work in industry. He was laid off at about the time that their first child was born, a difficult period for both of them. But he got back on his feet, graduated from school, and Marge became the kind of wife who was able to manage everything—the kids, the household, a job in the personnel department of a large company. The family looked upon her, she says, as the "Rock of Gibraltar."

By the time her eldest child reached the teen-age years, Marge was doing well in her job and her husband was working as a teacher, getting steady promotions. "We had a good, solid marriage, I thought," Marge says. Then one day, seemingly out of the blue, Tom came home from a teachers' workshop and told Marge that he didn't love her anymore; he had met a woman at the workshop and now was in love with her. Marge was devastated. "I thought we had a good marriage, everybody thought we had a good marriage. It was quite a shock to everybody."

Marge now believes that Tom had been stacking his job progress up against hers, and that her promotions made him feel like a failure. "He didn't think he had succeeded as I had, which is, of course, ridiculous. But he felt like he wanted to change his life completely. That's when he met this woman."

Marge was rocked by feelings of rage and anger. She tried to suppress her feelings, and plunged into what she remembers as a "black hole." She says, "I got to know the workings of a real depression. I think it was diagnosed as chronic depression. I did not want to live. The love of my children became nothing. Nothing was important. I managed somehow to work. When I started to plot how I could kill myself without bringing shame to the kids, that's when I realized something was very wrong because even though I really wanted to die I still knew that's not the way people should feel. I took myself to the mental health clinic where they were very helpful. The crisis team worked with me for a week and a half. I could barely move. My depression had gotten to the point where physically I was in very bad shape. I was hyperventilating constantly which resulted in a numbness in my hands and feet. I lost twenty pounds. I was unable to do anything. I couldn't take care of the kids, I couldn't cook. When I look back on it, it was very funny, the way I was trying to cook for the kids. Did you ever cook a meal that you couldn't stand to look at, touch, or smell? That's where I was at the time. I was nauseous all the time and I didn't eat any solid foods for three months. I lived on milk shakes, instant breakfasts, eggnog."

Marge's sister was the major force in turning the situation around. "She had gone through a very bad depression herself a few years ago and recognized what was happening to me. She's the one who insisted I get help—take antidepressant medication and get therapy every week for six months."

Slowly, Marge began to climb out of the "black hole." Her children rallied around her. "It was very scary for them, since they always considered me to be the rock, and then I fell apart for a little while. It was a difficult time for them, but it brought us closer, much closer."

Despite the trauma of the divorce and the wrenching time that followed it, Marge feels her life is better in many ways than it was when she was married. "I had been such a private person that I think I shut an awful lot of people out of my life, which tells me there was something wrong with my life and my marriage.

What I went through was an awakening to myself and my emotional needs and it made me aware of other people in a way I had never been before. It was a unique experience, a positive thing, and hopefully I'll never revert to the way I was before."

Marge is now able to think of her own emotional needs, and she sees this as a major change. "I always sacrificed myself and catered to Tom. I never really thought about my own needs and I allowed this to happen. I guess I enjoyed being leaned on, giving him support he didn't give back. But it's only because I have grown and changed that I can see that. I probably would have gone on just as I was."

Would she give up this personal growth for a chance to turn back the clock, to have her marriage intact? "Definitely not. I was happy then, but I wouldn't want that now. I'm a person, now, a whole person on my own. I wasn't then."

Marge feels that her daughter, now a young woman, will not fall into the "self-sacrificing" pattern that Marge believes was a disaster for herself. "I hadn't realized that I was bringing up my daughter very differently from the way I was brought up myself. The way I feel now about myself—about women—is the way she feels. In fact, she helped me. She was the one who said to me, 'Mama, you don't have to depend on somebody else for emotional support, you have your own security inside yourself.' I like her attitude. She'd like to spend her life with somebody, but she's going to retain her independence, and if anything happens to that relationship, she knows it could never devastate her the way it did me for a while."

The process of adjustment—the grieving process—spans a different time period for each woman. But sociologist Robert Weiss, who studied separation and divorce, points out[6] that it is basically the same process whether it was the woman who left, or the man, or whether it was a mutual parting of the ways. And psychological dynamics are much the same when a very bad marriage ends as when the dissolving marriage was a mixture of good and bad. Many women, and men as well, have been surprised by the sadness and pain they feel at the ending of a marriage they desperately wanted to escape. This is probably because they are not mourning the marriage itself, but the end of a dream—what might have been. Most marriages begin with promise and high hopes, and to lose those can hurt—even when the marriage itself has caused more pain than pleasure. This is one aspect of divorce that probably won't change. The stigma may vanish, more flexible court procedures may lessen the legal battles that can make the process a nightmare, but the pain that comes when you lose the "might-have-been" must still be lived through.

Lucille Frost,* the fifty-three-year-old architect, found the whole experience very painful, "even for me, and I'm a high-status person in a high-status job. I can see where it would be the end of the world for women who don't have much else in their lives. It's a very tough adjustment. . . . It took two complete years before I came to feel comfortable about myself and was able to tell people that I was divorced."

Lucille was married to a successful surgeon and was in a marriage that had been disintegrating for years. She says that she first felt unhappy in her marriage "the day after we were married. My ex-husband is a very complicated man with complicated needs, and I was not right for him. I still have guilt feelings—I don't know— it's a tangle of emotions. I don't owe him anything. He's got four nice children, he's achieved his career goals, and he's about to be married to a very nice woman. I don't have to feel guilty about anything. I think, if anything, I treated him better than he treated me. But I still have guilt feelings because I sometimes feel it was really me at fault. All I had to do was accommodate—but that's the position women are in and we can't resolve it."

We've seen that women feel that bad marriages bring out the worst in them. Lucille is an example of what happens when a husband doesn't approve of what a woman sees as the "best" in herself. "Jim always saw my talent to promote—which I always felt to be one of the best parts of me—as somewhat despicable. I have a need to talk. I'm not a compulsive talker, but the way I make decisions and really function is by talking everything out. We absolutely couldn't talk. He was always very silent, quite sullen, and also given to violent rages. I think he has learned to communicate better. The kids say that he does with his new wife-to-be, but he couldn't with me. He always used a lot of energy trying to get me to shut up. I always felt that what he disliked in me were the best things about me."

Since the divorce, Lucille feels that a great strain has vanished

* Lucille Frost was introduced in Chapter Seven, page 131.

from her life. Now, without constant criticism, she feels free to concentrate on her own development. "I feel more integrated and I think that's part of the divorce too. I was always trying to tear myself into little pieces to hide me because he didn't like parts of me. It's better now. I have an awareness of being at the peak of my powers, of knowing very well what I know and being able to do it well and easily. I'm aware of a kind of command I never had before."

Like Lucille, many women reported that they used so much energy trying to hold untenable marriages together that their own personal development got put on "hold." In such cases, a divorce brings about not only the relief of tension, but the opportunity for a woman to discover her own skills and talents.

For Janet Blake,* the staff member at a consulting firm, marriage was something that happened because it was supposed to. She remembers her mother's dying words: "I could die happy if only you were married." Janet was in college at the time. Years later, when her father died, "He said he was dying happy because he knew I was in good hands and I had a good husband. The marriage had been on the rocks for years and my father knew it."

But for the first ten years, the marriage was a generally happy one. A daughter was born and the couple enjoyed their lives as young parents. Soon, however, her husband's periods of depression—always evident—began to grow longer. The pressures in Janet's job were also growing, and while Joe would help out, Janet felt that she should be doing all the work at home as well as holding down a job. And, just as Lucille had felt guilty for not being able to be the person her husband seemed to want, Janet felt guilty and responsible for her husband's depressions. "I always felt that these fits of depression to which he was subjected periodically were my fault. I always blamed myself for them and then the blame permeated my life."

At the same time, Janet was becoming aware of the women's movement and the new possibilities it opened up for women's lives. Intellectually a feminist, she still was emotionally gripped by the "proper" role of wife and mother. "The result was that my husband received terribly mixed signals. On the one hand I was brought

---

* Janet Blake was introduced in Chapter Seven, page 135.

up to be a wife and mother, to feel that taking care of the house and children was a woman's job, but on the other I was becoming more enmeshed in my work, which involved a tremendous amount of travel and pressure. My husband really wanted to be 'with it,' part of this new movement. If I was working late, he'd make supper. I always took that as criticism, that I wasn't doing my job. It was my job to make supper, as far as I was concerned."

One day, when her husband was in one of his dark moods, he beat Janet after an argument. "He beat on me and stopped when my eye started to swell up. Then when I said I was going to the hospital, he blocked my way, kind of pushed me off into my study. That happened at about nine o'clock at night. At one o'clock in the morning I finally went for help. He didn't stop me and I stood on the corner of the avenue to get a taxi to go to the hospital. I died that night. I've heard of other people who have had a death experience—if you haven't had a death experience you don't know what it is, but it's a feeling of having died; you no longer have any fear of death. I stood there on that corner waiting for a taxicab, both eyes black and blue, and face all black, thinking that I had died. The taxi driver was a young man with a beard and he took me to the hospital and wouldn't accept a fare, which I thought was so kind. When I got there in the emergency room there was a group of women, all strangers, and they asked me to join them. They took me in, talked to me. I'd been rejected by my family. My mother-in-law was visiting at the time and she stayed out of it, which I guess was appropriate, so here my family had totally rejected me and that killed me. I realized I had no friends. In the hospital they asked me where I wanted to go. I didn't know where I wanted to go, I didn't have any friends, only acquaintances who were friends of my husband."

So Janet went back home. "But, you know, it was then I realized that I was really totally alone, that it was a myth and a delusion that there was something in the marriage and that I was going to be taken care of." She decided that there were three possible choices: "I could leave immediately, or I could go back to business as usual and resign myself to repeated beatings, or I could make it very clear every day of the week that I was not available for that kind of abuse. I chose the third method. I was never beaten again, but there was never anything in the marriage after that, except a defensive posture on my part. All my energy went into that, because clearly once physical abuse enters into a behavior pattern, it takes a lot of work to keep it out, and in subsequent times, he would bang his fist on the table when he got angry and then kind of pat himself on the back that he didn't beat me." Clearly, in the midst of this turmoil, Janet's thoughts could only be for her survival, not for her own personal development.

Finally the marriage was ended, by mutual consent. Janet is comfortable with her life now. She is not looking to remarry—as we'll see, this was true for many divorced women—but she does not rule out the idea of a relationship with one man—or several. She has grown comfortable, also, with herself. "That's one of the joys of the last few years, certainly since the divorce. I feel very good about myself. I was always trying for zero defects, just to be perfection itself in every way, and I don't do that anymore. I'm just the way that I am and that's it. Sometimes we make things happen, and sometimes they just happen to us. I believe that we can make things happen. For me—well, I haven't found the pathway yet to become president of a company, but that's what I'd like and I believe it's possible."

Divorced women, of course, are far from free of problems in their lives. Two major clusters of concerns emerged. The first we call "loneliness":

Not being able to find compatible companions
Lack of permanent intimate relationship
Problems meeting men
Being afraid of loneliness in later years
Problems in sexual relationships
Not having someone to share things with

In our interviews we found that the divorced women were in more conflict and were more concerned about intimate relationships with men than were single women. Perhaps this is because divorced women had been used to having such a relationship—however flawed and distressing it may have been—while single women were more accustomed to periods of aloneness and instability in their personal relationships.

Peggy, a forty-five-year-old teacher at a small college, is struggling with this loneliness cluster. Hers was one of the marriages that was a casualty of the "swinging sixties." She met her husband Phil when they both in high school and were married when he was nineteen, she was eighteen. "We were babies," she says. She helped support him through graduate school, and she had a life plan all set: "Idyllic marriage to a bright professor in a lovely Ivy League school." The couple had three children, planned and spaced and, as Peggy says, "We just bobbed along. I don't know whether we were happy, or if we were unhappy. We just didn't stop to think about it."

The first signs of cracks in the marriage came after her husband became caught up in "a very nasty tenure scene" and left academia completely. "I'm sure the crisis had a lot to do with the breakup of our marriage. I think it was the ungluing of a dream, one we both shared."

Peggy reacted by plunging into an affair which eventually caused the breakup of the marriage. The couple tried going to see a marriage counselor, but Peggy's husband was going through a metamorphosis of his own. "He went to Esalen and they sent him back unglued. He came back with his beard, long hair, and love beads—and he was a square Ivy League man. I think if times had been different, things would have been different for us. We got caught up in that whole sixties scene, when it became much easier to get a divorce than to stick with it. As I look back I keep wondering why somehow it couldn't have been stopped, because we do share a great deal. If I had it to do over again, I would have tried to pick up the threads of that marriage. I think we had probably more going for us than 90 percent of the people I know. We were done in by lack of self-awareness in terms of where we were at the time, and we were done in a little bit by a movement that I can only identify as psychobabble. I think that's my biggest regret."

Peggy sees herself as being at a crossroads as far as her relationships with men are concerned. "I have almost continually had a sexual partner since I was divorced. It might not have been an all-encompassing relationship, but there's been somebody whom I slept with maybe a couple of times a month. I'm in the process of giving that up. There's a lot going on in my head at this point to the effect that if a relationship isn't going somewhere, I don't want to bother with it. I'm going to live without it for awhile. I really want that feeling of commitment that makes a sexual relationship complete. I've been involved with two men, each of whom is living with a woman—just living together, they're not married and they're both unhappy. They are guys I've known for seven or eight years . . . these have been close male friends. They're coming here for their sexual relationships and I've finally decided to put that aside. I've already spoken to one of them and said I can't accept the crumbs from anybody's table anymore. And when I get a chance I'll say it to the other. I'll have a moment of fear of 'What am I going to do?' but I don't need to be validated that way anymore. That's really what it comes down to. I needed the validation for a long time, but I don't anymore. I want a man who's got his head together, taken care of his garbage. I'm looking for someone who is together enough to deal with closeness and space—who knows who he is."

In the past, Peggy has experimented with a number of ways to meet men. She has run ads in personal columns, tried dating services. "Most of the people I meet are losers. But I had a very nice relationship with someone for two years—he answered an ad and I answered his at the same time. My education rules out a lot of men who are threatened by it. I sometimes think that as we are getting stronger, men are getting weaker. These guys come out of divorces so damaged but they won't do anything about it. They just turn around and repeat their history with a much younger woman. I don't feel so good about myself in relationships with men, and that's what I'm struggling with in therapy. I do feel good about myself as a mother and as a professional. I'm getting to feel better about male-female relationships. I'm getting to the point where I can say it's not my fault. If I could live my life over, I'd be born with the self-awareness that I have now."

Ambivalence about relationships with men is a problem for many divorced women. The scars from a painful first marriage are taking a long time to heal for Ellen Dudley* the secretary in the sales department of a chemical company. The question of new relationships with men is problematic. Looking back on her marriage, she says: "The greatest delight now is being able to decide what I want to do, when I want to do it, even though I have the kids' schedules to work around. I was married to someone who didn't want to do anything and I felt guilty when I went out and did things. Often, I stayed home with him and was miserable. He wanted to be fed and taken care of, to bring home the money and

---

* Ellen Dudley was introduced in Chapter Six, page 114.

sit in his bathrobe and read and then go to bed and expect to make love every night. That was all I had to do. I went from being an open, energetic, vibrant, young person to someone who had lost all feelings. I was severely depressed and saw no future. I didn't have any dreams anymore. It was so sad—I want to cry when I think about it. I would never allow myself to be that unhappy again. I let it happen, but that could never happen again, not with anybody. That's a big change. I would not allow myself to be that unhappy again."

Her ex-husband has remarried, and that has stirred up some residual anger in Ellen. "I couldn't quite believe anybody would want to marry him. The anger was sort of at men in general—if a man decides he wants to get married again or to find someone to be his new slave, he can do it. There is always some woman somewhere willing to play the traditional games just to have the man, and that makes me angry as opposed to any direct anger at him."

Since her divorce, Ellen has had "one relationship you could call a love relationship and that was immediately after the marriage, which I find somewhat typical from most of the women I have talked to. Nothing since, nothing that has gone past the third or fourth date, or men wanting to sleep with me or me wanting to sleep with them because I know I can't get anything else. I've lowered my expectations down to just about zero. The latest three or four men in my life, each one is worse than the next. I mean, they're not even in the ballpark. I get angry at the society that has produced the games that men play—and they play them, of course, because it allows them to have power, and who wants to give up power? so they play the games. I understand that but it doesn't make me any less angry."

Ellen says she is not interested in remarriage. "I wouldn't even consider a traditional marriage, never again. I *can* envision myself, once the kids grow up, wanting to live with somebody."

She is concerned that an intense relationship with a man would interfere with her relationship with her children. "I don't want anybody else's input at this stage; all I would want is that somebody enjoyed some social time with the kids. But to have someone really involved with their upbringing, that would be more than they— or I—could handle."

So it is hard for her to envision someone in her life right now.

"I just can't picture myself with a man on a day-to-day basis. I want companionship . . . the perfect situation would be to find some guy who shared some of my interests, who is making a decent living, and I'm making a decent living, and any money that is extra is money that's just for fun things—vacation, luxuries—and not for support. We'd be available for each other, he'd live here some time, some times at his place. I don't see that it has to be totally apart or totally together. The men I've met either want nothing or they want to get married immediately, which I don't want. There doesn't seem to be the possibility of anything in between. Maybe I'm unrealistic—I don't know."

While Ellen is unsure about the role a permanent intimate relationship will play in her life, Sherri is certain such a relationship will not be central to her again. Years of an unsatisfying marriage had left her emotionally numb and unsure of her sexuality. "I had never kissed another man. I had been married for twenty-three years and I had no notion if I was attractive, if I was good in bed, if anybody would ever make a pass at me."

She had several quick affairs, and then met a man with whom, for the first time in her life, she fell deeply in love. "It was the most significant, caring, loving relationship—the only one that I ever had. He was the only human being that has ever been in the center of my soul. He wanted to be married and I wanted not to be married. I wanted to have my cake and eat it too. He wanted to live with me. I wanted him to live with me but have his own apartment too. He couldn't sustain that. It was much too difficult for him. He wanted to be married. He left a year ago."

Despite the depth of the relationship, Sherri could not live with his inability to let her have her own space, to continue the relationship without marriage. "I absolutely will not be married. I have known that from the day I got divorced. I think what I learned from this episode is that we are essentially alone and that's how I see where I am. I wouldn't make that sort of commitment of the soul again—not because I might get hurt . . . because it wouldn't make any sense. Some years ago, there was an earthquake study in Los Angeles that showed that kids were having some serious problems after the quake because, you know, if you can't stand on the earth, where is it that you're going to stand? Well, I have the feeling I'm going to stand on my own. It does put me outside the mainstream, I understand that, but at this time in history, I'm not so strange. People don't say, 'What's that lady doing?' I can go where I want, travel where I want. . . . I can invite people over to dinner who are married or unmarried, I don't feel at all like a fifth wheel."

It took Amy Faulkner,* the thirty-six-year-old magazine editor, a long time to feel comfortable without the constant presence of a man. She married her husband, Matt, when they were "right out of college and madly in love." But the marriage floundered and eventually ended. The sixties were in full swing, and everyone seemed free and uninhibited. "It seemed to me that all the while I was married, men were knocking on my door to have affairs with me, and I thought, Why should I be with this guy who is mute and uncommunicative if there are all those other guys out there? Then, suddenly, when you get out there, a lot of the men disappear."

Even though her marriage had not been a good one, Amy went through an intense grieving period. "It was really a shocker to me. And everything hits you at once, the grief and the panic. The loneliness was the hardest thing for me to deal with. I was desperate to get a man again. That whole desperation quality was what I felt most of the time."

The idea that she could be happy without a man came as a surprise to her. "Believing in the happiness that I do feel flies in the face of everything I was taught as a girl: you can't be happy by yourself; you can only be happy when you're dependent on a man. It's a really nice thing to find out that isn't so."

The sense of failure that Amy experienced when her marriage collapsed was due in part to her parents' idea of what success meant for a woman. Despite her considerable achievements in her career, Amy's parents judge her by only one criterion: Does she have a man? Any other achievement is ignored.

It was obviously threatening for Amy to feel good about being independent. "For a long time in therapy, everytime I started to feel independent I panicked because that goes totally against the grain of what I was taught, emotionally. But it's a much better way."

Amy says that therapy helped her to get out of what she sees as a destructive pattern in relationships with men. "For a while I

---

* Amy Faulkner was introduced in Chapter Six, page 119.

didn't have a man—then I'd get a man and sink back into a real emotional dependence, which I didn't like. But I didn't see any other way of relating to a man, so I was in a total bind. My therapist has really helped me see—and believe—that I have a stake in my own emotional independence. I don't have to abandon it when a permanent relationship with a man comes along. That's a real change in my thinking that makes me feel like there's a really solid course into the future."

Amy wants to make sure she holds onto her newfound independence. "I'm happy making my own decisions. I wouldn't want anybody making them for me now." One thing she would insist on in a new marriage, Amy says, is a prenuptial agreement in which the ownership of money was spelled out. "I don't think I'd be comfortable living on his money with my money being for frills and unimportant things. The person I'm going out with now has made a ton of money and that bothers me because money can be power. The person making more money thinks he can push the other person around and make the decisions, such as where you're going to live. But finding someone who doesn't want a dependent woman is a whole other thing."

Many divorced women today feel that there is a dichotomy between their own need for autonomy and the comfort of a stable intimate relationship. Terri, a thirty-eight-year-old commercial artist, is almost obsessed with this issue. Terri's marriage broke up because her husband Larry left her, but she says that all through the marriage she had repressed a great deal of anger at him. The couple's serious financial problems complicated what turned out to be a very tenuous relationship. When her husband left, Terri says, "That was proof that I was a leaveable person, that I wasn't worth staying with. But now I'm much clearer about who I am and what's real."

Terri feels much more like a whole person today, and she is eager for a good relationship with a man, but still she worries. "How would I move out of the wonderful space that I'm living in and let someone else in? Will there be enough room for me to be alone? Once, in a women's group session, there was a large circle on the table and a smaller circle and the question was where you'd put yourself if a man came into the larger circle? And I took the smaller circle to represent myself and I moved it completely out of the space and said I would completely disappear. That was my fear, that I would cease to exist, that I would give over so much to the man in the way of power that I wouldn't 'be' at all. I think I have to be careful with that now—I see in myself the tendency to do the reverse and try to prove that I am powerful." Terri's question, crucial to so many single and divorced women, is "Can I find someone who has a sense of himself and can let me mess up, and lean, and go away and be who I am, separate from whoever he is? Could I find a man with whom I could live, but not 'become as one' and all those ridiculous things?"

We were surprised at how ambivalent, even negative, so many divorced women were about remarrying. With less social pressure and stigma, with more opportunities for challenging work, the process of accommodation to the demands of a new marriage is less attractive to divorced women now, especially if there are children to complicate the process.

In fact, being too eager to remarry may be a sign of unresolved problems for a divorced woman. Those in our study who were very eager to remarry were those with severe financial difficulties. It seems that these women were seeking not so much a fulfilling relationship, but a way to bail out of a bad situation. Only 7 percent of the women in the sample fell into this category; 48 percent of the women said they were somewhat interested in remarriage, 27 percent were not especially interested in remarrying, and 18 percent said they did not want to remarry. So most women had what might be called a guardedly optimistic attitude about remarriage. They knew they didn't need a man to complete their identity, and they wouldn't marry again for what they considered the wrong reasons. If the right man came along, a person who would give them room to grow and who was capable of commitment, then they would consider remarriage. While an intimate relationship was often a high priority, a wedding ring was not.

The average number of years the women in our sample had been divorced was seven. Clearly, many of the women had been divorced for some time and had settled into a fairly stable life pattern. Our statistics on the number of women who were eager to remarry might therefore be low. Women who very much wish to remarry tend to do so quickly. It may be that the woman who remarries quickly does so when she is still "off balance"—still worried about how to support herself, threatened and unable to cope. Remarriage seems like a quick solution to the chaos in her life, but these are not, it seems, ideal conditions under which to launch such a critical venture as a second marriage.

The second cluster of concerns that can take its toll on divorced women includes these items:

Seeing the children upset
Having a difficult relationship with an ex-husband
Having problems going places alone

We've labeled this cluster "disruption" because it encompasses the changes and upheaval that are often the aftermath of divorce. As we've seen, the role of parent is the most crucial one to employed divorced women who are mothers. Concern about being a parent haunts many of them. Probably as a reflection of out-of-step anxiety, if the children are doing well, a woman feels like an "okay" person; when the children are upset, she is threatened.

Do divorced women actually have more difficulties in relationships with children than married women? One might suppose this to be the case, but our study shows it is not usually true for women who have been divorced for a while. Mavis Hetherington and other researchers[7] have shown that the first year or two after divorce or separation typically are troubled, and, of course, sometimes parent-child troubles continue indefinitely. For our subjects, however, child balance scores and the level of concerns divorced women had about children were about the same as those reported by married women. As we've noted, though, even if divorced women don't have more problems, having problems has more effect on divorced women's well-being. There are two sides to the vulnerability of divorced women to their children's ups and downs, however. Many divorced women take a special pride in knowing that despite some difficult periods, their children seem to be thriving, and they, as mothers, have had a lot to do with that happy outcome.

Ellen Dudley, the forty-one-year-old secretary, often experiences such feelings. She finds "a certain ego gratification that I'm doing it alone. It does something just for me. I know that I feel very happy when they are happy, especially if I in some way have led them into the thing that has made them happy. My older one is starting to be company for me, I've felt that in the last year. We'll sit here in the late evening and we'll talk about something and I suddenly realize that he is now more company than he is somebody I have to take care of. Both boys have become very independent. They cook for themselves, do laundry. Bill does the food shopping every other week for the whole family. They share in the cleaning. There's less time that I have to spend doing things for them. Seeing them become independent is really nice. I really like that and it makes me happy to feel that they have some preparation for the outside world because they've had to grow up a little faster. I think that's true for kids with divorced parents. In the end it will be a help to them, not a hindrance, because they've had to be independent more quickly. I feel it's positive, not negative, and I feel proud. When I introduce them to somebody new I always feel proud. I think they look terrific, they're bright, they're nice people."

Ellen has not been completely freed from anxiety, however: "Every month is a new worry. One of my fears is that there is hidden anger in there that they haven't gotten out, some directed at me, some at their father. And I fear that it needs to come out. I'm not sure when or where it will come out or what form it will take, and I don't feel as though there is anything I can do. I feel kind of helpless about that, and perhaps to talk about it might be more harmful than helpful, so I try to control that. I used to be afraid that they wouldn't have the ability to grow up and find a relationship with a woman and think about marriage and kids, but I don't worry about that anymore because I manage to get enough males into their lives. My father is close to them. My parents are very caring people and the kids have seen that and commented, 'Isn't it nice that grandpa and grandma care about each other.' I got Big Brothers for both of the boys, which has been going on for four years now. Bill, the oldest, has this lovely, sensitive, considerate sweet guy, just a doll, and I don't know which one loves the other more. It's beautiful and it's a reward for me, knowing I did that. I saw there was a need, and I went ahead, and it worked. I definitely provided something they need. I feel really good about that. Mark's Big Brother just graduated from Harvard last year, and he's got a new one he's even more excited about. I've tried to get male teachers for them whenever possible. There are a couple of male friends in my life, not lovers, but friends from when, or before, I was married. They come by periodically just to play chess with the kids and have dinner on their birthdays. So there are men in their lives. I've made sure they've been there."

Marge, the personnel administrator who went into a deep depression when her husband left her and then recovered, finds parenting better today than when her children were younger. She had her first baby when her husband had been laid off from his job. "It wasn't an ideal time to have a child, but at that time there was no choice—you got pregnant whether you planned it or not. I was very, very young and immature and so was my husband. One of us had to grow and I guess it probably was me. So I grew— I still have a long way to go. I didn't especially enjoy being a mother with my first child. It was too soon and the financial problems were terrible."

Now, she says she feels very happy when one of her three children succeeds at something that is important to them. "For instance, I'll tell you something that I love about my sixteen-year-old who has come full cycle now. He went through a period when he didn't have a mother. It was not manly to have a mother, so there was no physical contact. You know they still love you, but they go through that period of time. Now it's all right. He's bigger than me and it's all right on his terms. He loves to show off and hug me and throw his arms around my neck and pick me up . . . tell me that he loves me. My daughter has always been demonstrative. My thirteen-year-old is not very demonstrative physically, but he shows it in other ways. He is very loving."

In the domain of divorce, as in many of the domains we studied, there are single reward or concern items that do not cluster together, but that are individually very important. One concern item that was not part of a cluster but that has a very strong impact on divorced women is, in fact, their single greatest worry—finances. Worry about money has a major negative effect on Mastery. It is a concern that only the most affluent women escape completely, since income drops, two-thirds on the average, for women and children in the wake of a divorce. Ellen, for example, after four years as a divorcee, is only now starting to see the light at the end of the tunnel. It has been a *long* tunnel.

"Finances are my biggest concern, the cause of my stomach trouble. I'm sitting here now, and it's the first time in four years that I can say I'm paying all the bills. I've come up with all kinds of schemes to pay the bills in the last few years, mainly selling off parts of my house as time has gone on. The first two years I was managing on my child support plus my income from teaching and I've always rented one room, sometimes two rooms, to boarders. I got by—I had about $150 left at the end of the month. I considered that if there was $100 left after I had paid everything, I was doing pretty well. Then with inflation that was eaten away and my income went down from teaching. When I lost that job, I began to sink. I went through what little bank account I had at that point, which was only a few thousand dollars. I borrowed from friends; I took in typing at home, rented another room—God knows how I did it. I must have repressed it because I don't remember how I did it all. Then two years ago, in the spring, I couldn't make it anymore. I had $500 left in the bank. I took a part-time secretarial job because I still fight the issue of working full time because of the conflict in terms of kids. They were still young and I only wanted to work twenty-five to thirty hours a week. I wanted the other ten hours to keep everything together around the house. So I concentrated on finding a decent part-time job, which didn't happen. Then I decided I had to sell the house. Then I thought about selling half the house because it's a two-family that I own. I called my lawyer and accountant and we sat down and figured everything out and considered all the options and I put an ad in the paper. Within a week I sold the downstairs apartment. For the last two years I lived off that money, went back to school, and still had to work. I worked Saturdays and Sundays indexing and editing for a friend and typing at home. I had an internship at school, plus I worked fifteen or twenty extra hours just to make up the difference. I borrowed the money for the course, plus some spending money that I took from a loan, which I now have to pay back.

"I developed stomach trouble, as I say, because I wasn't paying the bills. I borrowed from friends with the promise that in the future I'd be able to pay it back. I was very angry. You're talking to me at the first point in my divorced life where I'm not quite so angry, but I probably will be in a few months again. When we got divorced in 1974, the support settlement was fair. It has not increased by a penny since then, so it's worth approximately 60 percent less. So my goal of financial independence in a job is prime—more important than satisfaction."

Ellen is pleased with herself and the things that she has accomplished, despite persistent financial pressures. But she says she wishes she had been raised differently. "There's one thing for sure. Every woman has to think absolutely like a man. She has to be prepared to support herself and others because the reality is that we still have the babies—and we will have to be able to support ourselves. But it's important not only for that reason, but for self-esteem, for feeling good about yourself."

Amy, the editor, tells a similar story of financial hardship.

"I remember one week, living with my son after the divorce, when we had one package of hot dogs for the whole week for both of us. The whole financial aspect of the divorce knocked me for a loop; I was really unprepared for that. I had a basic confidence that I could earn enough money, but the change in lifestyle was really radical. I couldn't go skiing, I couldn't go to the movies. Suddenly, all those sources of letting the steam out of the pressure cooker weren't there and that was a shock. Plus, my family was very unsupportive of the divorce and refused to help me out financially. That ended up making my financial situation much more punitive and added on to the burden. . . . They told me they'd buy me a car if I went back to my husband, and that if I left him they'd cut me out of their will and never give me any money, and that's been true."

For Marilyn Walker,* the thirty-eight-year-old clerical worker who has two children, a top priority is gaining more skills so she can command a better salary. Like most women, she wasn't prepared for the job of supporting a family.

"I know I'll make changes in my life. But what I'm going to have to go for is more secretarial skills, shorthand, dictation, where the money is. I have to brush up on these things and get so I'm good at them, so I can demand the money. That's my priority, first of all. I have to think of the money. I figured I'd be supported by a husband, I really did. I figured I'd do my job and he'd do his. I always did my job and I never could figure out how come he wasn't doing his when I was doing mine to the best of my ability. I'll have to educate myself further to meet my financial needs, I know that. I know, too, that I'll never sit back and think somebody is going to take care of me. I feel that nobody has ever taken care of me and I don't think they will. It would be nice, but I don't count on it."

Earning her own income is a reason for Marilyn's self-confidence. "I feel more secure now than I have in my whole life. I've lived in poverty and I know what it is. This is better than I've ever had in my life and whatever comes, I'll handle it. If we have to cut here and there I'm an old pro at that, I know what I'm doing so it doesn't bother me."

But the financial pressures are mounting. "My daughter will

---

* Marilyn Walker was introduced in Chapter Two, page 23.

be eighteen years old in a couple of months; neither of them will be getting child support much longer. Right now I'm not making any money, not at all. And I know that the only way I can do that is to further my education. But right now I can't find the time. And finance it? Forget it. There's just no way I can go to school right now. I think about it more and more. I look back and say where have the last five years gone, and I can get kind of panicky."

For most divorced women, the whole question of finances is intermingled with anxiety, resentment, and struggle. There is one group, however, who managed to escape this traumatic aspect of divorce. The women in high-prestige jobs talked very differently about finances than did other women. The fact that they could command very good salaries certainly did not make divorce a pleasant experience for them, but it did insulate them against the desperate struggle so many other women face. Well-paid women, when they discussed financial problems, were often talking about belt-tightening but rarely about survival. They weren't selling off parts of a house or doing typing at night or worrying about whether they could run a house when child support ended. Since money is the biggest concern of divorced women, it's clear that one great advantage for a woman of having a high-prestige job is that if she happens to wind up in the divorce courts, she has a good chance of escaping one of the most serious and distressing effects of the end of a marriage.

As we've noted, overall the employed women in our study who had high-prestige jobs were higher in Mastery than women whose jobs were less prestigious. But we found an intriguing difference between divorced women and other groups of women in this regard. The difference in Mastery scores between women in high-prestige jobs and those in moderate and low-prestige jobs was less for divorced women than for other groups. The "Mastery gap," as it might be called, is not so great for divorced women; being in a low-prestige job doesn't seem to be as distressing. How does one explain this?

The answer, we think, is that for many divorced women, just having a job and supporting themselves is a big improvement over their previous situation. Getting any job was something to cheer about when they had been unemployed and trying to find a way to support their children. The married woman who doesn't have to worry about where her next meal is coming from may indeed grumble about a job that is below her abilities. For the divorced woman, that same job may be like an island to a person adrift at sea—the fact that she can perform well and earn money does a great deal for her sense of competence.

At this point, the reader may be wondering how the rewards and concerns of divorce affect a woman's well-being. What impact do the "being in charge" and "personal growth" clusters have on Mastery and Pleasure? What about "loneliness" and "disruption"? And did the extent to which women had a positive balance of rewards over concerns make a difference?

The answers to these questions are very different for Mastery and for Pleasure. Mastery was unrelated to any of the reward and concern scores or to divorce balance. As a divorced woman, whether you are having intense problems meeting men doesn't affect your sense of Mastery, nor does the degree to which you like being in charge. Why is this?

Divorced women all have something in common—surviving a difficult experience that tested their personal strength. They seem to draw their confidence from the fact of their survival rather than from how much they are enjoying or not enjoying the state of divorce. Second, we believe that divorced women today are much less likely than before to blame themselves for the divorce, at least once it is over and behind them, or to feel stigmatized, worthless, or unfeminine because it happened. As we've seen, they feel like whole people, competent, successful, and female.

But Pleasure is a different story. To experience a high level of Pleasure in one's life takes more than surviving and feeling strong—particularly for a woman who did marry and expected to find happiness through that route. So, here's where divorced women can suffer. Not surprisingly, "loneliness" had a strong negative effect on Pleasure. "Disruption" did not. And "being in charge," but not "personal growth," had a positive impact. As we've seen, concern about finances—money—was the greatest single concern of divorced women, who typically find themselves responsible for their own economic survival. When a woman doesn't have an adequate income, all the other problems in her life pale by comparison, and not surprisingly her sense of Mastery is diminished.

Divorce is always, at best, a mixed bag for women. Women do not marry with the idea of one day "achieving" divorce. Looking back on divorce, they wish it were something that could have been avoided. But when it has happened and they have survived it, they often can look on it as a positive experience in their lives. Surprisingly, when the women in our study were asked how divorce had affected their lives—an open-ended question with no suggested answers—72 percent of the women mentioned positive growth in their sense of self, and 95 percent mentioned a positive effect on their career and/or education. Only one-third mentioned a negative effect as the main one—finances, relations with children, strain. When we asked if they saw their life as having had any major turning points, thirty-eight of the forty-six women mentioned their divorce as that turning point, but 80 percent of these said it was a turning point in a positive direction!

Of course, these women were not seeing divorce itself as a positive thing—and we must remember the human tendency to accentuate the positive—but it was often a healthy step for women caught in bad or borderline marriages. The fact that so many women experienced a sense of personal growth after ending a marriage raises some crucial questions. Did marriage hold a particular trap for these women in terms of dependency? Or is it tempting for *all* women to use marriage as a refuge, relinquishing personal growth to "let George do it"? Many divorced women spoke of not knowing how to handle money, not being prepared for the outside world, not testing their strength until forced to do so. Perhaps most married women if suddenly alone would face the same issues. Perhaps the problem is that while marriage can be either a hideout or a springboard to the world, it is often easier to hide than it is to venture. In today's world, hiding is particularly risky.

For the woman who found in marriage no safe haven, who lived through the wreckage of that marriage, the outside world is not necessarily an alien place, nor is she doomed to some kind of half-life as a failed person. As one woman says: "What I realize now is that I'm really the cause of everything that happens to me. I can't blame it on other people. I am the cause, that's what occurs to me, and that's what life is about. That's nice to know and I find it very liberating. I'm sorry my marriage didn't work—I would have liked it to work—though I really wonder if I would have learned as much about myself if it had."

MOTHERS AND DAUGHTERS

When I explain to students how to put a wire into something and how to screw it down, I'll say, "Do you know who taught me this?" They'll answer, "Your engineering professor?" And I'll say, "No, my mother!"

A fifty-five-year-old engineering professor

I have always lied to my mother. And she to me. How young was I when I learned her language, to call things by other names? Five, four—younger? Her denial of whatever she could not tell me, that her mother could not tell her, and about which society enjoined us both to keep silent, distorts our relationship still.

Nancy Friday, My Mother, My Self

NANCY FRIDAY'S BEST-SELLING BOOK presents a picture of mothers and daughters locked in loving but often near-mortal combat—the daughter trying to move toward independence, the mother holding her back. And indeed, many readers did identify with this portrait of an embattled relationship. In the wake of the book's success, mothers and daughters have been given renewed attention by the popular media. Unfortunately, that attention has focused almost exclusively on the problems in the relationship. This negative focus may have created a widespread belief that the mother-daughter bond is always a troubled, painful one, with conflict an essential component. Our findings show this dismal picture is not necessarily an accurate one.

It's not surprising that mothers are getting a "bad press" these days. "Mother" has been cast as the villain in a whole range of scenarios. In the fifties, she was accused of being overprotective and too indulgent toward her children, a monster who smothered them in an orgy of what author Philip Wylie called "Momism." In the days after the Korean War, some behavioral scientists claimed that American POWs who didn't resist "brainwashing" had been too pampered by their mothers. But then, when women tried not to be those awful, smothering "moms," new experts popped up to tell them that they were causing "alienation" in their children by too little mothering. It seemed that good old mom could do very little that was right, but lots that was wrong.

A review of the psychological literature shows that there can be some very real problems between daughters and mothers, especially during adolescence and young adulthood. But it's time to stop looking exclusively at the dark side of this relationship. It's nice to know there's some good news for a change. In our study, we found that the majority of relationships between women and their mothers are characterized by warmth, companionship, and compassion.

When we developed our rewards and concerns items in the domain of relationships with family of origin (parents and siblings), we included three items focusing just on women's relationships to their mothers. These items reflected what women had told us in our intensive interviews. We used them to create what we call our "maternal rapport" index, a measure of how positive women found their relationship with their mothers:

> I enjoy my mother's companionship
> I get along smoothly with my mother
> My mother is a good model of getting older

About half of the women in our sample had very high scores on the maternal rapport index, while only 25 percent reported low rapport. And a good mother-daughter relationship had a positive effect on the well-being of the adult daughter, contributing to both Mastery and Pleasure. While the impact on well-being is not the same for all our groups of women, often women do have the gratification of a warm, affectionate bond between mothers and daughters. Our study, we believe, provides a truer picture of the norm for this relationship than the tortured battles so often described in the popular media.

In our interviews we repeatedly found that by middle adulthood most women seem to have achieved a mature and objective view of their mothers, seeing them not as all-powerful figures with a controlling impact on their lives, but as human beings with understandable faults and virtues. These adult women view their mothers not the way children see them—through a magnifying glass as giants—but as people with whom they can, and have, come to terms.

Do these findings mean that all the angst we have been hearing about between mothers and daughters is nonexistent? Is the struggle of daughters to carve out their own lives, to win both independence and approval from their mothers, a figment of the imagination? Not at all. What our findings may tell us is another piece of good news—that relationships between mothers and daughters get better with age.

The mother-daughter struggles seem to center around issues of autonomy and identity—"growing up," in plain language—and they are usually resolved by the time a daughter is in her late twenties. Many younger women who are involved in conflicts with their mothers may be in the grips of "psychological adolescence"— a struggle that some theorists believe occurs later in life for women than it does for men.

For a young woman struggling with identity formation—finding out "Who am I?"—her mother can loom as the major force against breaking free. Many theorists have concluded, from looking at men's lives, that this sort of breaking away happens in adolescence. But we know from studies of adolescence that many women don't go through this important process until later.[1] Some women don't feel autonomous or independent until their twenties or thirties, or later, when they finally look beyond parents, husbands, and children as a source of identity. (For some women, of course, this never happens.) It is often not until this time that they realize that such borrowed identities as "Mary Smith's daughter" or "Bill's wife" or "Susie's mother" will not carry them through the rest of their adult lives. So it is not surprising that young women are often locked in conflict with their mothers at an age when they are supposed to be beyond all that. Many young women may still be seeing their mothers as giant figures—they haven't yet begun the process of "shrinkage" of their parents that is an essential part of maturing. But by age thirty-five, our study indicates, most women have completed this process. The angst of many mother-daughter relationships, then, need not doom the women involved to a permanent, ongoing battle. It may simply be part of the difficult process of growing up. As one thirty-five-year-old woman put it, "I never forgot, until I could actually follow it, a friend's advice. 'When you come to accept yourself, you will stop picking on your mother.'"

But for a young woman caught in the middle of the struggle, it may be difficult to arrive at an objective view of her mother. She tends to see every relationship through the eyes of the emerging self, seeing her mother only in relation to herself, not as other people see the older woman. Nancy Friday, in *My Mother, My Self,* recalls that once, when she broke up with a man, she telephoned her mother: "Her voice greeted me, free of the usual anxiety she felt for my sister. I did not tell her Ben and I were finished. I wanted to reverse the bargain, undo the shift in responsibility made so long ago when I had become the sharer of my mother's guilts, protector of her timidities. I wanted to be her child again. 'Why do you always treat me as if I could take care of myself?' I asked her. 'Why don't you ever worry about me?'"[2]

Here, the daughter expects the connection with her mother to be so intimate, so special, that her mother should be able to sense a personal disaster even when the daughter deliberately conceals it from her. The mother is expected to have mental telepathy, and the daughter is angry when she doesn't.

Compare the tone, the egoistic passion of those statements (one of the hallmarks of psychological adolescence is passionate self-absorption) with those of women in our study who were further along in the maturing process:

A forty-six-year-old married woman says: "My mother was not physically affectionate. She was a marvelous mother, I see that now, but I never thought she was. I didn't get along with her until I was thirty years old. My mother didn't play with us, my father did. My mother took care of us. . . . It was not until I had grown up myself that it dawned on me that she is a human being too and she has feelings, she isn't the tough lady I thought she was."

By thirty-five, a woman typically is able to look at her mother and sort out the good and the bad without anger or guilt. A forty-one-year-old single woman commented: "My mother is a wonderful, slightly manipulative, slightly dominant person. She's done what she had to do all these years; she has achievements that are quite a credit to her, she's come through many a storm, and she's done it her way and I respect and admire her. It's difficult to be a forty-year-old woman with her at times because she'd like to see things done the 'right' way. This past holiday that I spent there I had quite a conversation with her and she didn't necessarily like what she heard, but I more or less pointed out a few things in a kind way."

A mature daughter can view her mother objectively and with compassion, no longer being obsessed with whether she has lived up to all her mother's hopes, standards, or rules of conduct. One fifty-year-old woman says: "I know she'd rather see me go off looking like I had just stepped from a bandbox—the right weight and style— this is something that's very important to my mother. I wish it could be as important to me as it is to her for vanity's sake, but for some unknown reason it isn't."

Not all daughters attain an objective view of their mothers. For some women the struggle to win approval from a critical and "all-powerful mother" persists into their thirties, forties, and fifties, and it can impede their own psychological growth. They can seem stuck in the same old rut. When Rosalind Barnett sees such women in her clinical practice, she often asks the daughter to bring her mother to one of the therapy sessions. The gap between the daughter's image and the woman Rosalind sees can be striking. The daughter talks of a powerful, larger-than-life authority figure, and Rosalind sees a mild, sometimes frail, older woman.

Women can be too involved with their mothers in several ways. They can still be obsessed with trying to be a good daughter, trying to figure out what it is their mothers want—or be equally compulsive about being the opposite. Both extremes are different sides of the same problem.

Most women derive a sense of well-being through rewarding relationships with their mothers, although the effect is somewhat different for the various groups of women in our study, particularly in the area of Mastery.

The mother-daughter bond was especially important to women

who were not themselves mothers. Remember that when we looked at the variables affecting sense of Mastery for our six groups, we found that "parent balance"—how things are going with parents or siblings—was very important to never-married women. We interpreted that finding as a reflection of out-of-step anxiety, and speculated that women who had not married needed the support of their families to get that "I'm an okay person" feeling, so essential to self-esteem. We can add here that *all* women who are not mothers—married or unmarried—are affected more strongly by relationships with their mothers than are women who have children. They report higher levels of maternal rapport, and maternal rapport has a stronger impact on their well-being.

So being a mother seems to reduce the significance of one's own mother in one's life. It may be that becoming a mother gives a woman a sense of being an adult, and enables her to feel less dependent on her parents. Or, it may simply be that since motherhood adds another major role to a woman's life, it is this adding on of roles that makes the difference. That is, the more roles a woman occupies, the less important any single role—in this case her relationship to her mother—is to her well-being. Conversely, a woman with fewer roles tends to be strongly affected by the mother-daughter bond. For example, the correlation between maternal rapport and Mastery was very strong for married childless women at home but very weak for married, working women with children, perhaps because the latter group have lives crowded with husbands, children, and jobs.

This pattern echoes a theme that has emerged consistently throughout our study. The more sources of support a woman has, the less critical each one becomes to her well-being. For example, how parenting was going—child balance—was more important to women at home than to employed women. The same principle applies here. A woman whose sense of Mastery comes from several sources will not need to draw as much support from a relationship with her mother, however good it may be. That's important information for women who face their parents' old age with anxiety and concern. We found in our early long interviews with the women in our "snowball" sample that concern about aging parents was a major one for women in midlife. But when we looked at the data from our survey, we were fascinated and surprised by what the "numbers" showed. Among the women who reported concern about aging parents, it was the homemakers, not the employed women, whose well-being was diminished by this concern. As we've seen before, in the chapter on multiple roles (Chapter Eight), work seems to provide employed women with a buffer and relief, leaving less time and energy to dwell on personal problems. In contrast to the view that employment is just one more burden to a woman who must deal with her parents' aging, we believe that involvement in work can help a woman better tolerate this stress.

We were surprised at first to find that for one group of women there was a striking difference from other groups in the relationship between maternal rapport and Mastery. For most women, a good relationship with one's mother was associated with enhanced Mastery, but for divorced women, the opposite was true. The higher their maternal rapport score, the *lower* they were in Mastery.

What is going on here? We think our findings reflect ambivalence and distress that both mothers and daughters feel in the wake of divorce. When gerontologist Elizabeth Johnson studied mothers' perception of their child's divorce, she found that mothers of divorced women often retain feelings of dismay and disappointment for years after the divorce occurs.[3] They may feel that their daughters have somehow "failed" or not lived up to their expectations. For the daughters, therefore, the cost of staying close to mother may be that they incorporate into their own self-image the negative attitudes of their mothers. And perhaps it is those women who feel most devastated by their divorce who cling most closely to their mothers, risking their self-esteem for that closeness. So women whose daughters are divorced or are in the process of breaking up a marriage, should be aware that their disapproval or blame can hurt a daughter's sense of Mastery. Although it may be difficult, the mother of the divorced woman who can give her daughter strong support without communicating distress or disapproval can mitigate the threat to her daughter's sense of Mastery and create an opportunity for closeness.

The potential for strain in the mother-daughter relationship after a daughter's divorce also occurs in other situations. Changing lifestyles for adult children are often foreign to their mothers. In addition to leaving unsatisfactory marriages, adult daughters are pursuing higher education in nontraditional areas, are struggling to establish themselves in careers, are sharing child rearing of grandchildren with a variety of other caretakers. Some married daughters debate whether to have children, other daughters choose not to marry at all. Disappointment, concern, feelings of rejection—all these can easily come into play when a woman sees her daughter turn away from the pattern she herself has followed. The daughter who has moved away from her mother's pattern may also experience conflict and distress about her own motives, and about her chances for happiness in a life pattern for which she may have no models.

The question of whether a woman wants to be like her mother is a complex one. An important process in becoming an adult is identifying with one's parents, especially the parent of the same sex—modeling oneself on them, feeling similar to them. But what if your mother seems unhappy, or like a second-class citizen, or even just less interesting than your father? Theorists and researchers studying identification are asking these questions in new ways.[4] Does the fact that it's women who are assigned to the role of child rearing affect daughters differently from sons? Are mothers and daughters *too* identified with each other, so that daughters are bound to have trouble separating from their mothers and becoming autonomous? Do daughters inevitably resent this bond, and the mother who symbolizes it? And for sons, does the effort to establish their difference from the female parent force them to go too far in separating, creating problems with intimacy and empathy that diminish the quality of their emotional lives?

The theories of identification that emerged from psychoanalytic tradition have been focused on erotic development—perhaps because Freud was so concerned with issues of sexuality. But in recent years, a broader view of identification, one that looks at more than sexuality, has emerged, which takes into account the notion of women's power and status in analyzing mother-daughter relationships.[5]

Because women's lives have been so constricted, their daughters have sometimes taken as a goal *"not* being like my mother."[6] We know that children want to be like people who seem important, who are in charge of things. A major motive for wanting to be like a parent is that parents control resources of all kinds—money, respect, sexual pleasure. But too often the mother does not control any resources; she is subordinate to the father, never insisting on her importance as a person. She is part of the background of life rather than standing out in bold relief. But the daughter who rejects, even scorns this mother as a model nevertheless is still tied to her emotionally. The potential for emotional conflict and guilt is enormous. Here we believe is just one damaging legacy of the inequality of women. Fortunately, though, the new opportunities for women that have raised previously neglected mother-adult daughter issues also are moving us toward the conditions under which truly gratifying relationships are more likely.

For most of the women in our sample, the pleasures of the relationship between mother and daughter seem to outweigh the problems. One woman, asked about the words that came to mind when she thought about her mother, answered simply, "love and joy." She continued: "I will never forget the time when I was a freshman in college. I came from a small farming community and I didn't know much about what was going on—and I'll remind you again that my mother was a very devout Catholic. I'd been there until about Christmas time when a friend from down the hall came to me and said [about two classmates], 'Do you know those two girls are homosexuals?' I didn't even know what a homosexual was! My thought was to run to the dictionary, but the dictionary wasn't that helpful, so I went home with this and asked Mother. She explained it to me, and then she said, "Susan, there's so little love in the world, where we find it, respect it."

One woman, whose mother had died, said, "My mother and I were so alike—we had many of the same interests—books, theater, things like that. I really didn't need friends as long as I had my mother."

Another daughter said, "She's my favorite lady person, and we're very close." A thirty-eight-year-old woman said, "When my mother dies I think I'll miss her terribly and it will be a hard thing for me. I think in some ways my mother's being a kind and available person has had a lot to do with my being comfortable with myself." One woman, asked with whom she would most want to be when she's feeling down, said, "I hate to admit it, but my mother."

It is intriguing—and somewhat sad—to hear the note of guilt in that comment, as if seeking and finding support from one's mother were just a bit shameful. One's parents are, in fact, a great natural resource, but there seems to be a stigma attached to adults who value it. It's possible to overdo the "independence" notion, and thus to deny oneself the comfort of family ties and relationships. This may be a particular American tendency. We are a nation founded, the history books say, by people who cheerfully uprooted themselves to sail across an ocean or travel across a continent in a Conestoga wagon. Modern corporations expect their executives to play "musical homes," to transport a family back and forth across the face of North America in search of upward mobility. The illusion that one can be totally self-contained and self-sufficient is in accord with all this, but the human psyche also needs stability and connectedness. In an increasingly rootless, mobile society, one's parents can still be a profound source of support and comfort.

But to exploit that resource, we may have to find a whole new vocabulary to define the relationship between adult children and adult parents. How can one be a good parent to a child of forty? What is the role of a daughter at age fifty?

We are facing an historically new phenomenon. In the past, one's parents typically had died by the time one came to middle adulthood. If not, the parents were often frail and needed caring for.[7] Now, with people living longer, and retaining vigor and good health later and later, many of us will have a long stretch of years which includes a relationship with an adult parent or from the older person's perspective, with an adult child. The result is that the parent-child relationship may have to be renegotiated several times. As gerontologist Gunhild Hagestad and her colleagues point out, the woman who remains voluntarily childless is also making her parents "involuntarily grandchildless."[8] A daughter who has gotten a divorce may come home for help and support just at the time when a parent doesn't feel like getting into the nurturing role again. Adult children sometimes need to learn how to derive comfort from their parents without asking the parents to return to a role they no longer want. New issues, new expectations—and undoubtedly, new resentments—are bound to arise.

Not all the women in our study reported glowing relationships with their mothers. In any intimate human relationship there are disappointments and tensions, as well as rewards, and sometimes the problems predominate. A forty-three-year-old woman recognizes that in her case, it took absence to make the heart grow fonder: "My feeling is that I love my mother very much, but I could never live with her or have her live with me. She is a very strong individual and very opinionated, and still tends to think of us as her children— you know, she will tell me what I should do on my job. I think coming home to that would be pretty unbearable."

In most cases, however, women focus on aspects of the relationship that do work, and accept the rest. They seem to have outgrown the idea that their mothers should be perfect, or meet all of their needs. One forty-seven-year-old woman wishes her mother were able to share her feelings, but accepts the fact that this isn't in the cards. She describes a recent visit: "We did a lot of things together, gardening, canning, and freezing for the winter, picked blackberries, baked—we had a delightful time together. We didn't talk very much together. Probably in our family I am the one most concerned with feelings; they're somewhat mysterious to the other people in the family. When I got to the point that I wanted to talk with her about feelings, she had a hard time with that. But we did do a lot of things together. We're very close that way."

A forty-four-year-old woman said: "There's no question that my mother doesn't say a lot of the things that should be said, but she's a very intelligent person and she's very understanding. She is just the type of person who does not show her emotions. I've always tried to be very close to her and when I had my babies, she always came to New York and stayed there for weeks to make sure everything was rolling okay. She always has been a big help and I in turn am her support."

Change is a part of any relationship, and the mother-daughter bond is no exception. This is part of the good news for mothers and daughters, for often the change occurs on both sides. The daughter, as she matures, begins to appreciate the strains and the problems of her mother's life. She begins to understand certain behavior on the part of her mother that she once resented or felt was directed unfairly at her. The daughter often becomes more tolerant and forgiving. And the mother may change as well.

An example of this two-sided change, after a childhood shadowed by tragedy, is recounted by a forty-five-year-old woman who remembers: "I had a very hard time with my mother. When I was seven, I lost my brother at Normandy; he had just turned twenty-one. She took it very hard. There are two ways of taking death, either you immediately turn to the other child protectively or you turn her off. In her case, she turned me off. This was the second child she had lost and she was afraid of developing a relationship with me. I wouldn't say she was a bad mother by any means, but she was very aloof and cool. She didn't show a lot of emotion. Now that I'm older I can understand it, but I couldn't before. We were closer after I got married because she felt when I was grown, everything was fine and she didn't have to worry about me. From the day I married, our relationship improved a great deal. It was really strange, because we became close friends, and we'd talk a lot."

Although we didn't detect any solid evidence on this point, women often say that getting married brings them closer to their mother, and some researchers have also reported that this is so.[9]

While our study focused on the perspective of the daughter, we found evidence about the parents' view of why parent-child relationships improve over time in a study by Judith Wilen and her colleagues that examined changing relationships among three generations.[10] Wilen quotes a father's account of his relationship with his daughter, which illustrates the "plasticity" of older parents in their interactions with their children: "I did not approve of her marriage, so for a time, things were strained between us. Slowly over time she proved me wrong. She and her husband have made their marriage stay together and she finished school, so I was wrong. Slowly, things have improved with us."

The women in our study often marveled at the changes in their own mothers. A thirty-eight-year-old woman says: "I always remember my mother as a depressed woman with too much to do when I was growing up. She really got depressed in about, I guess, her mid-fifties. She cried a lot and just experienced no pleasure at all. She was very insecure about going out with people, she didn't want to go places. She was really very depressed and that seemed to peak about seven or eight years ago and she really had to do something."

The mother checked into a psychiatric hospital, and had treatment including a regimen of antidepressant medication. "She's just a different lady since then. She's been marvelous. She started playing golf, joined a couple of women's clubs, and she's a sociable lady, she's fun to be with—a total turnaround."

In addition to a growing fondness and admiration for their mothers, the adult women in our study often cited their mothers as important role models in a variety of ways. In the psychological literature on women, one missing consideration is how a mother can function as a model for her daughter in areas other than her erotic life or her capacity for mothering. In the past, women who achieved success in the world outside home and family most often singled out their fathers as vocational models.[11] This may be because so few of their mothers were able to achieve occupational success. In fact, only a small proportion were even in the workforce. But for women whose mothers were involved in careers, the mother often was the most influential model for her daughter.[12]

So mothers have not often been "mentors" to their daughters in the strictest sense since so few worked or were in a position to be helpful with careers. But many served as models of personal strength through such qualities as perseverance, courage, drive. Our subjects told us how important these qualities were in the world outside the home.

One forty-three-year-old woman remembers: "My mother was a woman who was a very up-and-coming, very involved woman. There were seven of us. After we were all settled, she went into politics and did very well on the school committee. She was always involved in mothers' clubs and things like that, so I think it kind of rubbed off on me."

If the mother-daughter bond is one that renews itself all through the life cycle, the father-daughter relationship is also very important. Fathers have often served as a "bridge" for their daughters into the adult world outside the home. We found evidence of this in our study, although only 110 of the 238 women in the survey had fathers who were living, and only 66 of these were described as in good health. Perhaps because of this women talked less about fathers than mothers. Nevertheless, the women in our sample often said that they identified with their fathers, and that their fathers encouraged them to achieve. One thirty-nine-year-old woman remembers: "I think my father had a lot to do with the confidence that I had as a kid, as a teen-ager. He always thought everything I did was terrific, and he pushed me to do more. With my mother, there were times of closeness but she was never a model for me. She wasn't involved in anything outside the home, and I used to wonder if she didn't get bored. She didn't push me one way or the other. My father was the one who said I had to go to college, had to get that degree. I modeled myself after my father. I was the daughter who sat next to him in the synagogue and wanted to be a rabbi—but, of course, I was a female, so while he thought that was nice, he didn't know how to do anything about it!"

Another woman, now forty-one, who grew up in a working-class neighborhood, had a father who was a teacher and who loved to write. She remembers: "I used to love to look over the typewriter and ask him what he was writing and he'd read to me at the end of the day." As a little girl she was with her father a great deal, and he encouraged her to strive to reach her highest potential. He told her she wasn't put on earth just to get married. He urged her to do what she loved most: "You hold true to that, whatever it is!"

We asked the women in our sample to what extent they had a good close relationship with their father that was rewarding to them. The more rewarding, we found, the higher their sense of Mastery, and there was an even stronger effect on level of Pleasure.

The quality of adult women's relationship with both parents, and with siblings too, was an important topic in our study. In examining the balance of rewards over concerns in this domain of life, we found a positive association with both Mastery and Pleasure. A good relationship with parents and siblings can make an important contribution to a woman's well-being.

Probably because their parents were near or in old age, women's concerns about them were great, and these concerns had a strong impact. There were two major concerns clusters. The first was "parents' decline." It included:

Worrying about how parents will manage
Figuring out arrangements for parents' care
Having to act like a parent to one's parents

It is painful for everyone when parents become frail and their health declines. Not surprisingly, then, this concern cluster has a negative impact on both Mastery and Pleasure. The effect on Pleasure is easy to understand, but why Mastery? We think it's because the problems an aging parent faces are beyond one's control and are often unpredictable; the sense of being in control is crucial to Mastery.

A second cluster of concerns centered around "guilt and conflict." The items making up this cluster were:

A poor relationship with a parent
Feeling uncertain or guilty about your obligations
Feeling that your parents don't approve of your life

This concern cluster had only a weak, negative effect on Mastery and Pleasure. As we've seen, by midlife, women typically have made their peace with their parents; even when a relationship is difficult or a problem, they can remain on an even keel.

Providing for the needs of a growing elderly population is a major national concern these days. Some social commentators see the movement of women into the workforce as a cause for alarm—who will care for the elderly? Is this justified? Do working women in fact abdicate care of elderly parents when they return to work? The evidence is that they do not.[13] But an employed woman may help in a different way from the woman at home. For example, if an aging mother wants to make a special holiday dish, a homemaker might drive her to her four favorite different stores to get just the right ingredients. The working woman is more likely to insist on one stop at the most convenient supermarket. But working women do not desert their aging parents.

Adult women often see their elderly mothers as role models of growing older. The ways mothers experience the aging process seem to have a strong impact on their daughters. On the negative side, a mother's illness is a major concern—will the same thing happen to me? One woman, now forty-nine, says that she didn't worry about hitting forty and isn't concerned about turning fifty, but, "My mother died when she was sixty-three so I imagine the year I'm sixty-two, I'll be sweating it out."

In contrast, our findings show that having a mother who is in good health and good spirits generates optimism about one's own future. A fifty-four-year-old woman says she thinks she will stay in good health. "My mother is seventy-six and so far—well, she has asthma problems, but she is also very healthy and also very happy. She likes to move. . . . She has energy and doesn't sit home and complain." Such examples may explain why most women in our survey, no matter what their life pattern, showed much less concern about aging than we expected. If your mother is "old" and thriving, you expect many more years of good living.

A professional, single woman in her late forties, says about her eighty-one-year-old mother: "My mother is in a very nice situation, and it wouldn't be something I would have anticipated a little earlier about getting old. Moving out to California certainly was a big transition for her, but I think she has done quite well with it. I think it's the fact that she lives in a very nice place, she's been very active there and seems to like her life better and better.

So I do not feel so pessimistic about getting older. It gives you a positive outlook!"

We find this to be true in our own lives. Grace's mother, Ruth Kestenman, is in her late seventies and impresses everyone by her vigor and youthfulness. Because of her, Grace doesn't associate growing older with deterioration and misery. Rosalind's mother, Dorothy Chait, who is also in her seventies, bought her first car in her sixties, travels extensively, and finds new adventures in the world of tournament bridge. Caryl's mother, Helen Rivers, died at sixty-nine but her sixties were a time of her greatest achievement and reward as a political activist. We have no doubt that our own optimism about the years ahead is due largely to these women.

CHAPTER ELEVEN

BY MYSELF

I used to feel really terrible about not being married. I used to think that marriage was in some way the prize that you measured yourself by, but the paradox was that I grew up knowing that I would not be married. When I tried to picture myself being married, I couldn't do it. It was always somebody else's measurement, not mine. I don't think that if I don't marry I will have failed at anything. I joined a reading group in an affluent suburb that was a real eye-opener. These were affluent, married women. Their husbands had good jobs, they lived in lovely homes. Every one of them had the American Dream—but there wasn't one of them I would have traded places with.

Pamela, 39, a nurse practitioner

PAMELA, AN ATTRACTIVE, ENERGETIC WOMAN, hardly fits the stereotype of the "spinster"—the dowdy lady who wears sensible shoes and puts the cat out every night, the pitiable creature who was not invited to life's banquet.

The never-married woman has been the victim of unflattering images in popular culture. Despite some recent "glamorization" of the single career woman, as in "The Mary Tyler Moore Show," the old images linger. The single woman is still the object of concern, pity, and anxiety. Just ask her parents!

If the image of the single woman has a long way to go in popular culture, is it any better among behavioral scientists? Unfortunately not. Theorists have suggested that because single women do not occupy the important female roles of wife and mother, their self-esteem should be lower than that of other women. (We're using the term "single" here to mean never-married, not widowed or divorced.) Behavioral scientists also thought that single women would have more "identity" problems, that they would be less happy and less well adjusted. And, as if all that weren't bad enough, single women were also assumed to be marital rejects who simply never got asked—the products of pathological families, or victims of some kind of physical or emotional handicap. As the authors of *The Inner American* recall about the climate of their earlier study: "In 1957 psychologists and the population at large assumed that not being married or not having children would make a person unhappy at least and probably psychologically ill-adjusted."

In these speculations, one hears the echo of the "Feminine Mystique"—which, bluntly put, says that a woman is nothing without a man. Not all of the gloom and doom about the state of single women came from social mythology, however. Some large-scale surveys have shown single women, especially those over thirty, to be more anxious and depressed and less satisfied with their lives than married women.[1] But the literature on single women was scant indeed. So little had been done until recently on never-married women—and men as well—that one researcher called unmarried adults "statistical deviants who have been virtually ignored in social theory and research."[2]

Happily, that situation has begun to change. The voices that are calling for a "revisionist" look at single women may be new, and still too few, but they do exist.[3] Our study offers important evidence that they are right and that many of the old stereotypes no longer apply, at least not to single women who are employed.

The map of well-being we introduced earlier showed how single women compare with other groups of women on both Mastery and Pleasure.

The scores of single women illustrate the fact that the two dimensions of well-being, Mastery and Pleasure, are indeed separate. Single women, like other working women, score higher on Mastery than do both groups of nonworking women (married with children and married without children).

Their Pleasure scores show a different picture, however. The Pleasure scores of the single women are the lowest in the sample. (Remember that these are group scores. Individual single women may score high on Pleasure, or low on Mastery, but single women as a

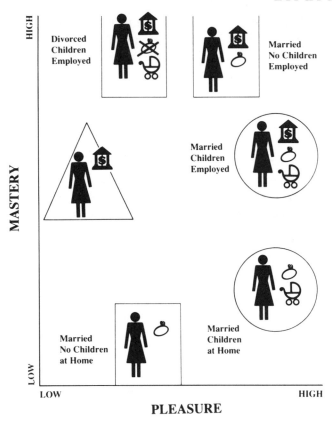

group do not.) Why is it that level of Pleasure of single women is relatively low?

First of all, we believe that this finding is tied in with the arenas of intimacy we talked about earlier. As we pointed out, women who are both wives and mothers have close relationships "built in" to their lives. Single women have to seek out these relationships that are so important to the Pleasure side of well-being. We've seen that both sexual satisfaction and money are important contributors to Pleasure, and in most cases, income is higher, and perhaps more secure and stable, for married women than for single women. In our society, access to the highest-paid jobs is hard to come by for women. And the double standard still makes it easier for men to find sexual relations outside of marriage. While sexual mores are changing, it may be difficult for many of the women in our sample to seek out intimate relationships in an active way. It's easy to see that single women can suffer in the area of Pleasure. They were members of what might be called a "transitional" generation. They were brought up in the shadow of the Feminine Mystique and encountered the feminist movement only as adults. Many may have been greatly influenced by the social mores prevalent in their formative years, when women were supposed to be passive, and "good" girls said No until they walked down the aisle. These women probably feel more constraints on sexual assertiveness than would younger women who grew up in a time of freer sexuality.

This transitional generation may also be experiencing the residue of the deeply rooted notion that the only happy woman is the married woman. Satisfaction, you may remember, is the sense you get from stacking your expectations up against what has actually happened in your life, and having the equation come out on the plus side. Many single women expected that they would be married—after all, nearly all the women of their generation were imbued with that notion when they were very young. Combine that expectation with the fact that women who are *not* married tend to exaggerate the happiness of women who *are* married—and it becomes clear that a single woman's beliefs and perceptions can cause her to regard her life as less rewarding than other women's, regardless of whether it actually is.

A lack of role models may also contribute to diminished Pleasure for single women. One of the components of Pleasure is optimism, the sense that things are going to turn out well. Many single women, even those whose lives are happy and full right now, are uncertain about what the future will hold. They see few successful, single professional women ten or twenty years older than themselves whose attitudes could reassure them that getting older will not be catastrophic. As increasing numbers of women opt for lives as single professionals, there will be more role models for younger women. Today's young girls may find it much easier than the women in our sample to feel optimistic about their future as unmarried women.

Given these considerations, the lower Pleasure scores of single women in our sample may reflect not inevitable problems of being single, but the particular circumstances of one group of women who grew up in a social climate that conveyed negative expectations for women about life outside marriage and that still exerts a "negative drag" on their feelings about their lives.

That's the bad news. The good news is that we didn't find a

similar effect on self-concept. The high Mastery scores of single women offer evidence that on the whole these women do not accept the notion that they are "failures" or that they are somehow inferior to other women. Mastery, we believe, is the primary key to well-being, and it's important to note that single women see themselves as competent and valued human beings.

Remember that all the single women in our sample are employed. One of the most important findings about these women is the crucial role that work plays in their lives. Their balance scores in the domain of work were strongly related to their well-being. The quality of their life at work affected Pleasure as strongly as Mastery, and this was the only one of the six groups for whom this was so. Work, we found, affects the two groups of unmarried women in our sample—the never-married and the divorced women—very differently.

Remember that there did not appear to be a huge Mastery gap between divorced women in low- and high-prestige jobs. The simple fact of having a job seemed an important ingredient of Mastery for divorced women. The picture is quite different for never-married women. They are the only group of women for whom occupational prestige had a particularly strong effect on the sense of Mastery. In other words, for a never-married woman, the type of job she has is strongly related to how good she feels about herself.

While divorced women in dead-end jobs seem able to feel quite good about their lives, the same does not hold true for never-married women. Of all the employed women in the study, only single women in low-prestige jobs had well-being scores that were as low as the nonemployed women.

Why this difference? As we've seen, the divorced women often had come from bad marriages, and for those who had not been employed, getting *any* job made things seem better than they were. The single women don't have this comparative perspective to help enhance their sense of Mastery. To them, having a low-level job isn't a step up—it's just having a terrible job.

This finding has important implications for young women. For an increasing number, marriage may not be "in the cards" because they will choose to remain single or because they won't meet anyone they really want to marry. Investing in marketable skills—going back to school, taking risks to move up the job ladder, making a serious professional commitment—will pay off in heightened well-being in the years ahead. Some people still feel that women shouldn't get too serious about work, because this will make them somehow less "feminine" and less marriageable. But it is a much greater gamble for a woman to neglect her work life and to risk ending up single in a low-level job. A single woman in a high-prestige job has a good chance of achieving high well-being, but a single woman in a low-level job has many of the cards stacked against her. The cluster of work concerns we labeled "dead-end job," remember, had a major negative impact on both Mastery and Pleasure for single women.

So it is inaccurate to say that being single is the major problem for women—it's being single and having an unsatisfactory job. It's a lethal combination, because it puts the most important contributors to both Mastery and Pleasure beyond your reach. It's not surprising that work plays so major a part in the life of the single woman; we've seen that the fewer roles a woman plays, the more central each one is to her well-being. To treat that area of her life casually places her at considerable risk.

The theme of "preference," of being where you want to be, that emerged with such significance throughout our study is particularly critical for single women. As we noted in Chapter Three, "The Well-springs of Mastery and Pleasure," the single women who said they preferred being single were high in well-being. Conversely, if a woman preferred to be married and she was not, she scored relatively low on both Mastery and Pleasure. This difference is a clear and strong illustration of the power of being "where you want to be" in your life. Another finding underlines this point: the more positive the balance of rewards and concerns never-married women report about being single, the greater their sense of Mastery and Pleasure. It makes a real difference whether the advantages of the single life feel right to the particular woman.

For Susan Gardener,* the cardiac surgeon, work has filled up much of her life. She doesn't regret it. "Surgery has been my life, and everything else has fit around that. Since I was so independent, I didn't stop along the way and decide that I needed a husband for an emotional crutch or for whatever wrong reason I might have married at that time. It wasn't in my mind. I never even considered marriage when I was going to medical school. I was

---

* Susan Gardener was introduced in Chapter Six, page 117.

going to become a doctor, period. I was going to college to get
an education so that I could go to medical school and I had very
full days, but the husband thing was always underneath everything
else. You have to meet the right person at the right time, I think,
and for me, that was the wrong time."

Susan realized that she could never have made it through medical school with a husband and perhaps a child: "I just couldn't
split myself that way. I just don't juggle three things at a time
well. And if I had a sick baby at home, I'd be home with the
sick baby and they'd be calling me from the O.R., 'Come on, it's
your turn now, what's the matter with you?' That would just tear
me apart, I just couldn't do it."

Susan thinks, quite realistically, that all lifestyles have their
good points and drawbacks, and that the one she has chosen suits
her well. "I never thought I'd be supported by a husband, never.
I've never put my fate in someone's hands. I'm going to take care
of me and I don't ever expect anyone else to. Fine if I marry a
millionaire, I'll be delighted. But I don't expect anyone else to support me. I look at other women who juggle families and a career,
and I think that's wonderful. But I wouldn't be able to do that. I
know what I have now and I know that I'm happier. If the knight
in shining armor comes running down the corridor, great, I'll look
at him, and if we can work things out, fine. But I'm very, very
happy, and I would need some emotional assurance that by getting
myself into another situation, I would be as happy as I am now,
and could make that person as happy as I am. That's the time I
would really think carefully because it would be a very, very major
move for me."

The picture of single women that emerges shows a sharp distinc-
tion between those who are thriving, enjoying their lives, and those
who are not. The women who preferred to be single—or those
who expected to marry but who have come to terms with the fact
that they did not—are generally doing well. But those women who
feel that their singlehood means they are rejected or "not chosen,"
suffer in terms of well-being. Pamela, the nurse practitioner, could
feel good about herself because she was finally able to understand
that not being married was, for her, an appropriate choice, not a
failure. Women who feel that singlehood is a stigma, who see themselves as second-class people, do not feel very good about their
lives.

Most of the single women in our study, however, did not seem to see themselves in the light of those unflattering social stereotypes. This finding dovetails with that of another recent study of the self-concept of single women by Lynn L. Gigy,[4] a researcher at the Human Development Program at the University of California, San Francisco. She compared attitudes toward the self of never-married women with those of married women, all over thirty. The single women saw themselves as more assertive and independent than did the married women, and they valued achievement and personal growth more highly. The married women valued interpersonal relationships more and the single women cared more about feeling independent and autonomous. As we'll see, such feelings were the best part of being single for our subjects. Gigy suggests: "Such a sense of independence may easily be seen as incompatible with the role demands inherent in a traditional marriage and thus may well account, in large part, for non-marriage in many women." She adds, "It also may account for the fact that these single women appear to be able to withstand the negative social sanctions they most probably have encountered for their non-conformity. They do seem resistant to them, for their morale and personal adjustment seem to indicate that the single women were really no more unhappy or pathological than their married counterparts."

The single women Gigy studied did tend to display such tendencies as being easily annoyed by others, wanting to keep a strict schedule, being bothered by little things. But these women also seemed more typical than the married women of what psychologist Abraham Maslow has called the "self-actualizing personality."[5] Such a person can set her own goals and determine her own priorities, can initiate and pursue actions in line with those goals, and can act with relative freedom from control by others.

This generally positive picture of single women in middle adulthood is also echoed by another study, one by psychologist Judith Birnbaum.[6] She found that the single professional women she studied were highly satisfied with their lives. The typical single professional, she reports, is a bright woman from a lower-class background who did well in school and found achievement as a way to make her way in the world without relying on feminine charm and wiles. "As an adult, she tends to be very work-oriented, depending on work for both personal satisfaction and economic independence. Often, she sees herself channeling her 'feminine' qualities of nurture into the world of work. The single professional often sees marriage as incompatible with her work life, fills her personal life with relationships with friends and co-workers, and sees her life as happy and productive."

The comments of women who are single, and who find their work life challenging and exciting, reflect a satisfaction with life and with themselves that would amaze those who believe that single women just can't be happy. The rewards of being single center around a series of items that comprise what we call the "independent lifestyle" cluster. They are:

Not being accountable to anyone
Being independent
The lifestyle suits you
Being able to do things spontaneously
Not having too heavy responsibilities

Cynthia, thirty-nine, a lawyer's assistant, expresses one aspect of this reward cluster. "I think the one advantage of being on my own and working is that I spend my money as I want, and I do with it what I want. I'm responsible only for myself and if I get a parking ticket for parking illegally, nobody's going to say, 'You were careless, you shouldn't have done it!' Forget it, that's it! You are accountable only to yourself."

Another independent, competent woman who is pleased with her lifestyle is Diane Wright,* the computer manager. She was the oldest of five children, the daughter of parents who took care to see that each child got proper attention. Her father had a stroke at forty-four that cut short Diane's plans for medical school, so she studied math instead. In her work she is in a position to command a good salary and she is in demand: "I'm a highly marketable commodity. I get telephone calls from headhunters once every two weeks. Fifty percent of that is because I'm a woman and 50 percent is simply the reputation I have in the field. So I guess that's one of the reasons I have confidence about the future."

Diane feels very good about herself. "I'm generally healthy— 75 percent of the time I feel happy, or content. I don't feel great depressions. Every once in a while I get discouraged, but I guess everybody does."

Unlike Diane, Pamela, the nurse practitioner whose comments opened this chapter, came from an unhappy family. "My mother started out okay but I think I'd agree with her that getting married,

---

* Diane Wright was introduced in Chapter Six, page 103.

for her, was a turn for the worse. Before her marriage, she taught, lived away from home, and I remember pictures of her with her Ford Roadster and friends with whom she'd spend summers on Martha's Vineyard. She married at twenty-eight. It was the Depression, and she wound up with several children, married to a man that she shouldn't have married. I wish she had separated. He was a very difficult man to live with. He had what I later learned were paranoid episodes and he always thought that my mother was fooling around and there would be horrendous scenes. He always had guns around. My mother and father stopped sharing a bed when I was in my teens, and it was around that issue that they had a tremendous fight and I remember waking up one night and he was trying to strangle her. I don't think my sisters or I were ever pushed toward marriage. My mother speaks openly of the fact that I'm better off not married."

Pamela graduated from secretarial school and went to work as a secretary in a large hospital. When she decided she didn't want to be a secretary, she went back to school to get a bachelor's degree. She got into a special federal program to train college graduates as nurse practitioners and then decided to go on to graduate school.

Today, she feels better about herself than ever before. "If someone had told me when I was twenty that I would wind up at thirty-eight single and living by myself, my expectation would be that it would make me unhappy. But it doesn't. I am feeling more comfortable with myself and somehow accepting and feeling okay about who I am. It's a good feeling and it only started arriving on the scene in the last seven or eight years. Somehow, turning thirty was a good thing for me. I would say my thirties have been my happiest years, the least conflicted years for me. Relationships with friends are rewarding and I have a better sense of well-being than I had before."

Parents' attitudes often remain a problem area for never-married women. Cynthia, the lawyer's assistant, says: "I guess I still do look for the supreme approval from them. It's never going to come. But my life is fine. They don't look at the trips I take, the things I can do: I've been to the Galapagos Islands, to the Amazon, schlepped through the jungle, I've watched whales from a ship, I've been to Paris. I have realized that I can have nice sheets and towels without being married. A friend of mine who is divorced said that when he was about to buy a house, it suddenly hit him that he could buy a house even though he was divorced. It was okay! You don't have to be married to have the things you want."

For many never-married women today, life feels quite full and satisfying. Edith Wheeler,* fifty-five, the chairman of a biology department whom we met earlier, finds her job challenging and her environment good. "I've often thought," she says, "that in terms of being a single woman the university is not only the place where you work but it's the place where your friends are. I considered very briefly when I finished my Ph.D. taking a job in industry and one of the reasons I didn't was that I didn't like the nine-to-five thing, coming in and going away. As a graduate student, your social life was involved with your fellow students and you were in the lab till all hours of the night and that was the greatest fun of it. So I just couldn't see myself in industry going back home at five o'clock."

Edith came from a small farming town, where she was a part of a close-knit community. Her mother always encouraged her to be economically independent. "My mother told me I should be a nurse, but I told her I couldn't nurse a grudge. I think my mother looked forward to my getting married, but she thought I should be able to support myself."

When Edith was in college, her serious interest in science blossomed and she realized that she would have to get an advanced degree to make any progress in her field. She was the first student from the town to get a Ph.D. While other women her age were marrying, "I didn't have time. That was the era when serious career pursuits and marriage for a woman were thought to be incompatible. I was determined to get the Ph.D. That was my goal and that was what I was going to do, and nothing else was going to get in the way. I was dating one young man who asked me to marry him. I said, 'Would you give up your career to marry me?' He said no. 'Then I won't marry you either.'"

Being single, Edith says, doesn't affect her social life at all. "There are enough people on the campus who are single and we get together all the time and do things with each other. When I go home, my sister and brother-in-law always include me in on parties. I've never had a problem."

Edith derives pride and satisfaction from assessing her life. "I'm a great teacher and that gives me great pleasure. I feel that

---

* Edith Wheeler was introduced in Chapter Six, page 118.

I'm giving something to the students and that I'm giving a great deal to the university. I think that I'm a good sister and a great aunt. I think I've respected my parents and I've done everything to take care of them through the years. I think my book is a great contribution to the field."

Not surprisingly, single women who score high in the "independent lifestyle" cluster of rewards are also high in level of Pleasure. Feeling independent, competent, and pretty much where they want to be in life, they are likely to be high in satisfaction, happiness, and optimism. In sharp contrast are women who feel stigmatized by being single, who have little sense of autonomy or control of their lives. Such feelings are not rare. Catherine, forty-eight, says: "Sometimes I say to God, 'Why don't you put something great in my life?' I mean, I'm sick of trying for things. I feel I'll just go along the way I am. I'm not going to try for anything else."

Catherine is stuck in a low-level job she hates, and her sources of support are few. She has a low estimation of herself. "I have no ambition. I just think that evidently I'm going to be the same cautious person, and not going to do anything great."

For Catherine, being single continually undermines her confidence. She does not find her independence rewarding: the lifestyle does not suit her. She feels unable to act spontaneously. "I would never go anyplace by myself. I think it's terrible, having to go someplace where it's all couples and be the single person. I find that a big stigma in my life, being single. You have the feeling of never having been chosen and it makes you feel you're worthless. I mean, if you're married, someone thought you were special and chose you. I think when you have that affirmation, you can really go ahead and do something. But if you haven't been, it leaves you all by yourself."

The major theme that characterizes the concerns of single women is related to need for others. We call this concern cluster "lack of intimacy." The items in this cluster are:

Not having a permanent intimate relationship
Difficulties meeting men
Sexual relations a problem

Concern about lack of an intimate relationship was a problem for both groups of unmarried women in our study, the never-married and the divorced. But there was a difference in the intensity of the concern. For the divorced women, this concern had a more negative impact on well-being. For never-married women, however, intimacy deprivation did not affect their sense of Mastery and had only a minor effect on Pleasure. The difference may be due to the fact that the divorced women once had such a relationship—they had chosen to marry—but now were deprived of an intimacy they once had.

Certainly, most single women aren't pining away because they are not married. There is often a rather wistful sense of "It might be nice, but it didn't happen," or "It's okay for others, but not for me." Single women, as a rule, seem to be less troubled about intimate relationships than divorced women. Some simply accept the fact that intimate relationships may be scarce at times. As one woman puts it, "Let's face it, there aren't all that many great men around!" Others, of course, do have a continuing relationship that is a source of satisfaction. Roseann Marshall,* an actress who is turning forty, says, "I've had the good fortune to have had an intimate friendship with somebody for three or four years, which has its frustrations too, but I think I am lucky in that respect because there are certainly a lot of single women who are not in that position. I sometimes toy with the idea of being married, but it's hard for me to face up to that. I had the opportunity to marry somebody who, I think, really wanted a motherly wife. And I felt I couldn't be that." She goes on: "I certainly do have a lot of ambivalence about the fact that I'm not married and I don't have a family. I think I have missed a lot of things. When I was in college, if anybody had said to me that I wouldn't be married two or three years out of college, I would have laughed. That thought never occurred to me. The reason I'm not married is because I didn't get married. It's really me that did it. I said no."

Roseann, despite the fact that she expected to be married, now realizes that she didn't see marriage as particularly glamorous or exciting. "I think marriage took its toll on my mother. She didn't get out in the world. She had too much steam to be stuck making three meals a day. I mean, it's boring. I think that's one of the things I was hesitant about when the question of marriage came up—that I was bored when I was growing up. I was bored with doing the same things all the time. I mean, I had the loveliest, most comfortable space—the cleanest childhood—and I was just

*Roseann Marshall was introduced in Chapter Three, page 34.

starved for a little risk. And I think that I really indulged that when I got out of college, and I'm still indulging it, and it's something I haven't faced up to in myself—that I want it both ways."

The problem Roseann sees is the loss of precisely that sense of independence many single women value. "If you ask me what the worst thing would be about marriage, I would say the loss of solitude. When I was a little girl, I loved to amble along, to lose track of time. I was up in New Hampshire recently on a visit to my parents and I was driving up this country road and there was a field full of barley or oats—beautiful, lovely, misty sort of thing. And I thought to myself, I've always liked to just muse. And I think that one of the things I enjoy is just being alone. There are times when I'm lonely, but usually I enjoy being alone—there are joys in that. And I've always had the feeling that it would be very hard to have both marriage and my performing. Although I have said I would like to do both things, I never quite figured out how you would do it. Perhaps it takes more flexibility than I've been able to muster.

"I went through a bad time last summer, when a lot of anger and resentment surfaced. I think I've apologized, for a long time, for not being married, for having career aspirations, for being interested in a great many things and not being single-minded about one of them. I was feeling very put upon, feeling very much like I had to apologize for my life, but then I thought, Hey, wait a minute! Now, just hold on! And I started to think. I began to essentially value what I had done more. I had been working for a long time. And I thought, I'm no disaster scene! I had undervalued what I had done."

For many single women, then, there is some regret, mixed with realization that marriage probably would have been a poor fit, given their goals and temperament. And being childless is less of a major concern than the lack of an intimate relationship. Perhaps women with a very strong desire to have children either choose to marry or take advantage of new adoption policies to become single adoptive parents. In contrast, Susan, the surgeon, says she does not buy the idea that life will be empty if she has no child of her own. "I cannot imagine having a child without being married to a man I loved so much we would want to have a child together. The cold, intellectual thought that I want a little thing on two legs running around because it looks like me has never occurred to me. I think it's hard enough for two people to raise a child, much less one person."

Cynthia, the lawyer's assistant, does not feel that being childless will have a major impact on her life. "My parents were very careful to preserve time for themselves together. My mother was not dependent on her children for her activities or companionship. At summer camp, I was the only one that didn't get letters from my mother saying she was lonesome for me. It wasn't that my parents didn't love their children, but they needed a break from us. So I never got the sense of needing children to fill a void. And I don't have that feeling that some of my friends have, that if you don't have children you are missing an enormous piece of life. Friends of mine who are single and in their late thirties, who know they are not going to have children, feel that it will be an enormous loss. And I don't have that feeling and I don't think I ever did. I've been pregnant twice and had abortions, and there was no conflict in making that choice. I had no response. I don't know if it was a repressed response, but it was an easy process. I knew just what I wanted to do. It was easy, no problems."

Perhaps because of a process of adaptation, perhaps because the climate for unmarried women has become more benign, many women reported that being single is easier to handle now than it was in their late twenties. Diane, the manager in the computer firm, says: "I don't know whether it's my age, or society changing. But nowadays nobody thinks about it. You're just invited places— if you want to bring somebody, okay. Nobody thinks everybody has to be a couple anymore. So it's easier in the past few years. I was definitely out of step in my twenties. I think the year after I graduated from college I was a bridesmaid eight times. Everybody was getting married and having children. And I found that by the time I was twenty-five or twenty-six, I had nothing in common with the girls I went to college with. All of them had married and had one or two kids, that was their life. At that time, most women didn't work, and I really had nothing in common with them as far as the children aspect of their lives was concerned. If I wanted to spend energy on children, I was much more interested in my own nieces and nephews than their children. All my college friends just disappeared at twenty-five or so; there was just nothing I had in common with them. I knew I was considered something of an oddball to be still working at twenty-seven, twenty-eight, when the rest of them had gotten married."

One reason that the quality of life has improved for single women is the greater acceptance of their sexuality, both by the women themselves and by society. Single women find many ways to attain sexual satisfaction. A long-term, intimate relationship may be the most highly desired context for sustained sexual pleasure, but it is not the only one. We have no evidence on whether a long-term relationship or a series of relationships have different effects on a woman's well-being. This depends on the woman herself, what else is happening in her life, and on her own expectations and desires.

Diane, for example, finds sex enjoyable, although she is really interested only in the context of a broader relationship. One-night stands are not her style. "I enjoy—have enjoyed—sex, but I've only enjoyed it in a relationship where I've actually enjoyed the other person. As a result of being with a person I liked, sex was a result of it and only a part of it. I guess I have difficulty understanding how it could be separated from the total relationship. I'm interested in it only with people I'm interested in and want to have sex with. Then it's fine. It's not regular, but the drive or the urge for me comes only in relation to one person. I've always enjoyed sex and been fairly open about it, but only with certain people. I like the intimacy that it brings. It becomes very important only because it is a symbol of the existence of something that's very intimate. But when there's a distance, a geographic distance, between us, the lack of sex doesn't bother me at all."

Single women who are lesbians have as varied feelings as do heterosexual women. One thirty-nine-year-old lesbian says that she would prefer to be in a permanent, intimate relationship with another woman for stability, sense of peace, and normality. "That's the most satisfying lifestyle for me."

Perhaps the hardest issue for single women to deal with is the possibility that they will never fulfill the fantasy "and they lived happily ever after." In our culture, the notion of being a fully female person is tied to attracting a man who will love you until the Rockies tumble, until the end of time, until the twelfth of never. In her clinical practice, Rosalind Barnett finds that many single women are upset, not because they feel miserable without a man, but because they don't! What does it say about their femininity, they wonder, that their lives are going well without a permanent intimate relationship? Is there something *wrong* with them? Are they less than complete women?

They often fear that someday the clouds will open up and they will pay the price for their "deviant" lifestyle. Well, I'm happy now, they think, but at some point will I be miserable?

The answer, in fact, is probably not. Most single women cope successfully with the happily-ever-after fantasy as they get older. The majority of women in our sample seemed to have done so; these struggles may be most intense among younger women. For a woman approaching thirty, the issue may be particularly salient since she is just realizing that she may in fact never live out the fantasy. The process may be akin to what happens with childlessness. We saw that many of the women in our sample who did not have children went through a period of anxiety or depression and wondered if they faced a permanent sense of inconsolable loss. They usually discovered that they did not. Women, it seems, can also come to terms with the fact that they are not going to live out a fairy-tale ending with a man, and eventually feel pleased that their lives can be full and satisfying without it.

Single women find a variety of arrangements that seem to suit them. Sometimes they find themselves in relationships that are not ideal, but acceptable. For Pat Spaulding,* the psychologist, a relationship that is stable, but not exactly what she wants, offers both satisfaction and some stress. Pat met a man ten years ago when she changed cities; he was married then and is now. For a time she dated other men as well, but finally decided to make a commitment to the married man, despite the fact that it seemed he would stay married to his wife. "It's turned out to be a situation where I am with him quite a bit—and I think really, everybody knows about it—even my family. They know him but we don't talk about the relationship, and his family knows me. It's sort of a strange situation. It's something I do feel very uneasy about, I'm not really totally comfortable about it.

"This man is a lot older than I am, but I think the relationship will go on forever, as long as he's alive. I hope it's a long time. The aspect of it that's nice is that he sees me as a lot younger

---

* Pat Spaulding was introduced in Chapter Seven, page 125.

and more attractive and as I get older, he does too. It's never been easy for me to go out and try to meet men, and I would be more concerned about it—about my looks—if I didn't have this relationship. I think that one of the reasons I stay in the relationship is that it would be too painful to try and go out and meet somebody else."

If it were possible, Pat would like to be married to this man. But that would mean pushing him to divorce his wife. "I have not wanted to do that," she says, "and I'm not sure that he would do it, because he does have some feeling that it wouldn't be right. So it hasn't seemed like a possibility, not without much distress. I think I would like to be married to him, but the relationship as it is is very gratifying because we don't have some of the conflicts we might have if we were living together. But I miss being able to do more things socially and to travel together. Getting involved in this relationship was a big turning point in my life. It's created a lot of stress; certainly it's something I would not have considered in my younger years. Perhaps I should have opted for a more traditional relationship, a marriage to someone, but that's hard to say. It's hard to say if anything different would have happened in terms of your life if you made another decision, so it's hard to know what would have been best. It seems to be that the women I know who are single in their thirties are all looking for men. That's their main interest socially, to put themselves into a situation where they can get married. They get so invested in trying to find a relationship that it keeps them from getting anywhere in their work."

Pat says that she does have regrets about not having children. "At one point, I even thought of having a baby without being married and I went through a lot at that time. I have decided not to. I feel that was the right decision for me to have made; it would have been too difficult. I think I might be in more of a place psychologically now to go ahead with it, but I think that now, at forty-four, I'm too old. I would have considered it up to age forty."

Pamela, in contrast, does not see herself as at all child-oriented. "The thing that I discovered about myself fairly early was that I love babies, but I don't like children. I remember saying, when I was in college, that I would raise kids until they were about six and then I'd farm them off to someone else until they were about 20. I've lived out a lot of my fascination with babies through my sister's kids. I can't stand them now. They're eleven, nine, and seven, and they're noisy and difficult and I don't envy her at all. One regret I have is that I didn't experience pregnancy and child-birth—I've always been fascinated by that. I would love to have experienced that, but to raise children—no!"

For Cynthia and Pat, being single is something that they did not expect but have come to terms with. Other women, like Susan and Edith, made early career choices that directed much of their energy away from a social life at an age when many young people were involved with the rituals of mating. No clear pattern emerged in our study that would seem to "mark" women for singlehood. Some come from happy families, some do not. Some had serious career ambitions early on, others did not. "Singlehood" for most women seems to be the result of a series of choices made over a series of years. One is not suddenly converted to the single state like Saint Paul being knocked off his horse by a bolt of lightning from above. As Pamela puts it: "There was no particular moment when I decided I wouldn't get married. It came on gradually. I was very seriously involved with a man who had kids—he was divorced—and there was a lot of talk and thought about marriage. He was very clear about not wanting kids and I began to visualize life in a different way. Up to that time—I was in my early thirties—I had always assumed marriage would mean children. I hadn't really thought about it very much, and with him I began to think of things in a different way. Even if I married now, I wouldn't have kids. I think I'm too old."

Single women, like other women, of course have their leftover problems from childhood, their personality weaknesses as well as strengths, and for some, as for Pamela, their relationships with men have reflected these. "I think in the past I was always afraid that being too close to a man meant getting into too many power struggles and I think the way I've reacted is to get conflicted. The last couple of times I developed psychosomatic symptoms and I just don't like myself very well when that happens. I suppose the pat answer is that whoever it is catches all the crap I never threw at my father, but I'm really hopeful that will mellow out. But I think I've accepted a lot of things about myself and I've stopped feeling so absolutely wretched about the fact that I didn't do so well with men.

"I think therapy was part of my understanding it—I think it helped me give up the idea of marriage—not as a goal, but as a measuring stick. I don't think that if I don't marry anybody I will have failed at anything. I think the women's movement helped me a lot. One of the women I looked up to when I was studying to be a nurse practitioner started it. For the first time I was able to look at a woman and say, 'This is someone for whom I have respect, and it doesn't have anything to do with men or measuring up in a male world.' I think also that seeing my friends get married, and realizing that it didn't change them, helped too. As far as I was concerned, it didn't add anything to their lives that I particularly wanted—with a couple of exceptions who married men with a great deal of money!

"In the best of all worlds it would be nice to share my life with a man and also to have done the things I have been able to do alone. I guess it would be nice if I could have accomplished everything I have done, but accomplished it within the context of a relationship with a man. I wouldn't trade it for my sense of self, though. What I'd like to do is feel good about myself and not have to give that up to relate to a man."

Relationships with men constitute only one aspect of closeness to others that is so critical to the well-being of single women. One of the best defenses against feelings of intimacy deprivation is the building of networks of friends; these relationships can function as important sources of both Mastery and Pleasure. This "network building" seems to be a skill that many single women are very good at. Not having the built-in companionship of husband and children, they create a web of friendships and extended family relationships to take their place. We believe this to be one of the most important steps a single woman can take to insure her well-being— perhaps second only to finding a challenging job. One woman says, "Since 1953 I have had Thanksgiving dinner with two couples that I met when I was in graduate school, and we still keep in very close touch. They're very dear friends."

Another says, "My closest confidantes, the ones with whom I share my inner feelings, are two women I've known for a long time who are single. It's odd, both of them are Jewish, and I'm not. I'm closest to them not in the day-to-day seeing each other kind of way, but in sharing those secrets you don't share with anyone else."

Pat, the psychologist, says: "If I want to talk things over, I do it with friends. That's been a problem because I don't fit in with my married friends as far as socializing, but I'm not in the same boat as my single friends. Most of my friends are a lot younger and I think it happened because of going to graduate school—I was older than my friends who were at the same level of training. I also belong to a women's organization that my mother was in, geared for educational philanthropy to help women get a college education. There are a lot of people who are my age or younger, most from the Midwest, and it turned out to be very nice for meeting women from different fields. Some friendships have grown out of it, one that is very close. One of the aspects of the group is to try to be very helpful to each other and it's a kind of backup group, where if you ever really needed any help for something, they would be available."

Many single women find that a special circle of friends stays together and supports each other over the years. Pat adds: "I see a lot of my friends, women friends that I'm comfortable being with and like to do things with. I've always seemed to have a group like that and the group was always the place where I could talk about what was happening in my life, rather than my family. I've known many of them for a long time. It's a real bunch of late bloomers. After I went to secretarial school, I went to live in an apartment with three friends from school and there was an apartment of girls right next door and we all became very close and friendly and the group expanded, until at one point when we were in our mid-twenties there were twenty-five to thirty women. Over the years it's boiled down to about a dozen. In the core group, the earliest marriage was at thirty-eight, and very few have kids, maybe three. There are several marriages that are childless by design and everybody has maintained their network of girl friends. So now it's a mixed group, single and married, with and without kids."

Because women traditionally have been able to build intimate, lasting friendships, they may have a real edge on men in this area. Earlier studies have shown that most men do not have confidants, and when they do, it is likely to be their wife. Yet married women who have confidants most often report this person is not their husband.[7] It is not surprising that when a man's wife dies, and he loses both his wife and the only person in whom he can confide, he is in bad shape. No wonder, either, that single men always show up near the bottom in large-scale surveys of well-being. While we have pitied the spinster and envied the bachelor, perhaps the reverse should be true. In a culture in which men often lack the pleasure of intimate, personal male friendships, the man without a woman may be the most bereft of all. Mothers who have traditionally worried about whether their daughters were going to marry or not, might more realistically be concerned about their sons.

We've saved for last what is perhaps the most neglected element in the well-being of single women. Although the negative stereotypes of single women in our culture center on the ring that she hasn't got on her finger—not on what she has or hasn't got in her wallet—our research shows that money, or the lack of it, plays an even more important role in well-being for single women than issues involving men or sexuality. Such items as how much money a woman made in the past year, how adequately she felt she could support herself, and how concerned she was about money, had a strong impact on her sense of Mastery. In our culture, girls are encouraged to daydream about the man they might marry, but are rarely told to think about how they might support themselves in the real world. As a result, many women have not had a very good idea of how to look after their financial interests over their life span. Roseann, the actress, puts it well when she says: "Money is a real issue for me, no doubt about it. I have worked for twenty years, but still, the concept of professionalism is very new to me. I just didn't have a model for long-term career building. And if you don't do that, and if you aren't lucky and inherit money, you are behind the eight ball financially, when you reach the point where you are no longer living a post-college life. And you want to own property, you want to put something aside for your old age, in case you are by yourself. To me that's a fundamental issue of being single and a woman."

Roseann's eyes were opened to the consequences of drifting—not making any serious plans for her future—when the apartment building she was living in was converted to a condominium. She couldn't afford to buy it. She realized she could literally no longer afford to see her work only as a vehicle of self-fulfillment, and decided to make an important change in her life. She got a degree in management in the arts field and now holds down an administrative position in a conservatory. She combines her performing with a job that gives her a steady income.

Roseann is also looking seriously at her future finances: "I have a friend who said to me, 'Roseann, you live as if you have a rich husband—and, you don't, so you had better do something about that.' She was very helpful to me. I've suddenly realized that I'm not going to be working forever, and I have to do something about that right now."

Such realizations are often sobering to single women. A woman may feel content with her life now, but wonders, what about the future? To our surprise, we must admit, we found single women to be no more (or less) concerned about growing older and about old age than were married women. Perhaps they realize that in a society where women outlive men by an average of nine years, and where the divorce rate is high, being married is no insurance against being old and alone. More important, many single women are deeply involved with a network of friends, and they don't see this as changing in the future. One woman laughs, "I have this fantasy of my friends and me, all sitting in rocking chairs on the porch of the nursing home together, growing old as a group."

Are these optimistic expectations about the future realistic, or will aging in fact be more difficult for these women than they now believe? Some encouraging data come from a 1977 follow-up study[8] of a group of gifted women, first studied in the 1920s, who are now in their sixties. The researchers, Pauline Sears and Ann Barbee, found the highest level of satisfaction among the unmarried women, particularly those who had been in paid employment for a significant portion of their lives. So there is every reason to believe that the positive side of singleness remains strong into old age.

An old woman who is frail, dependent, in need of care, is in a vulnerable situation, of course, but the question of who is alone in old age is a complex one, not determined only by whether one has ever married or had children. For Cynthia, the notion that marriage is an insurance policy against later loneliness seems absurd. She is aware of her parents' anxieties, though. "I know my parents would like to see me married, and I don't know whether for them it's a worry or an embarrassment or a combination of both. I feel badly that they would have gotten pleasure from me, had I been married and had children, that they are not getting now, but that's too bad. It would have been nice if it had worked out that way. But I try to assure them that my life is meaningful and I'm doing things and having a good time and I have a lot of friends. My mother will say, "Well, it's all fine now, but we worry about when you're older.' But I look at their friends, and I see all these people who are divorced or widowed in their fifties and it's clear that marriage is no guarantee that you'll have companionship for the rest of your life. And I think they agree that it's a lot easier being single now than it was half a generation ago."

If one were to draw a composite picture of the employed, single, woman in middle adulthood today, it would be of an active woman, seriously involved with her work, who maintains close ties with her own extended family, often including nieces and nephews. She is close to friends who give her support and comfort in time of trouble. She may be involved in an intimate relationship with a man, and if so, that most often is a source of pleasure and satisfaction in her life. If she is not involved in such a relationship, she feels some sense of deprivation, but it is usually not one that destroys her sense of self-esteem or her satisfaction with her life. And, as we've seen, if she is in a high-prestige job, her level of well-being is relatively high.

Given that no woman can predict her future marital status, the findings on single women are relevant to all young women. They don't have to fear that if they remain single, they have little chance for a satisfying life. Our findings also ought to be reassuring to the parents of such women, who are often panicky about the prospect of a daughter not getting married. Indeed, parents are often far more worried than the woman herself, and their matchmaking efforts or dire warnings certainly don't help her.

It is also important for a young woman to understand that the sources of well-being in the single life are not mysterious and unreachable but are in large part within the control of the woman herself. Since a life of "drift" can cost her dearly in terms of well-being, the unmarried woman should take care to get involved in a job that she finds challenging, where she can advance, and where she can earn a good salary.

The single woman also has to expend more effort than does the married woman in developing and maintaining friendships since she has less built-in companionship. But the effort she puts into her friendships has an important payoff: protection from feeling lonely and isolated, feelings that are a formidable barrier to well-being for the single woman.

It's important that so many single women in our study now feel good about themselves despite the fact that they spent their young adulthood in an era when the old stereotypes were in force.

If they are able to lead full and satisfying lives, even in the face of society's negative images of them, it should be much easier for women in the future to be both single and satisfied. No longer does society insist that people march two by two—to the supermarket, to dinner parties, to realtors' offices. Women are finding that walking "single file" doesn't have to be a lonely, unhappy journey. It can, in fact, be a singular path to the kind of full and happy life that is the goal of us all.

CHAPTER TWELVE

TOWARD A NEW
THEORY OF
WOMEN'S LIVES

The study of [human] development must also be a study of what exists and what changes in the social and economic environments of people. . . . The social and emotional development of adults does not appreciably follow in the shadow of biological development.

Sociologists Leonard Pearlin, and
Claire Radabaugh[1]

HOW DO PEOPLE GROW, change, and deal with life situations? Are they locked into an inevitable process determined by their age, their anatomy, and their unconscious? Or does what is happening in the world around them also determine their life experience? We believe that if we concentrate only on the psychological makeup of the individual, we will miss the significance of the forces that shape much of our behavior.

Leonard Pearlin and Claire Radabaugh, reporting their study of how people change over time, say: "Personality factors by themselves cannot provide a very useful explanation of how people develop unless such factors are viewed within the context of changing environmental circumstances." Woman, particularly, has too often been seen as oblivious to the world around her, as governed by her instincts, drives, and hormones, the Eternal Female.

The study of human development has too often ignored the world *outside;* that is, the world outside the individual. Since the days of Sigmund Freud, many psychologists and psychiatrists have tended to focus only on internal factors. This isn't surprising, since Freud made his voyages of discovery into an inner world of unconscious mechanisms and instinctual drives. Too often, however, many of those who followed him tended to lose sight of the fact that there is a very real world beyond the boundaries of the self, and that world exerts a constant and powerful influence on people. To say that your anatomy—or your chronological age—is destiny, is to ignore the forces of the social climate that surrounds us.

If there is one thing our study suggests, it is that a new understanding of women's lives is badly needed, one that doesn't ignore what is happening in society. Traditional theories of adult development don't do the job, and new theories of stages and crises of midlife aren't adequate either.

In the past, the "shadow of biological development" fell more deeply upon women than men. We've noted that in the nineteenth century concern over the proper functioning of a woman's reproductive system was so great that medical doctors cautioned against any rigorous intellectual pursuits for young women, because development of the brain should not compete with development of the ovaries. Explanations of who and what women were focused primarily on reproductive events—marriage, children, the empty nest, menopause. You could explain what was happening in a woman's life, it was believed, if you knew where she was in this reproductive cycle.

If a woman's emotional development is irrevocably tied to her reproductive functioning, then certain predictions follow. A woman should be high in well-being if she is a wife and a mother, and distressed if she is not. She should be happiest when her children are at home and dependent; when they leave, she should feel only sorrow and loss. Menopause should cause her great turmoil, because her reproductive life—and thus her core identity—is threatened.

Our study adds evidence to the case now being made by the "new wave" of social scientists that this approach is inadequate for explaining women's lives. A woman's level of well-being could not be predicted by whether or not she had children. Women did not feel devastated by "the empty nest;" and menopause caused so little disruption to the lives of most women that many saw it as a "nonevent." When you have data that contradict a theory, you ought to reexamine the theory! Our findings, together with those of our colleagues, do cast doubt on traditional ideas about women, but we're distressed at how persistent the tendency is to link women's lives mainly to their biology, both in explanations of their lives and in well-meaning prescriptions about how they *should* live.

A striking example is an editorial that appeared in the prestigious *New England Journal of Medicine* in 1982.[2] When researchers reported in the *Journal* that there appeared to be a drop in fertility for women over thirty, a younger age than had previously been believed, the *Journal* viewed the situation with alarm. It editorialized that women might have to devote their twenties to childbearing and put off career training and progress until their thirties and beyond.

But would such a course of action be helpful to a woman's well-being? Only if you assume that childbearing is so vital to a woman that everything else should be sacrificed because of the *possibility* that she might have fertility problems after thirty. A woman who follows this advice would be taking a great risk in terms of her future career development.

As it turned out, the importance of the fertility study, which received considerable attention in the press, was probably overstated. Critics point out that the statistics came from women who had been artificially inseminated, a very different process from conceiving naturally. To generalize from one to the other is a questionable practice.

But what if the statistics are accurate? What if women do face real problems with fertility after thirty? During their twenties do they then have to choose between a career and motherhood? Here, the *Journal* was operating, probably unthinkingly, under assumptions of an earlier time, ignoring the reality of women's new patterns of love and work. In the past, few women with young children were in the labor force, but today the majority of women hold paid jobs while they raise their children. And since our study found that married employed mothers were the women highest in well-being of all the groups in our sample, this pattern has a lot to recommend it.

So a more sensible prescription for young women today than early childbearing and late career entry is to fight hard for the social changes that will help women and men participate both in family life and in work: better child care services, more flexible schedules in the workplace, more involvement of fathers in raising children.

How did the idea that anatomy is destiny gain such a powerful hold on our society? A look at our history helps explain this phenomenon. Psychologist Joseph Pleck points out in *The Myth of Masculinity* that the Depression of the 1930s wreaked great psychological havoc on Americans—especially on men, who often found themselves unemployed, powerless to control their destinies, and unable to live up to the role of "breadwinner."[3] World War II saved the economy—and not a few psyches—at the same time. The years just before, during, and after the war also saw a mass migration of psychiatrists and psychologists, many of them disciples of Freud, from Europe to America.

The theories many of the Freudians espoused about women were introduced and popularized, Pleck points out, at a time when they fit precisely the mood of the country. There was the impulse to cherish home and hearth that is natural in the wake of a war; there was a need to displace millions of women from the workforce to make room for the returning males. The memories of the Depression made many men deeply uneasy about the security of their jobs, unwilling to add the worry of competing with women in the workplace. It is not surprising that the late forties and the fifties were the age of the Feminine Mystique.

But as we've seen, the women who bought the belief that their lives must center only on home and family (and most did) paid a price. Mental health data from the 1950s on middle-aged women showed them to be a particularly distressed group, vulnerable to depression and feelings of uselessness.[4] This isn't surprising. If society tells you that your main role is to be attractive to men and you are getting crow's feet, and to be a mother to children and yours are leaving home, no wonder you are distressed.

The data on the women in our study, as we've seen, present a startling contrast. Age had no relationship to well-being; women in their fifties felt as good about themselves as did women in their thirties. What happened?

It wasn't that the inherent nature of women changed—but

that the world around them changed. Psychologist Elizabeth Douvan, noting that a decline in women's self-esteem with age found in the 1950s did not show up in the 1970s, believes that it's social changes that have made it possible for women to cope better with growing older.[5] The women's movement, we would argue, not only is giving women permission to think about themselves in less limited ways than in the past, it also has led to real changes in opportunities. Inflation and the demand for more skilled workers have also catalyzed women into entering and staying in the workforce. Most women now nearing age forty who are at home plan to work once their "old" job of mothering fades away; older women have more to look forward to in the second half of life than canasta and minding the grandchildren. The changes in society that followed the women's movement, we believe, are a major reason so many women today feel better about themselves and their lives.

But if women's well-being is linked more to the social climate than to internal psychological forces, then confidence, optimism, and satisfaction all can be dissipated if the gains of the movement are allowed to slip away.

Our survey makes clear that most women do not see what is happening in their lives in social and political terms. On the whole, the women in our sample tend to say things like, "The women's movement hasn't had much impact on me *personally,*" and "I don't see what the fuss is all about." Their most frequent explanation of why they were happier now than when younger had to do with age: "It's turning thirty-five." "When you're forty you know who you are." "Being fifty makes the difference." But as we've seen, chronological age wasn't related to any of our measures of well-being. What was related was something much more connected to the women's movement—being in a good job. Yet even women in occupations only recently open to women fail to make the connection between their success and feminism.

A good example of this kind of thinking can be found in a *Boston Globe* article (January 9, 1977) headlined: "Four Harvard Women Enter All-Male Bastion, But Not as Feminists." The "bastion" referred to was the Rhodes scholarships, open to women for the first time that year. One scholar, asked whether she was a feminist said, "I guess I don't see myself as a feminist. I've never had to come to terms as a minority because I haven't been discriminated against." The other young women expressed similar sentiments.

These comments intrigued Columbia University professor Carolyn Heilbrun, the author of *Reinventing Womanhood*. She said:

> These were merely the latest in a long series of denials of feminism that began long ago to interest me. Why, I wondered, this compelling need to deny being a feminist, even on the part of those clearly intelligent enough to see that without the feminists the Rhodes scholarships would not have been opened to women. . . . No other group of people, anywhere, has ever felt impelled so persistently to deny their association with those who have won for them the opportunities they now insist on enjoying as their natural and inevitable right.[6]

This insistence on seeing achievement purely in personal terms is a very American way of thinking. Steeped in the myths of Horatio Alger, bred on the idea that every American can make it on personal merit if good enough, we tend to overlook the impact that social forces have on our lives. It may protect our egos to think this way, but it's a narrow view of reality that will hurt us deeply in the long run. This disinclination to think politically, to understand how the gains (or losses) of women as a group impinge on individual lives, may explain why so many women did not respond with enthusiasm to the Equal Rights Amendment. But this tunnel vision will ultimately work against the progress that has improved the situation for all women. Those women who do not see themselves as the beneficiaries of the women's movement in effect become allies of a growing backlash. If women in large numbers contribute by passivity to slowing the drive for equal status, they may find themselves in the position described by the late Walt Kelly, creator of "Pogo": "We have met the enemy and they is *us.*"

It's not surprising that when women fail to connect social change with their newfound pride and satisfaction, they assume it must be their age. The most popular current theories of adult development see crises and stages associated with chronological age as the key to understanding our lives. But as we've seen, new research shows that it just isn't so, and the latest theory is beginning to reflect this new understanding.

The famous "midlife crisis" is an example of an event that is supposed to be related to age. The term has become so much a part of popular jargon that anyone who reaches middle age and doesn't have a certifiable midlife crisis may feel somewhat deprived.

But does the midlife crisis really exist? Or more to the point, is it a necessary and inevitable midlife event?

When Yale psychologist Daniel Levinson and his colleagues did their study of forty middle-aged men, they found that many were wrestling with crises centering around assessing and "measuring" their lives.[7] Had they accomplished what they wanted to do? How could they come to terms with mortality? Was their dream of what they wanted to be in the adult world working out? The midlife crisis was related to the process of resolving these issues; unresolved, they would cause a man serious problems.

This research and the theory of the male midlife crisis were intriguing, but since Levinson and his team studied *only* middle-aged men, they had no way of knowing whether these issues were found as often in people of other ages, both younger and older. One study of men who were very successful at a young age found that by their early thirties they were wrestling with what were supposed to be midlife issues. They were asking themselves, "Was it worth it?" "What next?" and "What shall I do with the rest of my life?"[8] Many people may indeed face the kind of crisis Levinson described, but they may face it at thirty or sixty.

So it's a mistake to see a major crisis as an inevitable occurrence for all people at midlife. Our research found that the issues and upheavals Levinson describes are, in fact, rare in the lives of the women we studied. We found no evidence that these or the anxiety and depression that define the midlife crisis appear around the ages of forty to fifty. And women rarely spoke of measuring their accomplishments against their expectations, or of concern about "time running out." Of course, many women had no youthful goals to measure their performance against, except to get married and perhaps have children. Many were so involved in their earlier years in caring for others that they have only recently discovered ambitions of their own. Yet even those who were just beginning to build careers in midlife rarely expressed concern about time running out.

We were surprised at first that there was so little talk of mortality among the women in our sample. Why should this be so? As we thought about it, our surprise gave way to possible answers.

First, ours is a culture in which men are inoculated early in life with the goal of achievement in a form that constantly stresses the competitive nature of the career ladder. For many men, life is marked off like a football field, with gains and losses measured

all the way. It is not surprising that men tend to be constantly
sizing up their progress. Women's socialization has been different—
marry the right man, have children and thereby pretty much achieve
your goals. It's the fact that permanent happiness doesn't automatically follow that's given women troubles as they grow older. But
what if women become more career-oriented, if they begin to develop
vocational goals earlier in life? Will they then start to resemble
men as they approach midlife, brooding about having too little
time left to get to their goals?

We suspect they will not. As we thought more about this question, we began to realize that the male concern with mortality and
time running out at midlife is partly based on the physical realities
of being male. Men do not live as long as women—the differential,
in fact, is increasing—and they are more prone to life-threatening
diseases (heart disease, is the prime example) that strike at midlife.
Stories about a forty-five-year-old man who drops dead in his office
are all too common. Of course, women do get heart disease, but
usually much later.

The concerns women have about aging, we found, center not
on having too little time left, but on having too much. They know
they are likely to live well past seventy, and they worry about living
too long—becoming dependent, unable to function as active adults.
And while middle-aged men worry about being able to function
sexually, about loss of potency, midlife women typically report that
sexual satisfaction is increasing. In one study of women forty to
sixty, more than half said their sexual interest and responsiveness
had grown steadily since their twenties.[9] And recall that the women
in our sample showed no decline in sexual satisfaction with increasing age. So women in the middle years have a distinct edge over
men in terms of physical health and well-being and prospects for
the near future. This may be a reason why we detected so few
signs of any midlife crisis among the women in our sample. This
difference is one more warning that we must be on guard against
the tendency we pointed out earlier for researchers to study men,
ignore women, report their findings, and assume that these findings
apply to everyone. Men become the norm, and if women are considered at all, it is only to figure out how to squeeze them into the
male mold.

If we study women in their own right, as people whose experience is at least as central to the human condition as is men's, we

may well get a very different picture of the human life course.

There is already evidence that midlife, besides being a positive time for women, may be less stressful for men than "crisis" theorists think. Combined with the myriad images of carefree youth in the popular media, the gloomy image of middle age may give a distorted picture of the realities of the life cycle for most people—men and women. The very newest studies indicate that the idea of midlife as inevitably fraught with more problems than earlier years is erroneous. When Leonard Pearlin and his colleagues studied life experiences and stress in about 2,300 people of various ages, they looked at how people respond to change.[10] They found that the people showing the most signs of great stress were not the middle aged, but the young adults, who were wrestling with issues of becoming independent, coping with young children, and trying to carve out for themselves a place in the adult world. They point out that younger adults are also the people most vulnerable to economic problems, because "it is the period of life when there is commonly a great disparity between rapidly escalating material needs and actual earnings."

Women in our study typically reported that it was in their twenties, not at midlife, that they felt the most uncertain of their worth, the least pleased with their lives. If the study of midlife had begun with women, perhaps the midlife crisis would never have become part of our vocabulary! When you study women's lives, you see clearly the great variety of lifeprints among adults. You can't predict much about women's well-being from their chronological age. For example, a woman of forty reentering the workforce after twenty years at home will be wrestling with very different life issues than a single woman the same age who is fighting for tenure at the university where she teaches. While the lives of men today may be more homogeneous, they are not all alike either. A man of fifty who has just lost a job because his company went out of business may be more similar in the psychological issues he is facing to a thirty-five-year-old in the same boat than to another fifty-year-old who has just been named vice-president of a company. If you studied thirty-five-year-old unemployed men in the midst of the Great Depression, they would probably look psychologically quite different from employed men of thirty-five in the affluent sixties.

So for women the "age and stage" theories are not the answer to understanding the pattern of a life. Theories of women's lives that are now evolving take into account the fact that the times do change, and as environments change, people change with them. The women in our study, for example, didn't expect work to be central to their lives; yet for many it has turned out to be so.

The theme of achievement and work—jobs, education, career goals—dominated our interviews, especially when we asked women about their joys and regrets, hopes and frustrations. When we asked, "Thinking of your life as a whole, what things are the most reward-ing?" nearly half the women in the sample mentioned their achieve-ment in education or work. When we asked what major issues the women were dealing with in their lives, 47 percent mentioned career and economic issues, compared to 23 percent who mentioned issues of intimacy. And, when we asked, "If you could live your whole life over, what one thing would you most like to change?" the most frequent response was that they would seek better educa-tional or career preparation. Very few women mentioned marriage or children as things they would change if they could repeat their lives, and a scant 2 percent of women who had never married or were childless said they would marry or have children.

These answers were striking in the light of the commonly held belief that women's lives are dominated by issues of marriage and children. To a surprising degree, these daughters of the Feminine Mystique era are, as adults, concerned with work and achievement. The probability seems very high that today's young women will be even more involved in these pursuits as they move into midlife— certainly no less so.

We also asked women about major turning points in their lives. We defined turning points as "events that changed your life so that it was different afterward." Traditional theories suggest that such "marker events" should center around getting married, giving birth, menopause, children leaving home, and so on. The answers showed no such pattern. For example, only 20 percent of the married women mentioned marriage as a major turning point—half as a positive one, half as a negative one. For divorced women, however, the majority did see the marital split as a marker event. As we've noted, of the divorced women who did so, 80 percent saw it as a *positive* turning point. Even allowing for the human tendency to accentuate the positive, this finding is striking, and it is consistent with divorced women's descriptions of personal growth and increased competence following separation.

What women most frequently mentioned as turning points were events that seemed to come out of the blue, unpredictable, unexpected—a sudden job transfer, a car crash. Social scientists sometimes call these "life accidents" because they aren't part of the expected course of life. The second major category of turning points were events that were common but occurred at an unusual or "wrong" time, a time different from the norm. If a parent dies when you are fifty, you may suffer profoundly, but you are more prepared to deal with what happened than if you were fifteen. Events that can be anticipated are less likely to precipitate crises or feel like major turning points.[11] Many of the events previously thought to mark out the later stages of a woman's life—menopause, the empty nest, even widowhood—are in fact predictable. Most women expect to experience them and have some idea about when they are likely to occur. So we are prepared for such events, partly because of a process social scientists call "anticipatory socialization." If we know certain events are likely to happen, often we imagine them, rehearse in our minds what they will be like, how we will feel and act, what will happen next, and so on. Because of this mental rehearsal, we can often better withstand even tragedies such as widowhood or the loss of a parent, if they occur "on time"—more or less at the age they happen to everyone else we know. Whatever the pain or anxiety we feel, we will eventually cope and do not feel forever marked or changed by the event. It's very different, though, when a young woman of thirty-five loses her husband, or a child's parent dies. Such unexpected tragedies find us unprepared and often leave us feeling singled out by an unfair fate.

Divorce is a good example of an event that is rarely expected and predictable, in the sense that we rehearse for it and have in mind an appropriate age or time for it to happen. So here's one important reason why divorce, but not marriage, was so frequently mentioned as a turning point.

Beyond helping us to understand why some events cause crises and some do not, patterns of timing have a broader influence both on how we live our lives and on how we evaluate our lives. At any point in time in a society, there are dominant norms about when and in what order a woman takes on such roles as wife, mother, worker.[12] A woman who marries early, has children in her twenties, and only later builds a career, is likely to differ in her joys and sorrows, values and attitudes, from the woman who is in the workforce from young adulthood on, then marries at thirty and has one or two children without interrupting her career.

Why is this issue of timing so important? We have just come through an era when most women followed, or at least had as their ideal, just one pattern—early marriage, followed rapidly by childbearing and child rearing, with only intermittent employment during these years. When one pattern so predominates, it's hard to see it as just one possible lifeprint among many, or even to see how its effects might be different under different social conditions. We've said in discussing women and work that the temporary predominance of the housewife pattern blinded many observers to women's long-standing role as workers and economic providers.

Much the same thing has happened with our ideas about what is feminine behavior and what is not. Images of femininity that have dominated in this century were shaped by the particular historical era during which these images developed. The role of the economically dependent housewife went hand in hand with beliefs about the "eternal" nature of women, about their passivity and docility. Such traits were called "feminine," while assertion and independence have been seen as "masculine." Historical accident may be one reason for this false dichotomy. The behavioral sciences were in their infancy in the late nineteenth and early twentieth centuries. The scientists who first probed the dynamics of the human personality looked to their own societies for examples of human behavior, and most often bourgeois European or American women were the women they first observed. Freud, for example, drew many of his hypotheses about women from the study of patients who were affluent Victorian-era housewives. But the women of that time and that class were hardly typical of women in other times and other cultures; few women throughout history have been as sheltered and dependent as the women of the Viennese bourgeoisie. Anthropologist Marjorie Shostak introduced us (see Chapter Six) to the hardy !Kung women with their ability to be both assertive and nurturant, women far more typical of the world's women. If Freud and his colleagues had studied !Kung women, their notions about feminine behavior might have been profoundly different.

Until recently, most behavioral scientists assumed that what they called "masculine" and "feminine" characteristics were opposite ends of the same spectrum. This was what might be called a "seesaw" model of personality traits. If you were high in assertiveness, for example, then you automatically had to be low in nurturance. This model certainly wouldn't explain the !Kung women— or most of the rest of us, for that matter. New research and theory has helped us to understand that these traits are in fact independent of each other, not opposite ends of the same spectrum. We know that people not only can be, but need to be both nuturant and assertive; both tender and independent.

We all encounter situations in our lives which require us to act in different ways. An employee we are supervising at work who is chronically late must be dealt with very differently from a child who rushes to us, crying, after a bad fall. The old sex roles too often operate as a straitjacket, preventing men and women from acting in the most "adaptive" way—that is, the most effective way to deal with the situation at hand.

To many people the word that is used to indicate freedom from the straitjacket of sex stereotyping has an odd ring to it: *androgyny.* Too often it brings to mind images of uniformity, a world where everyone, male or female, dresses alike, acts alike, thinks alike. Many people are uneasy about feminism because, they ask, "Won't women become just like men? And won't it be a dull, gray, and uninteresting world?"

One fear they may be expressing is that tenderness and nurturance will vanish from the world. If men aren't tender and nurturant and women become more like men, then where will we go to satisfy our emotional needs? But these fears miss the whole point. If sex-role straitjackets disappear, tenderness becomes as much a part of men as of women. And when women become more assertive, it doesn't mean they lose their ability to nurture. Androgyny will, in fact, make people "more different," rather than more alike, freeing them to develop individual lifeprints, not simply conform to some preordained role. The fear of change, however, is a deep-rooted one, and the fear that *women* will change may be the deepest rooted of all. Our real nemesis may not be change itself but the fear of it. But change need not be destructive. It can get us away from oppressive sameness and alienation and help us to become more truly ourselves.

EPILOGUE

The life course is not fixed, but widely flexible. It varies with social change—not only with the changing nature of the family, the school, the workplace, the community, but also with changing ideas, values and beliefs. As each new generation . . . enters the stream of history, the lives of its members are marked by the imprint of social change and in time leave their own imprint.

Jessie Bernard, The Future of
Motherhood[1]

WHEN THE COLLEGE NEWSPAPER at a large eastern university recently asked students whether they planned to combine career and family, most of the women interviewed said no. The reason one young woman gave for not combining the roles of wife, mother, and career woman was that she wanted to give 100 percent to whatever she did. But one message that clearly emerges from our study is that to give 100 percent to just one part of your life, whether it's your family or your work, is to risk a great deal. Well-being requires working on developing both Mastery and Pleasure. To become "overspecialized," to concentrate solely on the traditional sphere of family—the "unbalance" women have typically chosen— is no more likely to lead to lifelong mental health than any other onesided life. For short periods of time, of course, being absorbed in any all-consuming interest—husband and children, a career— can be highly rewarding. But as a long-term lifeprint, it's a bad bet.

Why is it that in the case of women's lives the old folk wisdom that warns about putting all your eggs in one basket has been so totally ignored? One reason is that there seems to be a kind of time lag in our recognition of changing social conditions. The wife and mother role used to involve being an economic provider, doing productive, socially valued work. The loss of this function has only recently been recognized as a problem, rather than a privilege. The pattern that was supposed to shelter women and improve their lives, that of the economically dependent housewife, has for too many women failed to provide a firm foundation for personhood.

Another reason women haven't seen the danger of overinvesting in family responsibility is the myth of "You can't have it all!" The grain of truth here is that few women can in fact build a good life for themselves and for those they love by literally trying to have it all—a lifelong, high-powered, sixty-hour-a-week career; primary responsibility for raising several children; a romantic married life; friends; hobbies; exercise; and leisure. But not many men can have it all either, although some may have thought they succeeded by ignoring the emotional cost to wives, children, co-workers, parents.

Why then, haven't men asked themselves the question that so many women struggle with: "Can I have it all?" It's because this question, like code language, has a hidden meaning: "Won't a woman destroy her chances for happiness if she doesn't lavish all her attention and energy on those she loves?" Concentrating on your own development, investing in your own skills and interests, these questions imply, will prevent you from making a husband and children happy. And if your husband and children are unhappy, then you will have failed as a woman.

When men begin to think about changing the role patterns they have accepted, they tend to think in terms of adjustments and compromises—cutting down on hours at work, refusing a job transfer, taking on the grocery shopping, spending more time with children. No one seriously proposes that men relinquish marriage, choose not to have children, or, least of all, give up their work. What our study shows is that women too should stop thinking in "either-or" terms. As we've seen, a woman's well-being is enhanced when she takes on multiple roles. We saw that at least by middle adulthood, the women who were involved in a combination of roles—marriage, motherhood, and employment—were the highest in well-being, despite warnings about stress and strain. There is, of course, no lifeprint that is free of stress, nor is a life without stress either possible or desirable. What a woman needs is a pattern in which the rewards outweigh the problems.

The message here is that there is no pattern that is "hard" or "easy." Each life pattern will have different periods of maximum stress. An employed married woman who is trying to establish her career while coping simultaneously with young children may find that her twenties are a time of great strain. But the same woman may find that after thirty-five, life seems much easier. The children are getting older and more independent, her financial situation is better, and she is reaping the rewards of her earlier investment in her career.

A woman who stays home with her young children, on the other hand, and who reenters the job market later in life, may find that the years after thirty-five may be the most anxious ones. She is trying to play "catch-up" in the job market, wondering if she can compete, if she can find a job that will match her talents.

By midlife, as we saw, role strain—feeling pulled apart, overloaded—is more a problem for mothers at home than for women in the workforce. Employment seems to help a woman to cope with stress, while being responsible for raising children may be today's high-risk job. As sociologist Jessie Bernard has long argued, the wife and mother role can be hazardous to your health.

So rather than warn women only about the dangers of a highpowered career, we should also warn them about stress in the home, and we should point out the risks of low-level jobs. We saw that among the working women in our study, those in the high-prestige positions were highest in well-being. Contrary to the conventional wisdom, women who are employed are better off in challenging, demanding work than in the occupations long thought to be "suitable" for women.[2] A physician can earn a good income on a parttime basis, can arrange her professional life so she can get out to her child's school concert during the day, but a nurse can't. Professors don't ask a boss for permission to bring a child to work, if that's necessary; secretaries do.

A major emphasis in this book has been on work, because in our study we were able to examine women's lives as workers in great detail, and because theories of adult development have tended to view issues of work as more central to men than to women. But we think our findings have a great deal of relevance for homemakers, too. Being in the role you prefer is very important to wellbeing, and to many women being a homemaker seems to offer the best opportunity for developing and exercising their skills and interests. For some women the intense involvement of child rearing is a valued specialty; for others, volunteer activities, avocations, or sharing in a husband's career provides greater satisfaction than any paid job they could have. But we are concerned about how easily the homemaker role can become a trap. Divorce, the death of a spouse, economic need, changing personal or social conditions, can leave a woman in this lifeprint in an untenable situation. And homemakers today often must cope with feeling unimportant, left out, demeaned. But a paid job isn't the only remedy. Our study shows that there are other important sources of well-being too often overlooked by women, especially close relationships outside the circle of husband and children—those with friends, parents, siblings, fellow volunteers or enthusiasts. Women should not see these as competing with the role of homemaker but as making it more viable, less narrow. Employed women, of course, need to "invest" in these sources as well.

Another reason for our concern about homemakers is that we have just been through an era when, because the economy was expanding, a woman could decide to be at home with children for ten years or so and then find her way back to the labor force. This option is rapidly disappearing as the social and economic climate becomes less supportive. It was never easy to be a "reentry woman," but it's becoming even more difficult.

An important consideration for young women thinking about their futures is our finding that neither motherhood nor marriage per se automatically contribute to Mastery—to self-esteem and the feeling of being in charge of one's life. Some women find being a mother very rewarding, others find it more a source of distress. The quality of relationships with children varies, and it's not always within a woman's power to assure herself of a good experience. The arrival of a neat little bundle doesn't guarantee well-being.

Marriage, and particularly a rewarding marriage, can provide important ingredients of well-being, specifically, of Pleasure—an intimate relationship, sexual satisfaction, economic security. These are the elements that women who aren't married must struggle to find. But we also saw that for divorced women, this struggle seemed to result in a high level of Mastery. Despite the lower levels of Pleasure in both groups of nonmarried women, the gratifying parts of their lives, perhaps because they were all employed, tended to outweigh the problems. By middle adulthood, the process of shaping a lifeprint that fits, and of coming to terms with less positive aspects, appears to enable women to derive well-being from a variety of patterns.

A certain amount of anxiety is also part of the package, though. A complex society provides choices and options, but the price of an array of possibilities is uncertainty. In the 1950s, it was clear to almost every young woman what she "should" do, what would be good for her health and happiness. But did the automatic acceptance of the wife and mother role enable these women to escape anxiety? It did not, and when they arrived at middle adulthood, many were plagued with frustration and depression. Today's young women may feel plagued by the choices that face them in their twenties, but as we've seen, if they make challenging work a priority, they are likely to be able to attain well-being with or without marriage and motherhood.

It's important for us all—men and women—to recognize the importance of the Pleasure component of well-being, and of the life experiences that enhance Pleasure, particularly intimate relationships. How can we applaud the man who refuses to become a stranger to his child by working on weekends and passes up a promotion to advance his wife's career, and not applaud women who do the same? The problem, of course, is that men who put family first are courageously breaking the mold; women who do so are doing what's expected; and to date women have been all too ready to sacrifice everything else for the sake of their relationships. But we need to avoid a new double standard in which we look down on women who compromise their career goals while praising men who do so.

What we do warn against, though, is for a woman to set *no* limits to what she will do for others, while doing the absolute minimum for herself. In the past, this pattern at least carried with it social approval for doing one's duty, and many people act as though life would be better if only we would bring back those times. But the new social and economic conditions that have brought with them changes in values and behavior—birth control, a longer life span, modern technology—weren't created by feminists, and they won't be undone by antifeminists. When women typically live to be almost eighty there's no way that a life focused on motherhood can carry the same social value and meaning as it formerly did.

"Can a woman have it all?" Taking a careful look at what

underlies this question, we see an assumption that's often over-looked, that *all* women *want* it all. As we've seen, many women choose a lifeprint that does not include a husband and children, whether out of personal preference, or because they recognize the difficulties of managing more than one role under current social conditions, or because of particular circumstances. We've noticed a tendency for people to look very skeptical when they hear that women who aren't married or who don't have children are doing just fine. Reactions of "They're repressing their pain," or "Of course they won't admit they feel bad" are common. Why is it that there are few such reactions when married women with children say they're happy? Why don't people wonder whether these women are fooling themselves or lying to the researchers? We think the answer goes beyond a natural tendency to question unexpected find-ings. Rather, it's that women who are married and have children are supposed to be happy, but single women, divorced women, child-less women, aren't. However understandable these beliefs may be, they can cause problems for women in nontraditional patterns, who may begin to question themselves and doubt their feelings. "Am I really happy? What's wrong with me that I'm happy even though I'm divorced/don't have children?"

These attitudes are a holdover from the belief that there is only one right path for women, and that if they deviate from it, they are bound to suffer—if not now, then later. It would be a serious mistake to think that these attitudes have vanished; under new ideas and new words, old myths linger.

It may be hard to give up the idea that there is a ready-made blueprint for women's lives; choice is not easy. But the pain of self-discovery is productive pain, compared with the agony of con-torting oneself to fit a predetermined pattern.

As Carolyn Heilbrun says in *Reinventing Womanhood:* "Women have too long imagined only a constricted destiny for themselves, allowing the imagination of possibility to be appropri-ated for the exclusive use of men. It is time for women to claim an equal share in the ambitions as well as the frustrations of life."

It is our hope that the lifeprints of the women we studied will contribute to this task. Their lives, we believe, help define wom-anhood as Heilbrun envisions it—not as unchanging, rigid patterns, but as "a condition full of risk, variety and discovery; in short, human."

NOTES

INTRODUCTION

1. Erica Serlin, in a study of 384 women, forty to fifty-nine years of age, also found that the contributors to a woman's self-esteem and to her happiness were different. See E. Serlin, "Emptying the Nest: Women in the Launching Stage," in D. G. McGuigan, ed., *Women's Lives: New Theory Research and Policy* (Ann Arbor: University of Michigan, 1980).

2. Although we refer to the work of many researchers, we draw especially on the work of Joseph Veroff, Elizabeth Douvan, and Richard Kulka. In their recent book, *The Inner American: A Self Portrait from 1957 to 1976* (New York: Basic Books, 1981), they report findings comparing survey results conducted in 1976 on a sample of men and women over twenty-one years of age with results from a 1957 study on a similar sample. Since several of the questions central to our study were researched and reported by this team, their book provides a useful comparison at various points.

3. One interesting area of new research is how the presence of women in an occupation affects its prestige rating. There seems to be a negative relationship! For example, if people are told that a profession will soon have large numbers of women, the prestige rating they give that occupation tends to go down. See, for example, P. England, "Women and Occupational Prestige: A Case of Vacuous Sex Equality," *Signs,* 5 (1979): 252–65.

4. Harold Dupuy, "Self-Representations of General Psychological Well-Being of American Adults," paper presented at meeting of American Public Health Association, Los Angeles, 1978.

5. Technically, we used what is called a disproportionate random sampling procedure. First we decided on the criteria for inclusion into the sample, e.g., being never-married and employed; being divorced for at least a year and employed with children. Second, we determined that we needed forty-five women in each of the six groups formed by combinations of work and family status. Then we contacted each potential subject in order of the random number that was assigned to her—the lowest random numbers were contacted first. Thus the selection of subjects was random within the population of women who met the criteria for inclusion.

6. Two-earner families constituted over one-third of the sample. Among

them, one-third had wives employed in high-prestige occupations, and there is a correlation between income and occupational prestige. Thus the incomes of two-earner families were considerably higher than those of married one-earner families.

7. This is a debatable point. Geographical differences may be relevant to absolute level of well-being. We believe that the *relationships* we have found between well-being and other characteristics of the women, however, would be found if one studied women from other geographical areas. Previous research suggests that results would not differ in important ways if the study were done on a nation-wide basis.

CHAPTER ONE: Looking in the Wrong Place

1. Carolyn Heilbrun, *Reinventing Womanhood* (New York: Norton, 1979).

2. This is a major theme of Betty Friedan's recent book, *The Second Stage* (New York: Summit, 1981).

3. Self-esteem was measured by two indices. The first, the Rosenberg self-esteem scale (M. Rosenberg, *Society and the Adolescent Self-Image* [New Jersey: Princeton University Press, 1965]) is a widely used research instrument; the second was the balance score in the domain of the self—a measure we developed based on analyses of the first phase or "snowball" interview data.

4. The ingredients of Mastery—for example, self-esteem—are, of course, not completely independent of or unrelated to the ingredients of Pleasure—for example, satisfaction. People with high self-esteem do tend to be more satisfied with their lives. Rather, we're talking about how these ingredients cluster; in the sample we studied they grouped into the two clusters we've described.

5. The Mastery and Pleasure dimensions shouldn't be taken as true of all people at all times. Teen-agers today, for example, or women in the 1950s, may have derived great self-esteem from catching a man. We may also feel proud and competent when we help someone close to us cope with a personal problem. And for many people, intense Pleasure can come from completing a difficult piece of work. How men's psychological well-being is structured, whether Mastery and Pleasure are useful concepts, and if so, what affects them, remains to be seen. We need to examine well-being in different samples to determine the generalizability of the Mastery and Pleasure structure.

6. Factor analysis, the statistical procedure we used, allows one to determine the degree to which individual scales are in fact a measure of a similar underlying construct. An analogy is I.Q. testing where the various subscale scores of intelligence tests are combined because they measure aspects of an underlying characteristic, called "I.Q." Technically, all of the well-being indices assess Mastery, but some are much better indicators of Mastery than others. Self-esteem, sense of control, and low levels of symptomatology—anxiety and depression—are the measures that most strongly reflect the dimension we have labeled Mastery. The scores on the other three scales made only a marginal contribution to the subject's overall Mastery score. The same is true for Pleasure: satisfaction, happiness, and optimism are the three scores that most strongly reflect this dimension. For the technical

reader, each well-being index was weighted by its factor loading in arriving at factor scores for Mastery and Pleasure.

7. Maggie Scarf, *Unfinished Business* (New York: Knopf, 1978).

8. G. W. Brown, M. N. Bhrolchain, and T. Harris, "Social Class and Psychiatric Disturbance Among Women in an Urban Population," *Sociology,* 9 (1975): 225–54.

CHAPTER TWO: What about Me?

1. For a review, see Caroline Bird, "The Best Years of a Woman's Life." *Psychology Today,* June 1979.

2. Carol Gilligan, *In a Different Voice: Psychological Theory and Women's Development* (Cambridge, Massachusetts: Harvard University Press, 1982).

3. Lawrence Kohlberg, "Development of Moral Character and Moral Ideology," in M. L. Hoffmann and L. W. Hoffmann, eds., *Review of Child Development Research, Volume I* (New York: Russell Sage Foundation, 1964).

4. Jean Baker Miller, *Toward a New Psychology of Women* (Boston: Beacon Press, 1976).

5. A. Campbell, P. E. Converse, and W. L. Rodgers, *The Quality of American Life: Perceptions, Evaluations, and Satisfactions* (New York: Russell Sage, 1976).

6. M. Yarrow, J. Campbell, and R. Burton, *Child Rearing: An Inquiry into Research and Methods* (San Francisco: Jossey-Bass, 1968).

7. Melvin J. Lerner, *The Belief in a Just World: A Fundamental Delusion* (New York: Plenum Press, 1980).

CHAPTER THREE: The Well-Springs of Mastery and Pleasure

1. Gail Sheehy, *Pathfinders* (New York: Morrow, 1981).

2. Leonard Pearlin, talk presented to Social Ties Seminar, directed by Dr. Robert Weiss, Joint Center for Urban Studies, MIT, April 1982.

3. Jean Lipman-Blumen, "The Vicarious Achievement Ethic and Non-Traditional Roles for Women," paper presented at Eastern Sociological Society meeting, New York, 1973.

4. Walter Gove and Jeannette Tudor, "Adult Sex Roles and Mental Illness," *American Journal of Sociology,* 78 (1973): 812–35; and R. C. Kessler, and James A. McRae, "Trends in the Relationship Between Sex and Psychological Distress," *American Sociological Review,* 46 (1981): 443–52.

5. Preference for a role has consistently been found to be important. See, for example, Lois Hoffman, "Effects of Maternal Employment on the Child: A Review of the Research," in A. G. Kaplan and J. P. Bean, eds., *Beyond Sex Role Stereotypes: Readings Toward a Psychology of Androgyny* (Boston: Little Brown, 1976).

6. See especially, E. M. Hetherington, M. Cox, and R. Cox, "The Aftermath of Divorce," in J. J. Stevens, Jr., and M. Mathews, eds., *Mother-Child, Father-Child Relations* (Washington, D.C.: National Association for the Education of

Young Children, 1977); and J. S. Wallerstein and J. B. Kelly, "Children and Divorce: A Review," *Social Work,* 24 (1980): 468–75.

7. Abraham Maslow, "Dominance, Personality and Social Behavior," *Journal of Psychology,* 10 (1939): 3–39.

8. Debra Belle, *Lives in Stress: Women and Depression* (Beverly Hills: Sage Publications, 1982).

9. The role of sexual interest and activity in the lives of women in the middle and older years has drawn the attention of several researchers and scholars. The following are good examples of some of the work that has been generated in the area: Edward Brecher, and the editors of Consumer Union, *Love, Sex and Aging* (New York: Random House, forthcoming); Judith Long Laws, "Female Sexuality Through the Life Span," in P. Baltes and O. Brim, Jr., eds., *Life-Span Development and Behavior* (New York: Academic Press, 1980); Lillian Rubin, "Sex and Sexuality: Women at Midlife," paper presented at meeting of the American Sociological Association, 1978; Gail Sheehy, *Pathfinders* (New York: Morrow, 1981); and Samona Sheppard and Sylvia Seidman, "Sexuality and Midlife Women," paper presented at meeting of the Gerontological Society, November 1981.

CHAPTER FOUR: Marriage

1. J. Veroff, E. Douvan, and R. Kulka, *The Inner American: A Self-Portrait from 1957 to 1976* (New York: Basic Books, 1981).

2. W. R. Gove and J. Tudor, "Adult Sex Roles and Mental Illness," *American Journal of Sociology,* 78 (1973): 812–35.

3. Jessie Bernard, *The Future of Marriage* (New York: World-Times, 1972).

4. Abraham Maslow, "Personality and Motivation," *Journal of Social Psychology,* 16 (1942): 259–94.

5. For a discussion of changes in patterns of timing of first births, see Peter Uhlenberg, "Cohort Variations in Family Life Cycle Experiences of U.S. Females," *Journal of Marriage and the Family,* 36 (1974): 284–91; and Tamara Hareven, "The Last Stage: Adulthood and Old Age," *Daedalus,* 105 (1976): 13–27.

6. From a sermon preached by Samuel Miller, March 13, 1808, for the benefit of the Social Institute in the City of New York for the Relief of Poor Widows with Small Children. Cited by Barbara Welter in a chapter, "The Cult of True Womanhood," in Michael Gordon, ed., *The American Family in Social Historical Perspective* (New York: St. Martin's Press, 1973).

7. Talcott Parsons, "Family Structure and the Socialization of the Child," in T. Parsons and R. R. Bales, eds., *Family, Socialization and Interaction Process* (Glencoe, Illinois: Free Press, 1955).

8. Study done by David Winter, Abigail Stewart, and David McClelland of fifty-one college males who were given the TAT test to measure their need for power, affiliation, and achievement in 1964 and were questioned again in 1974

concerning current career, wife's career, and a variety of attitude items. See *Journal of Personality and Social Psychology,* 35 (1977): 159–66.

9. See *Psychology Today,* October 1977.

10. Peggy McIntosh, "Who Picks Up the Socks, or Notes on Choosing a Husband," *Brearley Bulletin,* Spring 1980.

11. John Kenneth Galbraith, "How the Economy Hangs on Her Apron String," *Ms.,* September 1974.

12. See L. Serbin, K. O'Leary, R. Kent, and I. Tonick, "A Comparison of Teacher Response to the Preacademic and Problem Behavior of Boys and Girls," *Child Development,* 44 (1973): 796–804.

13. Janet Lever, "Sex Differences in the Games Children Play," *Social Problems,* 23 (1976): 478–87.

14. Jean Baker Miller, *Toward a New Psychology of Women* (Boston: Beacon Press, 1976).

15. Dorothy Ullian, "The Development of Conceptions of Masculinity and Femininity" in B. Lloyd and J. Archer, eds., *Exploring Sex Differences* (New York: Academic Press, 1975).

CHAPTER FIVE: Children: and Baby Makes Three

1. Charlene Depner, "The Parental Role and Psychological Well-Being," paper presented at meeting of American Psychological Association, New York, 1979.

2. The impact on a couple both individually and jointly of the decision about timing of first births is discussed by Pamela Daniels and Kathy Weingarten in *Sooner or Later: The Timing of Parenthood in Adult Lives* (New York: Norton, 1982).

3. J. Blake, "Is Zero Preferred? American Attitudes Toward Childlessness in the 1970's," *Journal of Marriage and the Family,* 41 (1979): 245–57.

4. See A. Campbell, P. E. Converse, and W. L. Rodgers, *The Quality of American Life* (New York: Russell Sage, 1976).

5. Jerome Kagan and Howard Moss, *Birth to Maturity* (New York: Wiley & Sons, 1962).

6. David C. McClelland, C. A. Constantian, D. Regalado, and C. Stone, "Making it to Maturity," *Psychology Today,* 12 (1978): 42ff.

7. Lois W. Hoffman, "Early Childhood Experiences and Women's Achievement Motives," *Journal of Social Issues,* 28 (1972): 129–56.

8. Leonard Pearlin, "Sex Roles and Depression," in N. Datan and L. H. Ginsberg, eds., *Life Span Developmental Psychology: Normative Life Crises* (New York: Academic Press, 1975).

9. M. Guttentag, "Women, Men and Mental Health," in L. Cater, A. Scott, and W. Martyna, eds., *Women and Men: Changing Roles* (Palo Alto, California: Aspen Institute for Humanistic Studies, 1975).

10. Jean Baker Miller, *Toward a New Psychology of Women* (Boston: Beacon Press, 1976).

11. F. I. Nye and L. W. Hoffman, eds., *The Employed Mother in America* (Chicago: Rand McNally, 1963).

12. Angus Campbell, "The American Way of Mating: Marriage Si, Children Only Maybe," *Psychology Today,* 8 (1975): 37–43.

13. Depner, "The Parental Role and Psychological Well-Being."

14. G. Arling, "The Elderly Widow and Her Family, Neighbors, and Friends," *Journal of Marriage and the Family,* 38 (1976): 757–68.

15. N. D. Glenn and S. McLanchan. "The Effects of Offspring on the Psychological Well-Being of Older Adults," *Journal of Marriage and the Family,* 43 (1981): 409–21.

16. Campbell, Converse, Rodgers, *The Quality of American Life.*

17. J. G. Teicholz, "Psychological Correlates of Voluntary Childlessness in Married Women," paper presented at meeting of Eastern Psychological Association, Washington, D.C., 1978.

CHAPTER SIX: Finding the Challenge

1. These remarks come from Michael Gordon's introduction to his edited volume, *The American Family in Social-Historical Perspective* (New York: St. Martin's Press, 1973).

2. Marjorie Shostak, *Nisa: The Life and Words of a !Kung Woman* (Cambridge, Massachusetts: Harvard University Press, 1981).

3. Elizabeth Janeway, *Man's World, Woman's Place* (New York: Dell, 1971).

4. Helena Lopata, *Occupation Housewife* (New York: Oxford, 1971).

5. Rosalind Barnett and Grace Baruch, "Empirical Literature on Occupational and Educational Aspirations and Expectations: A Review, 1974," *JSAS Catalog of Selected Documents,* 6 (1976): 49.

6. Rosalind Barnett, "Sex Differences and Age Trends in Occupational Preference and Occupational Prestige," *Journal of Counseling Psychology,* 22 (1975): 35–58.

7. The work of Myra Feree shows that women value their jobs even when those jobs are routine and of low prestige. See "Working Class Job: Housework and Paid Work as Sources of Satisfaction," *Social Problems,* 23 (1976): 431–41.

8. Kay Deaux, "Self-Evaluations of Male and Female, *Sex Roles,* 5 (1979): 571–80.

9. "If I Were a Man," in *The Charlotte Perkins Gilman Reader,* Ann J. Lane, ed. (New York: Pantheon Books, 1980).

CHAPTER SEVEN: Risks and Dreams

1. This is the title of a recent book by Collette Dowling (New York: Summit, 1981).

2. Rosabeth Kanter, *Men and Women of the Corporation* (New York: Basic Books, 1977).

3. L. Baird, *The Graduates* (Princeton, New Jersey: Educational Testing Service, 1973); and L. Baird, "Entrance of Women to Graduate and Professional Education," paper presented at meeting of American Psychological Association, Washington, D.C., 1976.

4. I. H. Frieze, B. E. Whitley, Jr., B. H. Hanusa, and M. C. McHugh, "Assessing the Theoretical Models for Sex Differences in Causal Attributions for Success and Failure," *Sex Roles,* 8 (1982): 333–44.

5. Patricia Gurin, "Labor Market Experiences and Expectancies," *Sex Roles,* 7 (1981): 1079–92.

6. Pamela Daniels, "Dream vs. Drift in Women's Careers: The Question of Generativity," in B. Goldman and B. Forisha, eds., *Outsiders on the Inside: Women and Organizations* (New York: Prentice-Hall, 1980).

7. Daniel Levinson et al., *The Seasons of a Man's Life* (New York: Knopf, 1978).

8. R. Sears, "Midlife Development: Review of Daniel Levinson's *Seasons of a Man's Life,*" *Contemporary Psychology,* 24 (1979): 97–98.

CHAPTER EIGHT: Overload and Underload

1. On this issue see Carroll Smith-Rosenberg and Charles Rosenberg, "The Female Animal," *Journal of American History,* 2 (1973): 332–56.

2. There are several caveats to keep in mind. First, the relationship between role strain and the number of roles a woman occupies applies to the three roles we took into account. It is possible that role strain would increase if the number of roles a woman occupied increased or if the roles were different. Also, this finding might not apply if any one of the roles carried with it overwhelming demands.

3. F. Ilfeld, Jr., "Sex Differences in Psychiatric Symptomatology," paper presented at meeting of the American Psychological Association, 1977.

4. See Abigail Stewart, "Role Combination and Psychological Health in Women," paper presented at meeting of the Eastern Psychological Association, 1978.

5. Lois Verbrugge, "Women's Social Roles and Health," paper presented at Conference: Women, A Developmental Perspective, sponsored by NICH and NIMH, Bethesda, Maryland, 1980.

6. S. Haynes and M. Feinleib, "Women, Work and Coronary Heart Disease: Prospective Findings from the Framingham Heart Study," *American Journal of Public Health,* 70 (1980): 133–41.

7. An example of this theory is reflected in the work of William Goode, "A Theory of Strain," *American Sociological Review,* 25 (1960): 483–96.

8. S. R. Marks, "Multiple Roles and Role Strain: Some Notes on Human Energy, Time and Commitment," *American Sociological Review,* 42 (1977): 921–

36; and S. Sieber, "Toward a Theory of Role Accumulation," *American Sociological Review*, 39 (1974): 567–78, represent this revisionist viewpoint.

9. G. W. Brown, M. N. Bhrolchain, and T. Harris, "Social Class and Psychiatric Disturbance Among Women in an Urban Population," *Sociology*, 9 (1975): 225–54.

10. R. C. Kessler and J. A. MacRae, "Trends in the Relationship Between Sex and Psychological Distress," *American Sociological Review*, 46 (1981): 443–52.

11. Joseph Pleck, "Wives' Employment, Role Demands, and Adjustment: Final Report," NIMH #32620 and NSF SOC 7825695, NIMH 29143 and Time, Inc. Funds.

12. For a discussion of how women lawyers cope with multiple roles, see Cynthia Fuchs Epstein, *Women in Law* (New York: Basic Books, 1981).

13. Lester Thurow, *The Zero-Sum Society* (New York: Penguin, 1980).

CHAPTER NINE: Divorce: Coming Apart, Getting It Together

1. J. Veroff, E. Douvan, and R. Kulka, *The Inner American: A Self-Portrait From 1957 to 1976* (New York: Basic Books, 1981).

2. A. Campbell, P. E. Converse, and W. L. Rodgers, *The Quality of American Life* (New York: Russell Sage, 1976).

3. For a description of the lives of divorced women in different economic situations, see D. Belle, *Lives in Stress: Women and Depression* (Beverly Hills: Sage Publications, 1982).

4. Gail Sheehy in her book, *Pathfinders* (New York: Morrow, 1981), notes with surprise the large number of divorced women among "the pathfinders."

5. Dorothy Burlage, "Divorced and Separated Mothers: Combining the Responsibilities of Breadwinning and Child-Rearing" (Ph.D. diss., Harvard University, 1978).

6. Robert Weiss, *Marital Separation* (New York: Basic Books, 1975).

7. See especially, E. M. Hetherington, M. Cox and R. Cox, "The Aftermath of Divorce," in J. J. Stevens, Jr., and M. Mathews, eds., *Mother-Child, Father-Child Relations* (Washington, D.C.: National Association for the Education of Young Children, 1977); and J. S. Wallerstein and J. B. Kelly, "Children and Divorce: A Review," *Social Work*, 24 (1980): 468–75. Similar findings are reported by P. Brown, L. Perry, and E. Harburg, "Sex-role attitudes and psychological outcomes for Black and White women experiencing marital dissolution," *Journal of Marriage and the Family*, 39 (1977): 549–61.

CHAPTER TEN: Mothers and Daughters

1. Elizabeth Douvan and Joseph Adelson, *The Adolescent Experience* (New York: Wiley, 1966).

2. Nancy Friday, *My Mother, My Self* (New York: Delacorte, 1978).

3. Elizabeth Johnson, "Good Relationships Between Older Mothers and Their Daughters: A Causal Model," *The Gerontologist,* 3 (1978): 301–306. This issue is also discussed by Gunhild O. Hagestad and her colleagues. See G. Hagestad, M. Smyer, and K. Stierman, "Parent-Child Relations in Adulthood: The Impact of Divorce in Middle Age," in R. Cohen, S. Weissman, and B. Cohler, eds., *Parenthood as an Adult Experience* (New York: Guilford Press, 1982).

4. See, for example, Nancy Chodorow, "Mothering, Object-Relations, and the Female Oedipal Configuration," *Feminist Studies,* 4 (1978): 137–58; and D. Dinnerstein, *The Mermaid and the Minotaur: Sexual Arrangements and Human Malaise* (New York: Harper & Row, 1976).

5. See Beatrice Whiting, "Problems of American Middle-Class Women in Their Middle Years—A Comparative Approach" (unpublished paper, Harvard University, 1978); and Jerome Kagan and Judith Lemkin, "The Child's Differential Perception of Parental Attributes," *Journal of Abnormal and Social Psychology,* 61 (1960): 440–47.

6. Diana G. Kahn, "Daughters Comment on the Lessons of Their Mothers' Lives," Working Paper, Bunting Institute, Radcliffe College, 1980.

7. L. Troll, S. Miller, and R. Atchley, *Families in Later Life* (Belmont, California: Wadsworth Publishing, 1979).

8. G. O. Hagestad, "Problems and Promises in the Social Psychology of Intergenerational Relations," in R. W. Fogel, E. Hatfield, S. Kiesler, and J. March, eds., *Stability and Change in the Family* (New York: Academic Press, 1981).

9. L. R. Fisher documents how a daughter's relationship to her mother changes as she takes on the roles of wife and mother. See "Transitions in the Mother-Daughter Relationship," *Journal of Marriage and the Family,* 43 (1981): 613–22.

10. J. B. Wilen, "Changing Relationships Among Grandparents, Parents, and Their Young Children," paper presented at meeting of the Gerontological Society, Washington, D.C., 1979.

11. For example, see M. Hennig and A. Jardim, *The Managerial Woman* (New York: Doubleday, 1977).

12. Cynthia Epstein, *Women in Law* (New York: Basic Books, 1981).

13. E. Brody, L. J. Davis, and M. Fulcomer, "Three Generations of Women: Comparisons of Attitudes and Preferences for Service Providers," paper presented at meeting of the Gerontological Society, Washington, D.C., 1979.

CHAPTER ELEVEN: By Myself

1. Two such major studies are: A. Campbell, P. E. Converse, and W. L. Rodgers, *The Quality of American Life* (New York: Russell Sage, 1976); and R. A. Ward, "The Never-Married in Later Life," *Journal of Gerontology,* 34 (1979): 861–69.

2. Lynn L. Gigy, "Self-Concept of Single Women," *Psychology of Women Quarterly,* 5 (1980): 321–40.

3. Singleness has received recent attention as indicated by the following: Margaret Adams, *Single Blessedness* (New York: Basic Books, 1976); and Elmer Spreitzer and Lawrence Riley, "Factors Associated With Singlehood," *Journal of Marriage and the Family,* 36 (1974): 533–42.

4. Lynn L. Gigy, "Self-Concept of Single Women," *Psychology of Women Quarterly,* 5 (1980): 321–40.

5. Abraham Maslow, *Motivation and Personality* (New York: Harper & Row, 1954).

6. Judith Birnbaum, "Life Patterns and Self-Esteem in Gifted Family-Oriented and Career-Committed Women," in M. Mednick, S. Tangri, and L. W. Hoffman, eds., *Women and Achievement: Social and Motivational Analysis* (New York: Hemisphere-Halstead, 1975).

7. Two noteworthy studies on the choice and function of confidantes are: M. F. Lowethal and C. Haven, "Interaction and Adaptation: Intimacy as a Critical Variable," *American Sociological Review,* 33 (1968): 20–30; and R. B. Warren, "The Work Role and Problem Coping: Sex Differentials in the Use of Helping Systems in Urban Communities," paper presented at meeting of the American Sociological Association, San Francisco, 1975.

8. Pauline S. Sears, and Ann H. Barbee, "Career and Life Satisfaction Among Terman's Gifted Women," in J. Stanley, W. George and C. Solano, eds., *The Gifted and the Creative: Fifty-Year Perspective* (Baltimore: Johns Hopkins University Press, 1977).

CHAPTER TWELVE: Toward a New Theory of Women's Lives

1. Leonard Pearlin and Claire Radabaugh, "Age and Stress: Perspectives and Problems," in Hamilton I. McCubbin, ed., *Family Stress, Coping and Social Support* (New York: Springer, 1982).

2. The editorial was written by Alan H. De Cherney and Gertrud S. Berkowitz and appeared in the *New England Journal of Medicine,* February 18, 1982, *306,* 424–26. The article appeared in the same issue on pages 404–9.

3. Joseph Pleck, *The Myth of Masculinity* (Cambridge, Massachusetts: MIT Press, 1981).

4. Caroline Bird, "The Best Years of a Woman's Life," *Psychology Today,* June 1979, 20–26.

5. Elizabeth Douvan, Newsletter of the Committee for Gender Research, University of Michigan, Spring 1982.

6. Carolyn Heilbrun, *Reinventing Womanhood* (New York: Norton, 1979).

7. Daniel Levinson et al., *Seasons of a Man's Life* (New York: Knopf, 1978).

8. This finding came from an unpublished study conducted by Renato Taguiri and John A. Davis of the Harvard University Graduate School of Business Administration, 1982.

9. For a fuller discussion of sexuality see note 9, Chapter Three.

10. Leonard Pearlin and J. S. Johnson, "Marital Status, Life Strains and Depression," *American Sociological Review,* 42 (1977): 704–15.

11. For an interesting typology of life events, see O. G. Brim and C. D. Ryff, "On the Properties of Life Events," in P. Baltes and O. Brim, eds., *Life-Span Development and Behavior,* Volume 3 (New York: Academic Press, 1980).

12. B. L. Neugarten, J. Moore, and J. C. Lowe, "Age Norms, Age Constraints, and Adult Socialization," *American Journal of Sociology,* 70 (1965): 710–17.

EPILOGUE

1. Jessie Bernard, *The Future of Motherhood.* New York: World-Times, 1972.

2. S. G. Haynes, and M. Feinleib, Women, Work and Coronary Heart Disease: Results from the Framingham 10-year Follow-Up Study, in P. W. Berman and E. R. Ramey, eds., *Women: A Developmental Perspective* (Bethesda, Maryland: NICHD, NIMH and NIA, 1980).

APPENDIX: SURVEY

ON THE FOLLOWING PAGES, we have reproduced the questionnaire that was given to the women in our sample by our interviewers. Many of the questions in the survey were developed especially for this study. Others were developed by other social scientists in their own research and were incorporated into this survey. For example, the self-descriptions (question 78) were adapted from an inventory developed by Sandra Bem; the measures of anxiety and depression (question 85) came from an inventory developed at Johns Hopkins University; the seven items asking about the sense of having control over the things that happen to you (question 104) were developed by sociologist Leonard Pearlin; and the self-esteem items (question 113) were derived from the work of Morris Rosenberg. As the reader will observe, not all questions asked in the survey are discussed in this book.

We found that many women in our sample discovered that answering questions about their own lives was an illuminating experience, which they often used as a tool for looking at a whole range of issues in their own lives. How happy were they in their work? What were the problem areas in their marriages? What did they like about having children? What were the good things about being single? How important were parents and friends in their lives?

We invite readers to use the survey in much the same way. There are no "right" or "wrong" answers, no "standards" to live up to. But it may be a useful instrument for taking a close and honest look at one's own "lifeprint."

INTRODUCTION

When we talked on the phone you described yourself as ____. (*Insert appropriate category from telephone screening.*)

1. (*If R* is employed*) Could you tell me something briefly about your work as a ____?

* Respondent

In addition to (your regular work/being a homemaker), are there other regular activities that are important to you?

EMPLOYMENT

(If R is employed, continue on. If R is not employed, skip to question 9.)

We're interested in learning about both the good things and the bad things in different parts of women's lives—the gratifying or rewarding things and also the problems and difficulties.

2. In thinking about your current job, to what extent, if any, is each of the following rewarding: (1) not at all, (2) somewhat, (3) considerably, or (4) extremely?

   Hours that fit your needs
   Job security
   The appreciation and recognition you get
   The people you work with
   Helping others/being needed
   Liking your boss
   The sense of accomplishment and competence
   The variety of tasks
   The opportunity for learning
   The physical conditions
   Getting out of the house
   Being able to work on your own
   Helping others develop—bringing them along
   The job's fitting your interests and skills
   Good income
   Good support facilities and resources
   Opportunity for advancement
   Challenging/stimulating work
   Getting to make decisions

3. In thinking about your current job, to what extent, if any, is each of the following a concern: (1) not at all, (2) somewhat, (3) considerably, or (4) extremely?

   Having too much to do
   Job insecurity
   The job's causing conflicts with other responsibilities
   Not liking the boss
   Having to juggle conflicting tasks or duties

Not being given the advancement you want or deserve
The job's not fitting your skills or interests
The job's being too regimented—there's too much supervision
Bad physical conditions
Lack of recognition or appreciation
The job's dullness, monotony, lack of variety
Being dissatisfied with income
Problems due to your being a woman
Having to do things that shouldn't be part of your job
Lack of opportunity for career growth
Unnecessary busy work
Lack of challenge
The people you work with
The job's taking too much out of you—it's too draining

4. All things considered, how satisfied are you with your current job? Use a scale from 1 to 7, with 1 meaning completely dissatisfied and 7 meaning completely satisfied.

5. In general, how good would you say you are at work: excellent, better than average, just above average, or not very good?

6. If you were to get enough money to live as comfortably as you'd like for the rest of your life, would you continue to work?

   If so, would you continue to work at the same job as you now have?

   If not, what work *would* you do?

7. Is there anyone who has helped to guide, encourage, or inspire your work over a period of years?

   If so, who? Could you tell me about it?

   How would you describe your current relationship with that person?

(If R is never-married or divorced skip to question 33.)

8. We are interested in your husband's preference regarding your working outside the home. Which of the following five statements best describes how he feels?

   (1) He definitely prefers that I work for pay.
   (2) He somewhat prefers that I work for pay.
   (3) He has no preference.
   (4) He would somewhat prefer that I not work for pay.
   (5) He would definitely prefer that I not work for pay.

(If R is married, skip to question 14.)

HOMEMAKING

9. In thinking about your being a homemaker, to what extent, if any, is each of the following rewarding: (1) not at all, (2) somewhat, (3) considerably, or (4) extremely?

> Being free to make your own schedule
> Being there for your husband (and children)
> Having the amount of responsibility you can handle
> Doing creative things around the house
> Not having to go out and work
> Keeping the house looking nice and cared for
> Having enough time and energy to enjoy your husband (and children)
> The appreciation you get from your family
> A sense of competence, of being good at what you do
> Being able to pursue your interests
> Having other people enjoy your home
> Being available to do things for others

10. In thinking about your being a homemaker, to what extent, if any, is each of the following a concern: (1) not at all, (2) somewhat, (3) considerably, or (4) extremely?

> Having too much free time
> Not having your own money
> The lack of adult company
> Having to structure or plan your own time
> Disliking housework
> A lack of challenge
> Having to justify not having a job
> Lack of appreciation for all the work you do
> Having to divide yourself up in pieces and juggle things
> Not contributing to the family income by earning money
> Being too available to other people
> Boredom and monotony

11. All things considered, how satisfied are you with being at home rather than having a paid job? Use a scale from 1 to 7, with 1 meaning completely dissatisfied and 7 meaning completely satisfied.

12. In general, how good would you say you are at being a homemaker: excellent, better than average, just about average, or not very good?

13. If you could have someone to take care of things here at home, would you like an outside job right now?

> If so, could you tell me more?

MARRIAGE

14. Is this your first marriage?

If so, in what year did you get married?

If not, in what year did you get married the first time?

How many years were you married to that person?
In what year did you marry your present husband?

15. In thinking about your marriage, to what extent, if any, is each of the following items rewarding: (1) not at all, (2) somewhat, (3) considerably, or (4) extremely?

The companionship
Having someone to take care of you
Having a husband who is easy to get along with
The physical affection
(*If R has children*) Your husband's being a good father
Being able to go to your husband with your problems
The sexual relationship
Your husband's backing you up in what you want to do
The enjoyment of doing things for your husband
Your husband's seeing you as someone special, appreciating you
Having a husband who is a good provider
Having a husband whose personality fits yours
Your husband's willingness to share in the housework
Good communication
(*If R has children*) Your husband's willingness to share in child care

16. In thinking about your marriage, to what extent, if any, is each of the following a concern: (1) not at all, (2) somewhat, (3) considerably, or (4) extremely?

Your husband's being unavailable or not home enough
Poor communication
Your husband's physical health
Not getting enough appreciation or attention
(*If R has children*) Conflicts about your child(ren)
Your husband's job/career problems
Problems in your sexual relationship
Lack of companionship
Your husband's job instability
Problems for you caused by demands of your husband's job/career
Not getting along, personality clashes
Conflict over who does housework
Not getting enough emotional support—his not backing you up
(*If R has children*) Conflict over sharing child care

17. All things considered, how satisfied are you with your marriage? Use a scale from 1 to 7, with 1 meaning completely dissatisfied and 7 meaning completely satisfied.

18. In general, how would you rate yourself as a wife: excellent, better than average, just about average, or not very good?

19. Which of the following five statements best describes your employment history from the time you first married? By employment we mean working half-time or more.

   (1) I have rarely or never had a regular paid job.
   (2) I have worked from time to time.
   (3) I have worked about half the time.
   (4) I have had a paid job more of the time than not.
   (5) I have almost always had a regular paid job.

20. What are the good things, if any, that you find in combining work with marriage (and children)? (*R may answer separately for marriage and children.*)

21. What problems, if any, do you find in combining work with marriage (and children)?

22. What is your husband's usual occupation? (What sort of work does he do?)

23. How would you describe your husband's present health: excellent, good, fair, or poor?

24. What is the highest grade or level of education your husband has completed?

25. When important decisions have to be made in your family, who tends to make them: your husband always, your husband more than you, both of you equally, you more than your husband, or you always?

26. How satisfied are you with the way decisions are made in your family? Use a scale from 1 to 7, with 1 meaning dissatisfied and 7 meaning completely satisfied.

27. During the past six months, who usually did each of the following chores: (1) your husband always, (2) your husband more than you, (3) both of you equally, (4) you more than your husband, or (5) you always?

   Grocery shopping
   Paying bills
   Minor household repairs
   Laundry
   Lawn care/snow removal
   Cooking
   Cleaning

Taking out trash

Preparing income tax forms

(*If R has children*) Care of child(ren)

28. Is there anyone besides you and your husband who regularly does any of the tasks just mentioned?

If so, who?

29. How often during the last six months have you experienced problems in the sexual part of your marriage: almost always, much of the time, once in a while, or almost never?

30. How would you describe your sexual relationship: very satisfying, fairly satisfying, not as good as you would like, or very dissatisfying?

31. Would you say that your sexual activity is just about as frequent as you would like, more frequent than you would like, or less frequent than you would like?

32. Is frequency or anything else about your sexual life an issue for you now?

CHILDREN

33. Regardless of whether you have children or not, if you had things the way you wanted them right now, would you definitely not have children, probably not have children, probably have children, or definitely have children?

(*If R is married without children, skip to question 41. If R is never-married, skip to question 46. Continue only if R has children.*)

34. How many children do you have?

35. Starting with the first born, tell me the age and sex of each of your children, whether the child lives at home or not, and whether the child is yours naturally, yours by adoption, your stepchild, or your foster child.

Did you have any children who are no longer living?

36. Do you have grandchildren?

If so, how often do you spend time with them: once a day, once a week, once a month, or once a year or less?

37. In thinking about your children, to what extent, if any, is each of the following rewarding: (1) not at all, (2) somewhat, (3) considerably, or (4) extremely?

Being needed by them

The pleasure you get from their accomplishments

Helping them develop

The love they show
Feeling proud of how they are turning out
Liking the kind of people they are
Being able to go to them with problems
Enjoying doing things with them
The help they give you
The meaning and purpose they give your life
Being the best caretaker for them—being special and irreplaceable
(*If R has more than one child*) The way they get along together
Seeing them mature and change
The way they change you for the better
(*If R has grandchildren*) Enjoying your grandchildren's company
(*If R has grandchildren*) Knowing that your responsibility for your granchildren is limited

38. In thinking about your children, to what extent, if any, is each of the following a concern: (1) not at all, (2) somewhat, (3) considerably, or (4) extremely?

The financial strain
Feeling trapped or bored
Worrying about their physical well-being—health problems, accidents, and so forth
(*If R has more than one child*) Their fighting or not getting along with each other
The heavy demands and responsibilities
Worrying about the teen-age years—getting into trouble, drugs, sex
Not being sure if you're doing the right thing for them
Their not showing appreciation or love
Problems with their schooling or education
Feeling disappointed in what they're like—the kind of people they are
Not having enough control over them
Their needing you less as they get older
Your having too many arguments and conflicts with them
Their interference in your relationship with your husband
(*If R has grandchildren*) Worry about your grandchildren's well-being
(*If R has grandchildren*) Worry about how your grandchildren will turn out

39. In general, how good would you say you are as a mother: excellent, better than average, just about average, or not very good?

40. All things considered, how satisfied or dissatisfied are you in your role as a parent? Use a scale from 1 to 7, with 1 meaning completely dissatisfied and 7 meaning completely satisfied.

(*Skip to question 46.*)

CHILDLESSNESS

41. In thinking about your not having children, to what extent, if any, is each of the following rewarding: (1) not at all, (2) somewhat, (3) considerably, or (4) extremely?

   Being free to follow your own interests at home or at work
   The lack of heavy emotional demands children can bring
   Being able to do things spontaneously, on the spur of the moment
   Its being financially easier
   Keeping your relationship to your husband central and special
   Having a lifestyle that fits you
   Not being pulled in different directions

42. In thinking about your not having children, to what extent, if any, is each of the following a concern: (1) not at all, (2) somewhat, (3) considerably, or (4) extremely?

   The disapproval or disappointment of your family or your husband's family
   Not having anyone to take care of you in your old age
   Other people's seeing you negatively
   Feeling you may be missing out on a special experience
   Feeling you don't have a "real" family
   Feeling you are inferior or defective physically
   Feeling you are selfish

43. To your knowledge, are you physically able to have children?

44. To your knowledge, is your husband physically able to have children?

45. Are there any other factors that enter into your not having children?

   If so, what are they?

FINANCES

46. When you were seventeen or eighteen, how did you think your financial needs would be taken care of: did you expect to earn your own way, be supported by a husband, or what?

47. How much did you think about this: not at all, occasionally, fairly often, or very often?

48. How adequately could you support yourself now if you had to: not at all adequately, barely adequately, or quite adequately?

   How do you feel about that?

49. Approximately what was your total family income for the past year?

50. (*If R is employed*) About how much of this did you yourself earn?

51. In general, how do your finances work out at the end of the month? Do you usually end up with: a considerable amount after expenses, a small amount after expenses, just enough to make ends meet, or not enough to make ends meet?

52. How threatened do you feel financially from inflation: not at all threatened, somewhat threatened, or very threatened?

YOURSELF

53. How often do the things you do add up to being just too much: never, occasionally, often, or very often?

54. How often do you have to juggle different obligations that conflict with one another and give you a pulled-apart feeling: never, occasionally, often, or very often?

55. Some women feel they are not doing as good a job as they should in one or more areas. How often do you have this feeling: never, occasionally, often, or very often?

    If you've had this feeling, could you tell me about it?

56. Do you expect to make any of the following changes in the near future? (*Ask as appropriate.*)

    Getting married
    Having a baby
    Going back to school
    Getting a job
    Changing a job
    Stopping work
    Getting a divorce

57. When you were seventeen or eighteen, what kinds of expectations or goals, if any, did you have for your adult life?

58. How did things turn out compared to your picture?

(*If R is never-married, continue. If R is divorced, skip to question 67. If R is married, skip to question 78.*)

SINGLENESS

59. Do you prefer being single, or would you prefer being married?

60. To your knowledge, are you physically able to have children?

61. In thinking about your being single, to what extent, if any, is each of the following rewarding: (1) not at all, (2) somewhat, (3) considerably, or (4) extremely?

> Not being accountable to anyone else
> Being able to do things spontaneously—not being tied down
> Having a lifestyle that fits you
> Being independent
> Not having too heavy responsibilities
> Feeling able to take care of yourself and cope on your own
> Not being pulled in a lot of different directions
> Having satisfying sexual relationships

62. In thinking about your being single, to what extent, if any, is each of the following a concern: (1) not at all, (2) somewhat, (3) considerably, or (4) extremely?

> Finding companionship with compatible people
> Not having children
> Not having a permanent intimate relationship
> Not being part of a real family or really connected to people who need you
> Problems with sexual relationships
> Feeling not chosen, or inferior to married people
> Other people seeing you negatively, thinking something is wrong
> Difficulties meeting men

63. How would you describe the way things are going for you now sexually: very satisfying, fairly satisfying, not as good as you would like, or very dissatisfying?

64. Would you say that your sexual activity is just about as frequent as you would like, more frequent than you would like, or less frequent than you would like?

65. Is frequency or anything else about your sexual life an issue for you now?

(Skip to question 80.)

DIVORCE

66. Which of the following five statements best describes your employment history from the time you first married? By employment we mean working half-time or more.

> (1) I have rarely or never had a regular paid job.
> (2) I have worked from time to time.

(3) I have worked about half the time.
(4) I have had a paid job more of the time than not.
(5) I have almost always had a regular paid job.

67. Have you been married more than once?

    If so, how old were you when you first married?

    How old were you when you married for the second time?
    How many years were you married to that person before your separation/
        divorce?
    If you were married only once, how old were you when you got married?
    How many years were you married before your separation/divorce?

    For how long have you been separated/divorced?

68. In thinking about your life now, compared with when you were married,
    to what extent, if any, is each of the following rewarding: (1) not at all, (2)
    somewhat, (3) considerably, or (4) extremely?

    Feeling you have grown as a person
    The chance to develop and enjoy new skills and interests
    Having your privacy and independence
    More enjoyment of sexual relationships
    A better or closer relationship to your parent(s)
    Feeling able to manage
    Better or closer relationships with women friends
    Not having to answer to anyone
    Closer or better relationships with your child(ren)
    Freedom to be involved in your work
    Relief at not being torn between husband and child(ren)
    Freedom to be yourself and meet your own needs
    Less turmoil and more peace of mind
    Better or closer relationships with sibling(s)

69. In thinking about your life now, compared to when you were married, to
    what extent, if any, is each of the following a concern: (1) not at all, (2)
    somewhat, (3) considerably, or (4) extremely?

    Having less time for yourself
    Having to worry about money
    Difficulties finding companionship with compatible people
    Not having a permanent intimate relationship
    Problems in your relationship with your ex-husband
    Fears about being alone when you are older
    Difficulties meeting men
    Problems your children have because of your separation/divorce

Problems with sexual relationships
Having no one to share your responsibilities and decision making with
Other people's seeing you negatively, or disapproving
Fears about what will happen to you in the future
Loss of friends you had when you were part of a married couple
Discomfort about going places alone

70. How would you describe the way things are going for you now sexually: very satisfying, fairly satisfying, not as good as you would like, or very dissatisfying?

71. Would you say that your sexual activity is just about as frequent as you would like, more frequent than you would like, or less frequent than you would like?

72. Is frequency or anything else about your sexual life an issue for you now?

73. Which of the following four statements best describes your attitude about remarrying?

(1) I definitely do not want to remarry.
(2) I am not especially interested in remarrying.
(3) I am somewhat interested in remarrying.
(4) I am very eager to remarry.

74. What changes do you anticipate as your children leave home?

75. Thinking of your life as a whole now, what would you say are the main ways that divorce experience has affected you?

76. What are the good things, if any, that you find in combining working with having children?

77. What problems, if any, do you find in combining working with having children?

YOURSELF

78. Rate yourself on each of the following qualities. Use a scale from 1 to 7, with 1 meaning almost never and 7 meaning almost always.

Apt to defend your beliefs, stand up for your opinions
Affectionate/showing love readily
Moody/sullen
Independent/thinking or acting for yourself, not influenced by others
Sympathetic/understanding, caring about other people's feelings
Conscientious/faithfully doing what your conscience tells you is right
Assertive/insisting on your rights, standing up for yourself

Sensitive to the needs of others
Reliable/trustworthy
Having a strong personality
Understanding/tuned into others' feelings
Jealous
Forceful/acting like a strong, powerful person
Compassionate/feeling sorry about other people's problems
Truthful/honest
Possessing leadership qualities
Eager to soothe hurt feelings
Secretive/keeping things to yourself
Willing to take risks
Warm/having loving feelings for others
Conceited/vain
Dominant/acting bossy or important
Tender/softhearted
Adaptable/able to adjust or accommodate to others easily
Willing to take a stand
Loving children
Tactful/able to say or do things without offending others
Aggressive
Gentle/kindly
Conventional/following accepted standards and rules

79. How would you describe your present health: excellent, good, fair, or poor?

80. How often does your health get in the way of things you want to do: all the time, often, sometimes, rarely, or never?

81. Have you ever felt that you were going to have a nervous breakdown?

If so, could you tell me about when you felt this way? What was it about?

What did you do about it?

82. Is your menopause completed, is it going on, or has it not started yet?

83. Have you had a hysterectomy?

84. Have you had or are you having Estrogen Replacement Therapy?

If so, for how long?

85. How much has each of the following symptoms bothered or distressed you during the past week including today: (1) not at all, (2) a little, (3) quite a bit, or (4) extremely?

Sweating
Feeling low in energy or slowed down

Having trouble getting your breath
Feeling lonely
Suddenly feeling scared for no reason
Feeling critical of others
Feeling no interest in things
Hot or cold spells
Feeling trapped or caught
A lump in your throat
Blaming yourself for things
Feeling fearful
Crying easily
Headaches
Trembling
Having trouble concentrating
Feeling nervous when you are left alone
Temper outbursts you cannot control
Nervousness or shakiness inside
Feeling hopeless about the future
Poor appetite
Faintness or dizziness
Loss of sexual interest or pleasure
Feeling afraid in open spaces
Thoughts of ending your life
Heart pounding or racing
Feeling blue
Constipation
Difficulty falling asleep or staying asleep
Having to avoid certain things, places, or activities because they frighten
   you
Hot flashes

86. When you were growing up, what was your father's usual occupation?

87. What was your mother's usual occupation?

88. Which of the following four statements best describes your family's finances
    during your childhood?

    (1) Money was very bad.
    (2) We always had enough for essentials.
    (3) We had most things we wanted.
    (4) We were well off.

89. When you were growing up, who earned the money to support the family:
    your father only, your mother only, both parents, or someone else?

    If someone besides your father earned money, explain the circumstances.

90. Did you always live together with both of your real parents up to the time you were sixteen years old?

If not, explain what happened and when.

91. What was the highest grade or level of education your mother completed?

92. What was the highest grade or level of education your father completed?

93. Which of the following five statements best describes your mother's employment history since you were born? By employment we mean working half-time or more.

    (1) She rarely or never had a regular paid job.
    (2) She worked from time to time.
    (3) She worked about half the time.
    (4) She had a paid job more of the time than not.
    (5) She almost always had a regular paid job.

94. Regardless of whether your mother worked or not, do you think she would have preferred to work? Would you say definitely yes, probably yes, probably no, definitely no, or that you don't know?

95. Is your mother alive?

If so, how would you describe her present health: excellent, good, fair, or poor?

96. Is your father alive?

If so, how would you describe his present health: excellent, good, fair, or poor?

97. Do you have any brothers or sisters?

If so, tell me the age, sex, and marital status of each sibling (including any who have died), and whether each has any children.

98. In thinking about your parents, siblings, and other close relatives, to what extent, if any, is each of the following rewarding: (1) not at all, (2) somewhat, (3) considerably, or (4) extremely?

    The feeling of family closenesss or togetherness
    Being able to count on your parent(s) to help out financially
    A good close relationship with your father
    Good close relationships with siblings
    Being able to talk over problems with your parent(s)
    Enjoying your mother's companionship
    Having a mother who is a good example/model of getting older
    Getting along smoothly with your mother

Your parents' getting along well with important people in your life—children, husband, friends

The help sibling(s) or other close relatives give you

99. To what extent, if any, is each of the following of concern: (1) not at all, (2) somewhat, (3) considerably, or (4) extremely?

Too many demands or obligations from siblings or other close relatives

The financial support of aging parent(s)

Difficult or poor relationships with parent(s)

Feeling guilty/uncertain about obligations to parent(s)

Having to act like a parent to your parent(s)

Being personally involved in physical care of your parent(s)

Parents' disapproval of or not understanding your way of life

Seeing your parent(s) decline and worrying how they will manage as they get older

Figuring out arrangements for your parents' care—nursing home, help, etc.

Difficult or poor relationship with sibling(s) or other close relatives

(If R is never-married, skip to question 104.)

100. Is your (former, *if R is divorced*) mother-in-law alive?

If so, how would you describe her present health: excellent, good, fair, or poor?

101. Is your (former, *if R is divorced*) father-in-law alive?

If so, how would you describe his present health: excellent, good, fair, or poor?

102. How would you describe your relationship with your (former, *if R is divorced*) mother-in-law and father-in-law?

103. What responsibilities, if any, do you have for their care?

104. For each of the following statements, tell me if you strongly agree, somewhat agree, somewhat disagree, or strongly disagree.

There is really no way I can solve some of the problems I have.

Sometimes I feel that I'm being pushed around in life.

I have little control over the things that happen to me.

I can do just about anything I really set my mind to.

I often feel helpless in dealing with the problems of life.

What happens to me in the future depends mostly on me.

There is little I can do to change many of the important things in my life.

105. Thinking of your life as a whole, what things are the most rewarding—what gives you the most pleasure?

106. If you could change one thing in your life as it is now, what would that be?

107. If you could live your whole life over, what one thing would you most like to change?

108. Do you see your life as having had any major turning points—events that changed your life so that it was different afterwards?

If so, what were they? How was your life different afterward?

109. All things considered, would you say that, these days, you are very happy, pretty happy, or not too happy?

110. Right now what issues, if any, are there in your life that you are dealing with—things you have to make a decision about, or settle, or make your peace with, that you think about quite a bit?

111. How satisfied are you with your life as a whole these days? Use a scale from 1 to 7, with 1 meaning completely dissatisfied and 7 meaning completely satisfied.

112. When you think about the future, how do you usually feel: extremely hopeful, somewhat hopeful, or not at all hopeful?

113. For each of the following statements, tell me if you strongly agree, somewhat agree, somewhat disagree, or strongly disagree.

On the whole, I am satisfied with myself.
At times I think I am no good at all.
I feel that I have a number of good qualities.
I am able to do things as well as most other people.
I feel I do not have much to be proud of.
I certainly feel useless at times.
I feel that I am a person of worth, at least on an equal plane with others.
I wish I could have more respect for myself.
All in all, I am inclined to feel that I am a failure.
I take a positive attitude toward myself.

114. To what extent, if any, is each of the following a rewarding part of your life: (1) not at all, (2) somewhat, (3) considerably, or (4) extremely?

Religious faith
Volunteer or service activities
Interests or hobbies (music, crafts, sports, groups)
Good close friends

Relationships with children not your own—children of relatives, or friends of your children

Social activities and groups

115. To what extent, if any, is each of the following a concern: (1) not at all, (2) somewhat, (3) considerably, or (4) extremely?

Not having enough free time for yourself
Health worries
Loneliness
Money problems—not having enough money
Dissatisfaction with volunteer work
Not enough social life

116. When you have a problem, what do you do?

117. When you want to talk about a problem, is there anyone in particular you confide in?

If so, whom?

Would you confide in that person if the problem concerned your children?
What if it concerned your work?
What if it concerned your marriage?

If you generally do not confide in anyone, could you tell me why not?

118. To what extent, if any, is each of the following rewarding to you: (1) not at all, (2) somewhat, (3) considerably, or (4) extremely?

Feeling able to cope with problems
Knowing your own strengths and limitations
Having pride in your accomplishments
Feeling that you are a good person
Feeling that you are attractive
Liking yourself
Feeling you are changing for the better
Feeling good about the sexual part of your life
Feeling good about your ability to be a good friend

119. To what extent, if any, is each of the following a concern: (1) not at all, (2) somewhat, (3) considerably, or (4) extremely?

Feeling inferior—not being self-confident
Feeling your accomplishments are inadequate and don't measure up
Feeling a need to justify your way of life to yourself and others
Feeling your education or training is inadequate
Not feeling as competent as you would like
Feeling different or deviant

Feeling unattractive

Feeling guilty about wanting more for yourself, wanting to meet your own needs more

Not being able to say no when you want to

120. What is the highest grade or level of education you have completed?

121. What is your religious preference, if any?

122. Who, if anyone (besides your husband and children), lives with you?

123. When you think about your getting older, what are the things, if any, that you look forward to?

124. When you think about your getting older, what are the things, if any, that worry you?

125. Some people's ideas about what is okay for women have changed quite a bit in the last few years. How would you say you have been affected by these ideas?

126. (*If R has children*) These new ideas have affected how some women bring up their children. How about you? Could you tell me about this?

INDEX

Agoraphobia, 162–163
Allport, Gordon, 17
Anger, sexual dysfunction and, 71–73, 75
Anticipatory socialization, 243
Anxiety:
  childbearing decisions and, 79
  defined, 17
  homemaking role and, 161–163
  midlife crisis and, 239
  out-of-step syndrome and, 14–15, 40–41,
    43, 45–46, 47, 48, 93, 209, 251
  relationship disturbances and, 21–22
  well-being vs., 17, 18, 250
  (See also Depression)
Arenas of intimacy, Pleasure and, 38–40, 44,
  46, 51, 166, 176–183, 210–211, 250

Barbee, Ann, 230
Barnett, Rosalind, 101, 123–124, 196, 223–
  224
Bernard, Jessie, 57, 246, 248
Birk, Ann, 72–73
Birnbaum, Judith, 215–216
Boston Globe, 237–238

Campbell, Angus, 95
Chesterfield, Earl of, 12
Childlessness, 14, 44, 47, 152
  changing views on, 78–81, 95–97, 242, 251
  decision making on, 78–80, 95–97, 101–
    102, 221–222, 225–226
  in freedom cluster, 97–100
  in missing out cluster, 95–96, 100–101
  old age and, 99, 101
  work satisfaction and, 96–100
Children, 78–102
  as adolescents, 88, 90–92, 193
  as cause of conflict, 88–92
  child balance scores, 184
  childlessness vs., 47–48, 78–81, 95–101,
    242
  in daughter-mother relationship (see
    daughter-mother relationship)

of divorced women, 50–51, 171, 184–186,
  191
effects of mothering style on, 85–87
fathers and, 203, 204–205
married, 92, 196–197, 203
of married working mothers, 16, 45–46,
  81, 87, 93, 94, 147–148
mother's income and, 94, 146, 165–166,
  167, 182, 183, 186–190, 191
preschool, 89–90
(See also Motherhood, mothering)
Control, sense of:
  being in charge cluster and, 168–170, 181–
    183, 190, 215
  daughter-mother relationship and, 193,
    196, 197, 198, 205–206
  defined, 17
  depression and, 19–22, 24–25, 236
  divorced women and, 38, 50–51, 166–167,
    170–183, 186, 189, 190, 198
  homemaking and, 38, 40, 42–44, 54, 154–
    156, 158, 159, 161
  marriage status and, 58, 59
  at middle age, 24–25, 236–237
  motherhood and, 80, 82–83, 85, 88, 93–
    96, 99–102
  never-married women and, 49, 104, 209–
    221, 230–232, 251
  occupational prestige and, 49, 50, 53–54,
    108, 117, 212–214, 215
  risk-taking and, 31–33
  role strain and, 140, 144–150, 248
  self-esteem and, 19–22, 237
  well-being and, 17, 18, 236–239
  work and (see Work)
Culture of Narcissism, The (Lasch), 28

Daniels, Pamela, 129
Daughter-mother relationship, 85, 101, 192–
  207
  adolescence and, 193
  aging parent and, 197–198, 205–207
  childlessness of daughter and, 197

Daughter-mother relationship (cont.)
  concern clusters in, 194–200, 205–207
  daughter with children and, 196–197, 203
  divorce and, 198–199
  fathers and, 203, 204–205
  guilt and conflict in, 205–206
  identity formation and, 194–195, 199–200
  Mastery and Pleasure levels and, 193, 196,
    197, 198, 205–206
  maternal rapport and, 193–194, 197, 200,
    202
  role models and, 193, 199–200, 203–205,
    206, 207, 217
Deaux, Kay, 114
Depner, Charlene, 96–97
Depression:
  defined, 17
  divorce and, 171, 179
  love relationships and, 13, 15, 19–22
  marriage status and, 14, 57, 58
  Mastery needs and, 19–22
  midlife crisis and, 239
  motherhood and, 88, 147
  1950s conditions and, 24–25, 236
  role strain and, 143–144, 147
  self-interest vs. self-sacrifice and, 28–29
  sexual problems and, 75–76
  single women and, 209
  well-being vs., 17, 18, 32
Discrimination, sex, 134–138
Divorce, 164–191
  financial concerns after, 165, 167, 182, 183,
    186–190, 191
  grieving period after, 171–173
  parent-child relationship after, 184–186
  self-esteem and, 168–170, 173, 176, 178
  short-term vs. long-term effects of, 165–
    166, 167, 171–174, 178
Divorced women with children, employed,
    36, 49–51
  being in charge cluster and, 168–170, 181–
    183, 190
  concern clusters of, 176–191
  dependency concerns of, 165, 166, 181–183
  disruption cluster of, 184–189, 190
  financial problems of, 50, 165–166, 167,
    182, 183, 186–190, 191, 247
  intimate relationships of, 166, 176–183
  loneliness cluster of, 166, 176, 181
  Mastery and Pleasure levels of, 38, 50–51,
    166–167, 170–172, 174, 176, 178,
    181–182, 186, 189–191, 198
  occupational prestige and, 50, 189
  personal growth cluster and, 170–176, 190,
    191
  relationship with children of, 50–51, 166,
    171, 179, 184–186, 191, 198–199
  remarriage of, 165, 179, 180, 182–183

sexual relationships of, 176–178, 180
  work and (see Work)
Doll's House, A (Ibsen), 57
Douvan, Elizabeth, 4, 237
Dupuy, Harold, 5

Education, women's focus on, 242
Emotional life, as women's domain, 12–16
Empathy, development in girls of, 69–70
Equal Rights Amendment, 238

Family of origin, as source of support, 48–
    49, 193–194, 197, 200, 202, 231
Fathers, daughters and, 203, 204–205
Fels Institute, 84–85
Feminine Mystique, The (Friedan), 19
Femininity issue:
  changing social conditions and, 244–245
  work and, 117–119
Feminism (see Women's movement)
Finances, 3
  divorced women and, 50, 165–166, 167,
    182, 183, 186–190, 191, 247
  economic provider role and, 105–106, 114,
    236, 247
  femininity issue and, 244–245
  girls' career choice and (see Younger
    women)
  Great Depression social changes and, 236
  homemaker's guilt feelings about, 42–43,
    106, 143, 151, 160–161
  husband's job problems and, 73–75
  marriage and, 54, 74–75
  Mastery and Pleasure levels and, 49, 50,
    51–52, 53–54
  as midlife concern, 242
  multiple role strain and, 146
  never-married women and, 216, 229–230,
    231
  parenting satisfaction and, 94
  sexual satisfaction linked to, 53–54
  two-career marriage and, 65
Framingham Heart Study, 144
Freud, Sigmund, 2, 15, 199, 234, 236, 244
Friday, Nancy, 192, 195
Friedan, Betty, 2, 19
Future of Motherhood, The (Bernard), 246

Galbraith, John Kenneth, 65
Gigy, Lynn L., 215
Gilligan, Carol, 26, 27
Gilman, Charlotte Perkins, 119–120
Girls (see Younger women)
Gordon, Michael, 105
Gove, Walter, 57
Gurin, Patricia, 127–128
Guttentag, Marcia, 88

Hagestad, Gunhild, 201
Health:
    aging and, 240
    multiple role strain and, 140–145, 147,
        150, 173–174
    well-being and, 16–17
Heart disease:
    in men vs. women, 240
    type of job and, 144
Heilbrun, Carolyn, 13, 29, 238, 251
Hetherington, Mavis, 184
Homemakers, homemaking:
    aging parents and, 197–198
    agoraphobia of, 162–163
    boredom and isolation cluster of, 159–160
    college-educated, 30–31
    concern clusters of, 150–156, 159–163, 247
    demands made on, 153–155
    emotional availability cluster of, 158–159
    freedom cluster of, 153–158
    lack of structure and, 19, 106–107, 153
    liking the work cluster of, 159, 248–249
    Mastery and Pleasure levels of, 38, 40, 42–
        44, 54, 154–155, 156, 158, 159, 161
    mothering role of (see Motherhood,
        mothering)
    not earning money cluster of, 42–43, 106,
        143, 151, 160–161
    role strain, 141–143, 145, 147, 247, 248
    satisfaction and, 30–31, 40, 156–159, 161
    self-esteem and, 19, 27–28, 40–44, 106–
        107, 112, 146, 150–153, 155–156
    sexual satisfaction and, 54
    underload strain of, 150–153
    well-being balance score of, 161
    "work" function of, 4, 106–107, 153
    (See also Married women with children,
        at home; Married women without
        children, at home)
Husbands:
    communication problems with, 66, 68–73
    dependency on, 31–32, 40–44, 45, 168
    family conflict and, 93
    as fathers, 203, 204–205
    household tasks shared by, 43, 64–65, 142
    in new "caring" role, 61–63, 64, 65
    occupational prestige of, 43–44
    role strain and, 142, 247
    in two-career marriages, 64
    work problems of, 66, 73–75
    (See also Divorce; Marriage; Men)

Income (see Finances)
Inner American, The (Veroff, Douvan, and
    Kulka), 4, 20, 51, 57, 60, 65, 66, 79,
    81, 82–83, 104, 109–110, 112, 113, 209

Janeway, Elizabeth, 106

Kanter, Rosabeth, 122
Kelly, Walt, 238
Kohlberg, Lawrence, 26–27
Kulka, Richard, 4
Kung women, 105–106, 244

Lasch, Christopher, 28
Lever, Janet, 69
Levinson, Daniel, 129–130, 239
"Lifeprints," defined, 7
Lipman-Blumen, Jean, 43
Lonely Crowd, The (Reisman), 56
"Looking in the wrong place" syndrome, 19–
    22, 87, 101
Lopata, Helena, 106–107
Love, as women's realm, 12–16, 20–21 (*See
    also* Nurturant imperative)

McClelland, David, 63–64, 87
McIntosh, Peggy, 64
Marriage, 55–77
    arenas of intimacy and, 38–40
    caring husband cluster in, 61–63
    childlessness and, 99–100, 102
    college-educated women and, 30–31
    communication in, 66, 68–73
    concern clusters in, 60, 66–77, 249
    cooperation cluster in, 64–65
    emotional distance cluster in, 66–70
    family size and, 60
    high-pressure jobs and, 67, 148
    husband's job problems cluster and, 66,
        73–75
    income and, 54, 74–75
    mental health and, 54, 57, 58
    multiple role strain and, 139–163
    new expectations for, 57–59, 60, 66
    in 1950s vs. present, 55–57, 60, 61
    Pleasure levels and, 38, 43–48, 54, 59–60
    Pleasure vs. Mastery in, 58, 59
    power issues in, 70
    reward clusters in, 60–65
    sexual dysfunction in, 72–73
    sexual satisfaction in, 46, 54, 72–73, 75–
        77, 95
    working mother and, 16, 45–47
    working wife and, 45–48
    (*See also* Divorce)
Married women with children, employed, 36,
    45–47, 235
    children of, (see Children)
    high well-being scores of, 143
    marriage balance and, 46
    Mastery and Pleasure levels of, 38, 40, 45–
        47, 54, 143, 246
    mothering role of (see Motherhood,
        mothering)

Married women with children (*cont.*)
  prestige of job and, 143
  role strain and, 139–150, 247–248
  social ties of, 46, 249
  work rewards of, 46–47, 144–145, 248
Married women with children, at home, 36,
    42–44
  college-educated, 31
  dependence on husband of, 42–44
  Mastery and Pleasure levels of, 38, 40, 42–
    44, 54, 154–155, 156, 158, 159, 161
  mothering role of (*see* Children;
    Motherhood, mothering)
  rewards of, 30–31, 156–159
  (*See also* Homemakers, homemaking)
Married women without children, employed,
    36, 47–48
  marriage and (*see* Marriage)
  Mastery and Pleasure levels of, 38, 40, 47–
    48, 54, 246–251
  out-of-step anxiety and (*see* Anxiety)
  work rewards and (*see* Work)
Married women without children, at home,
    36, 44–45
  Mastery and Pleasure levels of, 38, 40, 44–
    45, 54, 246
  role strain and, 141–143, 145, 147
  self-esteem and, 45, 150–153
  (*See also* Homemakers, homemaking)
Maslow, Abraham, 52, 53, 54, 57, 215
Mastery, 34–54
  changes in social climate and, 25, 233–238
  as dimension of well-being model, 1, 18–
    19, 36–38, 246
  rise in middle age of, 24–25, 236–237
  (*See also specific headings*)
Men:
  attribution patterns of, 122–123, 127, 129–
    130, 237–238, 247
  divorce and, 172, 177
  economic provider role and, 105–106, 114,
    236
  as fathers, 203, 204–205
  friendships of, 228–229
  marriage and (*see* Marriage)
  mental health and, 145, 241
  "midlife crisis" and, 239–241
  mortality concerns of, 239–240
  mother-son relationship and, 199
  never-married, 228–229
  parenting issue and, 81
  power-driven, 63–64
  scarcity of, for older women, 53
  work satisfaction and, 115
Menopause, 234, 235, 243
Middle age:
  "midlife crisis" concept and, 238–241

1950s conditions and, 5, 24–25, 236
  well-being increased in, 24–25, 236–237
Miller, Jean Baker, 27, 70, 92
Monroe, Marilyn, 53
Moral decision making:
  dependency vs., 31–32
  self-sacrifice and, 27–29, 41
  by women vs. men, 26–27
Mother-daughter relationship (*see* Daughter-
    mother relationship)
Motherhood, mothering, 78–102, 192–207
  autonomous cluster in, 83–84, 85, 87
  child balance in, 94
  conflict cluster in, 88–93
  coupled cluster in, 84, 85–86, 87
  depression and, 88, 147
  feminity and, 102
  fertility studies and, 235–236
  "good" conflict and, 92
  guilt feelings in, 86, 87, 92, 93
  marital relationship and, 95, 99–100, 102
  Mastery and Pleasure levels in, 80, 82–83,
    85, 88, 93–94, 95–96, 99, 100, 101,
    102, 246
  rewards of, 83–86
  role strain and, 141
  "selfishness" in, 84–85
  social supports in, 93
  traditional views of, 78–79, 80–81, 84–85,
    87–88
  (*See also* Childlessness; Children;
    Nurturant imperative)
Multiple role strain (*see* Role strain)
My Mother, My Self (Friday), 192, 195
Myth of Masculinity, The (Pleck), 236

National Institute of Mental Health, 31, 88
Never-married women, employed, 36, 48–49,
    208–232
  aging and, 230–231
  arenas of intimacy and, 210–211, 219–229,
    231
  childlessness and, 221–222, 225–226
  concern clusters of, 209–213, 219–224
  high-prestige work and, 49, 212–214, 215
  income and, 49, 210, 216, 229–230, 231
  independent life-style cluster of, 215–219,
    221
  marriage as viewed by, 20, 211, 215–216,
    219, 220, 221
  Mastery and Pleasure levels of, 49, 104,
    209–213, 220, 230, 231–232, 251
  mental health of, 209, 215, 226
  parents and, 48–49, 217–218, 230, 231
  Pleasure levels of, 209–211, 219
  preference as issue for, 213–214
  reward cluster of, 215–219
  role models and, 211

Never-married women (*cont.*)
self-esteem of, 49, 209, 212, 214–215, 217, 219
sexual satisfaction of, 53, 210, 223–225
social networks of, 217–219, 227–228, 230, 231
social stereotypes of, 208, 215, 231–232
as "transitional generation," 211
work and (*see* Work)
New England Journal of Medicine, 235
Nurturant imperative:
concern for loss of, 245, 247
parent-child bond and, 92
self-esteem and, 26–31
at work, 117–119
(*See also* Motherhood, mothering)

Occupational prestige:
definition of, 4–5
Mastery and Pleasure levels and, 49, 50, 53–54, 108, 117, 212–214, 215
role strain and, 143–144, 146
sexual satisfaction linked to, 53
Optimism, well-being and, 17

Parents (*see* Children; Daughter-mother relationship; Fathers)
Parsons, Talcott, 61
Pearlin, Leonard, 88, 147, 233–234, 241
Pleasure, 1, 34–54
definition of, 2, 18
as dimension of well-being model, 1, 18, 38–40, 246, 249–250
rise in middle age of, 24–25
(*See also specific headings*)
Pleck, Joseph, 145, 236

Quality of American Life, The, 30–31

Radabaugh, Claire, 233–234
Reinventing Womanhood (Heilbrun), 29, 238, 251
Reisman, David, 56
Research design, 3–11
age range in, 5
characteristics of women in, 7–8, 35–37
model developed in, 18
purpose of, 3–4
subjects of, 5–6
survey method of, 8–11
Rhodes Scholars, 237–238
Risk-taking, 121–134
avoidance of, 127–129
career change and, 126–127
challenge cluster of rewards and, 121
dependency and, 31–32
"getting ahead" syndrome and, 122–124
job advancement and, 121–125

passivity and, 125, 129
self-assessment and, 122–124
sexism and, 134–138
Roles:
changing patterns of, 25, 104–106, 247–248
as choice, 16, 30–32
differentiation in, 34–35
femininity and, 117–119, 244–245
men's view of, 12–13
as models for younger women, 5, 35, 46–47, 193, 199–200, 203–205, 206, 207, 211, 212
multiple (*see* Role strain)
1930s Depression as cause of changes in, 236
personal design of, 149–150
stereotyping of, 244–245, 247
women's traditional view of, 13, 26–28, 40–41, 48, 57, 122–124, 211, 223–224, 236, 244
Role strain, 139–163
depression and, 143–144, 147
finances and, 146
high- vs. low-prestige jobs and, 144–145, 146–149, 248
homemakers and, 141–143, 145, 147, 150–153, 247, 248
husbands and, 142
limited resource model and, 140–141
married, employed mothers and, 139–163, 247–248
Mastery and Pleasure levels and, 140, 146, 147, 148, 150
mental health and, 140, 143–145, 147, 150, 173–174
at midlife, 146–148
number of roles and, 140, 141, 143
physical health and, 144
"underload" and, 150–153
Rubin, Zick, 64

Scarf, Maggie, 21
Sears, Pauline, 230
Self-esteem:
age and, 237
definition of, 17
of homemakers, 14, 19, 27–28, 40–44, 106–107, 112, 146, 150–153, 155–156, 161, 168–169
husband's approval and, 40–44, 45
marriage status and, 58, 214–215
mental health and, 18, 21, 27–29
nurturant imperative and, 27, 29
parenting and, 85, 93
parents' approval and, 49, 181, 196, 197, 198–199, 217–218

Self-esteem (*cont.*)
  social support and, 41, 93
  well-being and 17, 18, 19–22
  work life and, 21–22, 46, 49, 50, 53–54,
    108, 117, 212–214
Self-interest:
  changing attitudes toward, 25–33, 84–85,
    172, 250
  self-sacrifice vs., 28–29, 163, 247, 250
Sexism, in workplace, 134–138
Sexual satisfaction, 46, 47
  earning power linked to, 53–54
  marriage and, 46, 54, 72–73, 75–77, 95
  in midlife, 53, 75–77, 240
Sheehy, Gail, 38
Shostak, Marjorie, 105–106, 244
Social ties, Mastery-Pleasure levels linked to,
  44, 46, 51, 93, 99, 109, 197, 217–219,
  227–228, 249
Stewart, Abigail, 63–64, 143–144
"Superwoman" model, 2–3, 143, 247

Teicholz, Judith G., 102
Thurow, Lester, 149
Total Woman concept, 2
Toward a New Psychology of Women (Miller),
  70
Tudor, Jeanette F., 57
Turning points:
  life accidents as, 243
  theories vs. actual events as, 242–243

Ullian, Dorothy, 71
Unfinished Business (Scarf), 21

Veroff, Joseph, 4

Weiss, Robert, 172
Well-being:
  age and, 24, 236, 237, 238–239
  "balance" and, 10, 15, 18, 20–22, 46–47,
    246–251
  components of, 1, 2, 14–19, 36–54
  defined, 16–17
  as focus of research, 1, 17–18
  happiness vs., 17
  maps of, 37–44
  prediction of levels of, 234–235, 241
  social change and, 233–237, 242, 247, 250–
    251
  (*See also* Mastery; Pleasure)
Wilen, Judith, 203
Winter, David, 63–64
Women:
  aging concerns of, 24, 239–240
  developmental theories on, 234–235, 238–
    242, 244–245, 248
  education sought by, 242

emotional life as realm of, 12–16, 20, 21
  in Freudian theories, 234, 236, 244
  male models applied to, 240
  media's portrayal of, 13–14, 21, 28
  men's traditional view of, 12–13, 234–236
  "midlife crisis" and, 238–241
  midlife well-being of, 5, 24–25, 236–237
  reproductive events as "definition" of,
    234–236, 242
  as scapegoat for social ills, 16, 28, 33, 122,
    236
  as servant class, 65
  social changes now affecting, 233–237,
    242, 250–251
  socio-political consciousness of, 237–238
  stereotyping of, 52–53, 244–245
  women's traditional view of, 13, 26–28,
    31–32, 40–41, 48, 57, 122–124, 211,
    223–224, 236, 244, 251
Women's movement:
  ambivalence toward, 152, 174–175
  career choices and, 14, 31–32, 127, 149,
    152–153, 237–238
  Equal Rights Amendment and, 238
  gains in social climate due to, 25, 237
  personal views of, 237–238
  single women and, 211, 226–227
Work, 103–138
  advancement barriers in, 121–125, 134–
    138
  attribution patterns and, 122–124
  as buffer and escape, 144–145, 154, 198,
    248
  burnt-out feelings in, 112
  challenge cluster of, 109–112, 116–117,
    121
  change in commitment toward, 109–112,
    237, 242
  childlessness and, 96–100
  clerical, 111, 144
  dead-end cluster of, 114
  defined, 4
  dissatisfactions with, 112–116
  dull-job cluster of, 114, 115–116
  expectations and ambitions in, 104, 113,
    130–134
  family planning issues and, 149
  in female ghetto jobs, 74
  femininity issues and, 117–119, 244–245
  homemaking as, 4, 106–107
  initial experience of, 127
  marriage and (*see* Marriage)
  Mastery levels and, 22, 38, 40, 45–51, 54,
    103–120, 129, 143–144, 166, 170,
    189–190, 212–215
  midlife start in, 133–134, 241, 248, 249
  mothering role and (*see* Motherhood,
    mothering)

Work (*cont.*)
   multiple role strain and, 139–163
   national economic conditions and, 236,
     237
   nurturant imperative and, 117–119
   Pleasure levels and, 104, 108, 109, 114
   prestige and, 49, 50, 53–54, 103, 108, 117,
     144–145, 147, 148–149, 245, 247, 248
   professional, 113–114, 117–118
   recognition and, 115–116
   rewards of, 14, 108–112, 114, 144, 146–
     149, 246–251
   risk and, 121–134
   self-esteem and (*see* Self-esteem)
   sexism at, 134–138
   socialization and, 108, 122–131
   social relationships cluster of, 109, 116–
     117
   stress reduced by, 21–22, 144–146
   traditional views of, 14, 105–108, 113
   women vs. men in, 19, 115, 117–120, 122–
     123, 127, 129–130, 239–241
"Wrong place" syndrome, 19–22
Wylie, Philip, 193

Younger women:
   career choices and work life of, 52, 74,
     108, 113–114, 116, 134, 138, 148, 242,
     249–251
   change in attitude toward marriage of, 58,
     224, 242

childlessness at issue for, 79–80, 95, 101–
   102, 242, 251
early conditioning of, 69–71
models for, 5, 35, 46–47, 52, 193, 199–200,
   203–205, 206, 207, 211, 212, 231
new life pattern for, 236
as subject to stress, 5, 46, 241
women's movement and, 14, 29, 237–
   238
(*See also* Daughter-mother relationship)

Zones of vulnerability:
   dependence on husband's approval as, 42–
     44, 45, 168
   after divorce, 165, 176–191
   in homemaking role (married women with
     children, at home; married women
     without children, at home), 19, 150–
     156, 159–163, 247
   love relationships and, 21, 42–43, 45
   in marriage, 43–48, 60, 66–67, 168
   for married women with children,
     employed, 45–46, 139–150, 247
   for married women without children,
     employed, 47
   in mother-daughter relationship, 194–200,
     205–207
   of never-married women, 48, 209–213,
     219–224
   parenting as, 46, 48–51, 82–95, 194–200